Medicine and Society in Early Modern Europe

Medicine and Society in Early Modern Europe is the latest contribution to the highly successful series of New Approaches, and offers undergraduate students a concise introduction to a subject rich in historical excitement and interest. Bringing together the best and most innovative recent research, Mary Lindemann examines medicine from a social and cultural perspective, rather than a narrowly scientific one. Drawing on medical anthropology, sociology, and ethics as well as cultural and social history, she focuses as much on the experience of illness and on patients and folk healers as on the rise of medical science, doctors, and hospitals. Mary Lindemann is a distinguished scholar in the history of medicine and writes with exceptional clarity on this fascinating subject; her book will be essential reading for all students of the history of medicine, and will provide invaluable context for historians of early modern Europe in general.

MARY LINDEMANN is Professor of History at Carnegie Mellon University. Her publications include *Patriots and Paupers: Hamburg, 1712–1830* and *Health and Healing in Eighteenth-Century Germany*. The latter was awarded the 1998 William H. Welch Medal Book Prize from the American Association for the History of Medicine.

New Approaches to European History

Series editors
William Beik *Emory University*
T. C. W. Blanning *Sidney Sussex College, Cambridge*

New Approaches to European History is an important new textbook initiative, intended to provide concise but authoritative surveys of major themes and problems in European history since the Renaissance. Written at a level and length accessible to advanced school students and undergraduates, each book in the series will address topics or themes that students of European history encounter daily: the series will embrace both some of the more "traditional" subjects of study, and those cultural and social issues to which increasing numbers of school and college courses are devoted. A particular effort will be made to consider the wider international implications of the subject under scrutiny.

To aid the student reader scholarly apparatus and annotation will be light, but each work will have supplementary bibliographies and notes for further reading: where appropriate, chronologies, maps, diagrams, and other illustrative material will also be provided.

For a list of titles published in the series, please see end of book.

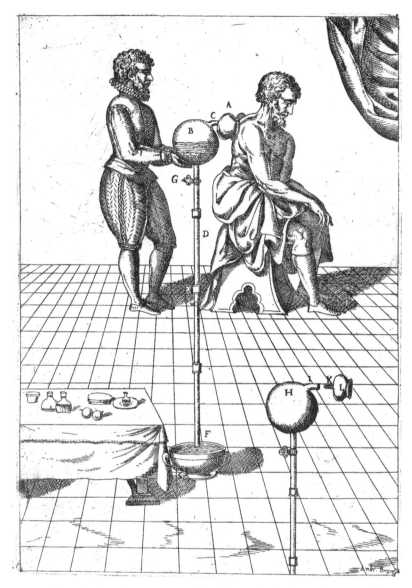

Frontispiece: A surgeon applying the method of cupping to a patient.

Medicine and Society in Early Modern Europe

Mary Lindemann

CAMBRIDGE
UNIVERSITY PRESS

PUBLISHED BY THE PRESS SYNDICATE OF THE UNIVERSITY OF CAMBRIDGE
The Pitt Building, Trumpington Street, Cambridge CB2 1RP, United Kingdom

CAMBRIDGE UNIVERSITY PRESS
The Edinburgh Building, Cambridge CB2 2RU, UK http://www.cup.cam.ac.uk
40 West 20th Street, New York, NY 10011-4211, USA http://www.cup.org
10 Stamford Road, Oakleigh, Melbourne 3166, Australia

First published 1999

Printed in the United Kingdom at the University Press, Cambridge

Typeset in Plantin 10/12 pt in QuarkXPress™ [SE]

A catalogue record for this book is available from the British Library

Library of Congress Cataloguing in Publication data

Lindemann, Mary.
    Medicine and society in early modern Europe / Mary Lindemann.
        p.   cm. – (New Approaches to European history)
    Includes bibliographical references and index.
    ISBN 0 521 41254 4 (hbk.) – ISBN 0 521 42354 6 (pbk.)
        1. Social medicine – Europe – History.   2. Medicine – Europe –
History.   3. Medical care – Europe – History.   4. Public health –
Europe – History.   5. Medicine – Social aspects – Europe – History.
    I. Title.   II. Series.
    RA418.3.E85L55   1999
    306.4′61′094 – dc21   99-17819 CIP

ISBN 0 521 41254 4 hardback
ISBN 0 521 42354 6 paperback

For Michael, again

Contents

Illustrations

All illustrations courtesy of the Wellcome Institute Library, London.

Tables

Acknowledgments

These acknowledgments begin on a sad note. Unfortunately I can only thank Bob Scribner posthumously. Bob first suggested that I write *Medicine and Society in Early Modern Europe*. His untimely death caused a great loss to all early modernists.

Several institutions supported work on this volume over a number of years and in several capacities. A Fulbright Regional Research Grant for the United Kingdom, Germany, France, and the Netherlands allowed me to pursue research in several countries and do extensive reading in numerous libraries during spring semester 1994. During that time I enjoyed the hospitality of the Wellcome Institute for the History of Medicine (London) and exploited the facilities of Henry Wellcome's great medical library and its splendid iconographic collection. I returned there in early 1998 where I wrote the last chapters of the book. I would like to thank all my friends at the Wellcome and my fellow denizens of the Twentieth-Century Room for their friendship, advice, and scholarly expertise, all freely given, and also for their unfailing sense of humor: Sally Bragg, Bill Bynum, Gordon Cook, Alex Goldblum, Natsu Hattori, Rhodri Hayward, Michael Neve, Vivian Nutton, Kim Pelis, Roy Porter, Chandak Sengoopta, Tilli Tansey, and Andrew Wear. The Falk Medical Historical Library at the University of Pittsburgh was a valuable source for secondary literature, and its librarian and my friend, John Erlen, made me feel especially welcome there.

I owe special debts of gratitude to three other friends and colleagues. Tom Broman and David Harley went over the entire manuscript with a finetooth comb and made many excellent suggestions about how to improve the overall presentation, writing style, and general approach. Caroline Acker, Department of History at Carnegie Mellon University, read some early chapters and offered useful advice about how to improve them. Michael Miller also read the manuscript in its entirety. Of course, none of these helpers is responsible for any remaining flaws.

Finally, working with Cambridge University Press has been a pleasure. The general editor of the series, Richard Fisher, was extremely patient, waiting until I finished another book before expecting me to deliver this one. My two editors at the Press, first Vicky Cuthill and then Elizabeth Howard, were models of courtesy and efficiency. My copy-editor turned out to be an old acquaintance and ex-student, Karen Anderson Howes, who worked cheerfully and rapidly to produce a finished manuscript.

Introduction

Medical history has changed almost out of all recognition over the past twenty-five years. This rather astonishing metamorphosis has made it possible to write a book on *Medicine and Society in Early Modern Europe* that is contextual, historiographic, revisionist, and, I hope, provocative.

First, this book is contextual in trying to weight equally the two halves of the title: "medicine" and "society." The primary goal has been to "mainstream" the history of medicine. Mainstreaming takes a historical subspecialty, like the history of medicine, lifts it out of the confining limits of a disciplinary channel, and refloats it in broader historical currents. Doing so requires us to write medical history in new ways. No longer is an epic or romantic story of spectacular breakthroughs and embattled pioneers enough. Medical history must now account for all the greater social, political, cultural, and economic forces affecting Europeans from 1500 to 1800. If we fail to grasp these sweeping issues, we will never fully appreciate the role of medicine in society.

The approach taken here is, moreover, historiographic and argumentative. *Medicine and Society* resolutely avoids telling a story of progress. Instead, it presents interpretations up front and deals with scholarly controversies head on. No event, no discovery, no idea is ever uncontested and even the losers in history deserve their day. Simple parables of right and wrong, truth and error obscure historical realities rather than revealing them. Thus, this volume sedulously avoids a *whiggish* interpretation. "Whiggish" is academic shorthand for a version of history that postulates a single passage into the modern world leading resolutely from the dark ages of ignorance, superstition, and suffering into a brighter world of knowledge, science, and abundance. This "things-are-getting-better-all-the-time" school has been rightly condemned for its hindsight, although it would be equally foolish for us to deny the undoubted progress medicine has made since the middle ages. Nonetheless, the path toward improvement was neither straight nor narrow, and Europeans made many detours and bumped up against many dead-ends in traveling it.

Finally, this history is revisionist. It belongs to what is now called the *new history of medicine* and to the equally new *social history of medicine*. To understand the difference, it is necessary to review briefly the history of the history of medicine. First, a caveat. The "new" history of medicine differs from the "old" in several ways and we, its practitioners, tend to assume its superiority. It is prudent, however, to bear in mind that each age remains a prisoner of its own prejudices. And if we today are less willing to accept the march of progress uncritically, perhaps our successors will find our certainties equally false.

How then has the writing of the history of medicine been transformed over the past quarter-century? For a long time the history of medicine could be accurately described as *iatrocentric*. That is, physicians wrote medical history as a hobby and followed well-trodden paths, concentrating on biographies, bibliographies, medical theory, and practice. These histories were essentially *internalist*. At its worst, internalist writing produced exultant chronicles of medical progress and equally celebratory biographies of medical pioneers. "Great men" and "great ideas" dominated. Yet internalist history was not always bad history. Many early studies were carefully done and meticulously researched. Moreover, it amassed a store of knowledge upon which we all still draw. Nor did all those laboring in medical history's old regime satisfy themselves with a rosy view of the present compared to a ghastly past.

Still, in the 1960s and 1970s, things changed. New ideas as well as fresh faces entered the field and eventually revolutionized the writing of medical history. George Rosen (an M.D. and a Ph.D.) bridged the two eras. In his 1967 presidential address to the annual meeting of the American Association for the History of Medicine, Rosen called upon scholars to redefine the "matter and manner of medical history." He proposed an agenda for research into the social context of medicine, into demography, into the history of emotions, and into responses to disease. Above all, he insisted that "the patient deserves a more prominent place in the history of medicine."[1]

Disenchantment with late twentieth-century health care also profoundly affected the course of medical history. Critics of modern, technocratic medicine assailed the prerogatives of a professional medical elite, while abhorring the dehumanized character of modern medical treatment. As early as 1963, Ivan Illich stressed the *Limits to Medicine*. Several authors, including the eminent physician and medical sociologist,

---

[1] George Rosen, "Levels of Integration in Medical Historiography: A Review," *Journal of the History of Medicine* 4 (1949): 460–67; Rosen, "People, Disease, and Emotion: Some Newer Problems for Research in Medical History," *Bulletin of the History of Medicine* 41 (1967): 8.

Thomas McKeown, noted that improvements in nutrition, rather than advances in medical science or public health, accounted best for the decline of mortality since the eighteenth century. Doubts about modern medicine multiplied, with many deploring the manipulative character of the dominion of doctors in the modern world. Psychiatry seems to have borne the brunt of these attacks. Thomas Szasz, for one, launched bitter jeremiads against the abuses of modern psychiatry and psychiatric institutions, arguing that the diagnosis of "mental illness" was just another way of imposing a bourgeois mentality and code of behavior on people termed "deviants." The French philosopher Michel Foucault chimed in with his basically pessimistic view of the results of the rise of scientific medicine at the end of the eighteenth century.[2]

New historians of medicine were generally not as censorious as the culture critics, but they were certainly skeptical of straightforward stories of scientific progress and of the "great men in white" presented by their predecessors. These new players took an *externalist* approach sensitive to the broader context in which medicine moved. They focused, moreover, on persons traditional medical historiography had slighted or scorned. Feminist historians, post-colonialist scholars, and medical anthropologists contributed their perspectives, directing historians to the study of women in medicine, to non-European medical experiences, and to folk healers.

Increasingly since the 1960s and 1970s, professional historians, rather than physicians, have dominated the field. A large number of these trained as social historians. In Britain, the flourishing Society for the Social History of Medicine publishes its own journal, *Social History of Medicine*, and thus provides a scholarly outlet for historical analyses of medicine and society. Older journals, such as the *Bulletin of the History of Medicine* (Baltimore) and *Medical History* (London), devote ever more space to the social history of medicine. Indeed, social history now rules the medical historical roost, at least in the Anglo-Saxon world.

The British and the Americans (from the United States and Canada) have been in the vanguard of this movement. Departments of history in the United States often employ a medical historian, and student interest in the history of medicine, as well as in bio-ethics, seems quite lively. In Britain, the Wellcome Trust funds a number of academic units dedicated

---

[2] Ivan Illich, *Limits to Medicine: The Expropriation of Health* (Harmondsworth, 1977); Thomas McKeown, *The Role of Medicine: Dream, Mirage, or Nemesis?* (Princeton, N.J., 1979), and McKeown, *The Modern Rise of Population* (London, 1976); Thomas S. Szasz, *The Myth of Mental Illness: Foundations of a Theory of Personal Conduct* (London, 1972), and Szasz, *The Manufacture of Madness* (New York, 1970); Michel Foucault, *Discipline and Punish: The Birth of the Prison* (New York, 1977), and Foucault, *The Birth of the Clinic: An Archaeology of Medical Perception* (New York, 1973).

to medical history. British and American scholars have produced works that embody the new history of medicine and that attract an increasingly large general readership. It is an exciting moment to be a medical historian, especially as the flood of publications shows little sign of cresting.

Still, the social history of medicine has its own blemishes and blindspots. For instance, the desire to recapture the experiences of women healers, folk practitioners, and their patients has led some scholars to rather dubious conclusions. Instead of viewing previous medical practices as unscientific, irrational, superstitious, and simply bad (as many internalists had done), these historians endow it with a preternatural wisdom and a coherence that it probably never possessed. It is possible, for instance, that the whole idea of a popular medicine conveyed by oral tradition through the centuries might be the figment of an overheated historical imagination.

Too much of the new medical history (and this was also true of the old) centers on the British and especially the English past. This orientation has often imposed a tyranny of Anglo-Saxon models or forced questionable comparisons to a paradigmatic England. This prejudice is slowly fading, but the asymmetry persists. European scholars have not, in truth, taken up the social history of medicine as enthusiastically as their British and American colleagues. The Italians, with their innovative microhistorical techniques and their strong emphasis on the history of mentalities, have produced intriguing (if also sometimes odd) perspectives on plague, bodies, and pain. In Germany, the home of medical historiography, younger scholars are now questioning the analytic validity of concepts of professionalization and medicalization that once guided research there. France, despite the Annalist tradition (with its emphasis on the sea changes in history, on climate, demography, and secular population shifts), has lagged behind and been rather slow in accepting the new medical history. Much of the innovative work has centered on the nineteenth century. The French have, however, long been deeply involved in large-scale demographic projects with relevance, for instance, to cause-of-death investigations. These French trends pertain to a large degree to the Scandinavian countries as well. The Dutch historians of medicine, once mired in the history of great men like Herman Boerhaave, have become extremely active participants in the new history. One can point to a series of fine Dutch studies on patients and practitioners, on religious beliefs, and on alternative medicines and healers. The Spanish have made significant contributions to the history of hospitals, diseases, and public health.

Finally, the new history of medicine has not spread as widely in chronological and geographical terms as many of its advocates wish. Most work is still Eurocentric, and centers, moreover, on western Europe or the north American colonies. Africa, Latin America, and Asia remain relatively neglected. Chronologically, coverage has concentrated on the nineteenth and twentieth centuries and the early modern period (for England, especially). Medieval and ancient historians have moved more sluggishly into the field, perhaps because the sources for the social history of medicine in those early periods are thinner and more difficult to exploit. Yet here, too, and especially for the middle ages, progress in the writing of medical history is obvious.

No existing general survey of medicine and society in early modern Europe fully incorporates the exciting and innovative work in the social history of medicine that has appeared since the 1970s. Early attempts to define and synthesize the social history of medicine for students remained fairly orthodox in their selection of topics and, of course, benefited only little from the literature that has done so much to revivify and refurbish medical history.[3] One recent survey by Lawrence Conrad, Michael Neve, Vivian Nutton, Roy Porter, and Andrew Wear, *The Western Medical Tradition*, which covers an almost 2,000-year period from 800 B.C. to A.D. 1800, more successfully integrates the new medical history. It provides an excellent guide to a medical tradition that stretches back to the Greeks. It is, however, principally concerned with medicine and thus centers less on society than does the present volume. An eminently readable and broadly interpretive work that ranges over the whole of medicine throughout time and in all places is Roy Porter's *The Greatest Benefit to Mankind*, but it offers, understandably, only a brief overview of early modern developments.

In composing the current volume, some basic problems had to be solved. Unquestionably the subject was medicine, but the text was also intended to appeal to those interested in early modern history more generally. A second challenge was to establish borders to a subject that proffered myriad seductive opportunities for spinning out connections. How can, for example, a history of medicine *not* deal with famine and poverty, and yet also not stray too far from the path of *medical* history by roving off into the territory of the demographers and family historians? The solution followed in these pages has not been a very rigorous one. I have not hesitated to trespass on the "turf" of other scholars; such encroachment seems to me a splendid and appropriate way to demonstrate the centrality of medicine to larger themes in European history.

A strong accent on recent work in social history, cultural history, and mentalities characterizes *Medicine and Society*. Careful attention is paid to

---

[3] For example, F. F. Cartwright, *A Social History of Medicine* (London, 1977).

socioeconomic and cultural structures throughout. These preferences, however, in no way dictate the slighting of more orthodox subjects such as medical theory and education. Still, the book pursues themes different from those which have guided more traditional surveys. It devotes as much attention to patients as to practitioners; to "general" practitioners as to physicians; to community and family care as to hospitals; to artisanal and empirical training as to formal or university-based medical education; to medical mentalities as to conventional medical philosophies; and, finally, to the cultural and societal significance of medicine as to scientific meaning. Wherever possible, the volume exploits interdisciplinary perspectives drawn from anthropology, sociology, feminism, and literary criticism.

It was also necessary to decide whether to adopt a thoroughgoing *social constructivist* view of disease. Disease is very difficult to define. One can take an essentially positivist approach and argue along with the *Oxford Concise Medical Dictionary* that disease is "a disorder with a specific cause and recognizable signs and symptoms." That seems clear enough until we start to think about afflictions that have no discernible cause and the signs and symptoms of which often fluctuate, sometimes radically. Chronic fatigue syndrome, for example, has sometimes been diagnosed as a "real disease" (myalgic encephalitis) and sometimes dismissed as "yuppie flu." On the other side, even though the origins of alcoholism, hysteria, and juvenile hyperactivity remain unclear, they are frequently labeled "diseases." Clearly one cannot deny that these diseases are to a large extent socially constructed and that their explanations shift with changing social and cultural expectations. "'Disease' is an elusive entity." It is more than a biological thing and "in some ways disease does not exist until we have agreed that it does, by perceiving, naming, and responding to it."[4]

Social constructivism links up with *historical relativism*. Most historians accept that knowledge is relative. What people "knew" in the past was "true" whether we believe it now or not. Whereas we might search for the "germ" cause of syphilis, people of the sixteenth century constructed a disease in their minds and from their experience that they recognized as the "Great Pox" or the "French Disease." In this volume, the importance of the social construction of disease and historical relativism will come out in many ways, for example, in showing how early modern peoples held attitudes toward various afflictions that differ from ours. This divergent awareness, however, did not make them more superstitious or more gullible than we are. Yet, not everything is socially or culturally con-

---

[4] Charles E. Rosenburg, "Framing Disease: Illness, Society, and History," in Rosenburg and Janet Golden, eds., *Framing Disease: Studies in Cultural History* (New Brunswick, N.J., 1997), xiii–xv.

structed and it is hard to accept that "reality does not exist." There is much value in Margaret Pelling's argument that the social construction of disease "cannot be applied universally . . . [for] some diseases are more socially constructed than others." Pelling quite rightly points out that social constructivism and historical relativism when carried to the extreme hinder a subtle understanding of others by suggesting that only people in their own time and place can have accurate perceptions of "their" illnesses.[5] This book, while avoiding a whiggish, positivist stance that elevates twentieth-century over previous wisdom and ways of knowing, also accepts that "real things exist." Thus, chapter 2 does not hesitate to discuss the "diseases" of smallpox and plague, although it also warns of the dangers of confidently diagnosing diseases in the past as if we possess some superior and more scientific understanding of them.

This book concentrates on the three centuries between 1500 and 1800. The general layout is topical, with each chapter addressing a group of related issues. Within chapters, chronological confines are quite elastic. For instance, it is absurd to discuss epidemics without examining the plague experience of the fourteenth century. This temporal pliancy holds true for other subjects, especially for public health, medical education, and hospitals. In some chapters, such as those on hospitals and education, the medieval background is more luxuriant because it is essential.

The volume makes no pretense about being comprehensive in scope. Gaps in descriptions or analyses generally reflect the lacunae in historical research, as well as page limitations. Geographically, the book tries to be as evenhanded as possible. The secondary literature is simply more voluminous for certain areas and periods than for others: early modern England has been the subject of a great deal of research; France in the eighteenth century and Italy during the Renaissance have received more notice than other countries; and central, northern, and eastern Europe, Spain, and Portugal (again with some significant exceptions) have enjoyed less attention. Many of these gaps cannot be closed here, although the author hopes that her research interests, in central Europe and the Low Countries, rectify this imbalance somewhat.

[5] Jon Arrizabalaga, John Henderson, and Roger French, *The Great Pox: The French Disease in Renaissance Europe* (New Haven, Conn., 1997), pp. 16–17; Margaret Pelling, *The Common Lot: Sickness, Medical Occupations and the Urban Poor in Early Modern England* (London and New York, 1998), 6–7.

1   Sickness and health

Of each 1,000 people born, 24 die during birth itself; the business of teething disposes of another 50; in the first two years, convulsions and other illness remove another 277; smallpox . . . carries off another 80 or 90, and measles 10 more. Among women, about 8 perish in childbed. Inflammatory fevers cause another 150 [deaths]. Apoplexy [kills] 12, dropsy 41. Therefore, of each 1,000 born, one can expect that only 78 will die of old age, or die in old age . . . It is apparent enough that at least nine-tenths [of humankind] die before their time and by chance.[1]

Definition of "health" by the World Health Organization (WHO): "complete physical, mental, and social well-being and not merely the absence of disease and infirmity."[2]

Thinking about sickness and health

Sickness and health are the antipodes of human existence, but perhaps no two terms are more difficult to grasp. The definition WHO accepted in its 1946 constitution remains an unattainable goal for many people even in the most prosperous countries of the world today, and such a definition would certainly have perplexed early modern people whose lives were repeatedly blighted by disease and ill health.

Common usage tends to conflate the terms *disease* and *illness*, or to employ them synonymously. At least at the outset of this chapter, however, we should differentiate between the two. Disease is a biological entity; illness is a perceived condition. One way of looking at disease and illness is to deem both of them medical facts and ahistorical realities, i.e., as having real existences and real causes (either somatic or psychological). Accordingly, one would say: "The microorganism *Yersina pestis*

---

[1] Christoph Wilhelm Hufeland, *Die Kunst des menschlichen Lebens zu verlängern* (Jena, 1797), 365–66.

[2] "Constitution of the World Health Organization," *Chronicle of the World Health Organization* 1, nos. 1–2 (October 1946), quoted in Margaret Mead, ed., *Cultural Patterns and Technical Change: A Manual Prepared by the World Federation for Mental Health* (Deventer, 1953), 28.

causes plague." Those who stress the central importance of history and culture in shaping perceptions of bodies and diseases would, however, disagree. These scholars, known as *social constructivists*, focus on how social and cultural milieux determined the language used to describe illness; how different societies (and groups in society, such as elites and peasants or men and women) held disparate perceptions of disease and developed varied strategies for coping with illness; and how bodies functioned as signs or symbols.

In addition, we should distinguish between two different theoretical perspectives on disease: the *ontological* and the *functionalist* (or *holistic*). The ontological view of disease regards each disease as a real entity with an independent existence. The ontological model carries major implications for therapy in suggesting that the same methods of treatment will work in all cases. The functionalist approach, however, sees disease as existing only within a specific organism and as resulting from a dysfunction that may be attributed to an individual's personal habits or to various environmental effects on him or her.

The ontological view of disease gained favor from about the middle of the nineteenth century onward partly as a result of triumphs in public health, discoveries in bacteriology, and – in the early twentieth century – the development of sulfa drugs and antibiotics. Such successes significantly augmented the social and cultural status of physicians and their overall influence. Before the nineteenth century, however, functionalism dominated lay and academic medicines alike. Healers selected and applied treatments that would restore the "proper working" of the organism as a whole.

The Hippocratic/Galenic tradition, dating from the works of the Hippocratic writers[3] (Hippocrates lived from c. 450 to c. 370 B.C.) and Galen of Pergamum (A.D. 129–c. 200), remained influential throughout the middle ages and well into the eighteenth century. This doctrine tied disease chiefly to the environment but also incorporated concepts of pollution and impurity in explaining what caused disease. At least until the seventeenth century, and probably much later, a mixture of *environmentalism* and *humoralism* dominated interpretations of disease. For most people, lay and learned alike, health rested in the proper balance of the four *humors* – black bile, yellow (or red) bile, blood, and phlegm – and disease arose from their imbalance, a general state of disequilibrium that the environment could affect or influence. Thus, in Galenic and Hippocratic medicine, diseases were unique to individuals and *specific*

---

[3] Hippocrates left no writings identified as his and his alone. The "Hippocratic corpus" is composed of several works (*Airs, Waters, and Places, Epidemics, Aphorisms,* and *Prognostic*) attributed to Hippocrates, but possibly written by others.

diseases or *disease entities* as we normally speak of them (e.g., influenza, plague, AIDS) did not exist. Attaining and preserving a state of health, therefore, required balance, and that equilibrium was inherently elusive and easily forfeited. Environmental changes – a particular condition of the air or water, an especially hot or wet summer, or an unfavorable conjunction of the planets, for instance – could upset the body's internal hydraulics with predictably pernicious results.

The Hippocratic/Galenic tradition, moreover, postulated a continuum between health and illness and located each individual somewhere on that band. Health was, in fact, "an unattainable ideal" and most people hung "forever suspended between health and illness."[4] Too much of one humor, or too little of another, could cause disease, as could the "corruption" or "putrefaction" of one or another of the body's humors. Any alteration in the nature of a humor spelled danger for the individual. Even minute oscillations had to be dealt with expeditiously to avert illness. Standard therapies and preventives depended on readjusting perceived imbalances either by siphoning off a humor that had grown too strong or become corrupt, or by bleeding, purging, vomiting, or setting *artificial issues* (i.e., lesions). Indeed, according to the eighteenth-century physician Samuel Tissot, there was no reason to worry about a slight looseness or diarrhea. This was the body's own attempt to cleanse the system by "carry[ing] off a heap of matter that may have been long amassed and then putrified in the body [and] which, if not discharged, might have produced some distemper."[5]

In humoral medicine, prevention (or *prophylaxis*) was as important as treatment (or *therapeutics*). The best means of maintaining health was to practice moderation in all things, especially in the use of the *six non-naturals*: (1) air; (2) sleep and waking; (3) food and drink; (4) rest and exercise; (5) excretion and retention; and (6) the passions or emotions. A healthy regimen was predicated on observing these rules of nature and avoiding exhaustion, overheating, overeating, excessive consumption of spirits, and immoderate desires. Such ideas were prevalent, and informed not only medical theories but more popular versions of health and illness as well.

Linked ideas of equilibrium as health, disequilibrium as illness, and the individual character of each person's sickness did not alone shape people's perceptions of health and illness. Ancient ideas of disease as an invasion of the body or as a form of pollution also persisted throughout

---

[4] Georg Hildebrandt, *Taschenbuch für die Gesundheit auf das Jahr 1801* (Erlangen, 1801), preface.

[5] Samuel August Tissot, *Advice to the People in General with Regard to Their Health*, trans. by J. Kirkpatrick (Boston, 1767), 104.

the early modern period. People accepted immorality and vice as causes of disease, both collectively (in terms of epidemic outbreaks) and individually. Leprosy, for example, could be viewed as a punishment for concupiscence, although also, conversely, as a mark of special religious merit and moral virtue. In effect, naturalistic explanations of the Hippocratic and Galenic traditions competed and combined with religious viewpoints, with the result that each possessed the power to mold responses to disease. Thus, while communities cast out lepers and quarantined plague patients, they simultaneously sought expiation of sins and did penance. In addition, the sixteenth-century Swiss physician Paracelsus (c. 1493–1541) broke with the humoral tradition in conceiving of disease as caused by an entity – the *archeus* – that invaded the human body. Indeed, since classical times, arrows loosed by the gods symbolized the external source of disease, as Apollo's shafts slew Niobe's children. For Paracelsus, as later for Joan Baptista van Helmont (1579–1644) and Thomas Sydenham (1624–89), diseases became specific and the diseased state qualitatively differed from the healthy one.

What interests us here is the currency of these notions. How did people regard disease (or illness) and health? To what extent did "popular" and "academic" ideas on such crucial human conditions correspond or conflict? Historians once wrote confidently about the obvious contrasts between lay and academic conceptions of health and illness. Historians of medicine once spoke slightingly of "popular errors" and superstitions, and constructed a teleological epic based on the march of scientific progress. This interpretation underpinned the equally accepted dichotomy between competent medical men and pernicious "quacks." Then, censure of modern medicine and its whiggish historiography arose in the 1970s and continued throughout the 1980s. Some critics stressed the *iatrogenic* character of modern medicine, i.e., the ability of medicine and physicians themselves to cause disease. Many scholars rejected older interpretations of the history of medicine that focused advancing medical progress. As a result, studies of nonelite forms of medicine and of nonprofessional or nonacademic healers proliferated. Medical historians began to take seriously the whole range of practitioners and practices existing outside, and alongside, official medicine. New analytical terms arose to accentuate and cope with these differences, such as "elite/ popular," "orthodox/unorthodox," "academic/lay" medicines, practices, and perceptions. Gradually, however, it became clear that the dichotomies themselves were suspect and that the overlap of "popular" and "elite" medicines – or rather the presence of a broad substratum of common beliefs about health, illness, and therapeutics that most members of society shared – truly characterized early modern medicine. This perception informs the following discussion of sickness and health. I do not intend to imply, however, that there was no conflict and no diversity within the world of early modern medicine (conflict was bitter and endemic). Rather, a sharp division between "popular" and "elite" medicines fails to capture the medical reality of early modern Europe and is misleading. Both the lay and the learned shared medical practices and perceptions in the early modern period and accepted a basically similar view of how their bodies worked.

Experiencing the body

The science of human physiology concerns itself with the functions of the human organism and its parts. In this section, however, we will not be so much concerned with early modern physiological theories (see chapter 3) as with a common pattern of belief concerning how bodies performed or failed to do so. This focus is linked to what has over the past decade come to be known as "the history of the body," itself closely allied to new cultural history and to feminist theory. Obviously not everyone experienced physicality in the same manner. Crucial differences between males and females, as well as among social groups, conditioned a variety of beliefs and attitudes.

Most early modern people, however, accepted several basic concepts about bodies, even if they did not articulate their ideas systematically. First, the old notions of the *naturals* (including the complexions and the humors), the *non-naturals* (discussed above, p. 10), and the *contra-naturals* (or diseases) prevailed almost everywhere. Most people understood the body as composed of a mixture of the four humors – blood, phlegm, black bile, and yellow bile. The four ancient *elements* – water, fire, earth, and air – constituted the humors. Humors themselves had *qualities*: phlegm was cold and wet; black bile was cold and dry; blood was hot and wet; and yellow bile was hot and dry. Each individual possessed a *complexion* or *temperament* that reflected a unique blend of qualities and that also differed according to age and sex. The young tended to be hotter and moister than the aged, who were dryer and colder. Men, as a rule, were hot and dry, while women were inclined to be colder and moister. In addition, each part of the body had its own characteristics: the heart was hot and the brain was cold, for example.

The humors played a central role. The human body was held to be a seething mass of fluids rather than an assemblage of discrete organs or cells. Even in the seventeenth century, when ideas of the body as a machine or as a chemical distillery – *iatromechanics* and *iatrochemistry* –

became more popular, the older humoral physiologies and pathologies endured, especially in everyday life. People routinely spoke of humoral relationships and accepted the intimacy of the bond between humors and temperaments. The sixteenth-century clerk Bartholomäi Sastrowen remembered that his father "was rather rash" and "when the *colera* [yellow bile] got the upper hand, he could not control himself." The eighteenth-century cameralist administrator and publicist, Johann Jakob Moser, described his own temperament as one in which "the choleric was strongly in the ascendant," although, in his case, mixed with the sanguine. When Moser surveyed the traits of the choleric personality, he listed, among others, impatience, suspiciousness, quickness to anger, garrulity, glory-seeking, sneakiness: in short, a person possessing both a "subtle understanding" and a tendency toward reckless and quixotic actions.[6]

The humors exhibited their own distinguishing characteristics and a preponderance of one or another helped determine a person's physical and mental make-up. Phlegm was a white, clear humor and individuals with an overbalance of phlegm tended to have dull, phlegmatic temperaments. Yellow (sometimes red) bile was produced in the liver and stored in the gall bladder; an excess resulted in a bilious and quarrelsome nature. Black bile was associated with the spleen and determined the gloomy melancholic personality. In fact, "spleen" was an early modern synonym for melancholy and the phrase to "vent one's spleen" indicated ill temper. Blood ranked as the most critical and elevated of the humors, the "noblest" humor, so to speak. Blood was the vital juice of life, and it also played fundamental, if poorly understood, roles in the utilization of nourishment and in reproduction. Blood, as well, governed the sanguine temperament.

The fluid humoral system underlay ideas of conception and gestation as well. Two classical theories of reproduction – the Aristotelian and the Hippocratic/Galenic – continued to determine how people reasoned about sexuality and reproduction in the early modern world. Aristotle believed that both men and women produced what he called "sperma." In men, sperma was seed and, in women, menstrual blood. Women lacked seed because their quality of "coldness" did not permit them to produce enough warmth to stimulate germination. Moreover, male sperma was active, while female sperma was passive. At conception, the male seed animated menstrual blood to produce life. More influential than the Aristotelian tradition, however, was the Hippocratic/Galenic theory in

---

[6] *Deutsche Selbstzeugnisse*, vol. V, *Aus dem Zeitalter der Reformation und der Gegenreformation* (Leipzig, 1932), 19, and vol. VII, *Pietismus und Rationalismus* (Leipzig, 1933), 227.

which both sexes contributed in equal measure to conception. Now the two sexes became complementary in that both produced seed. This two-seed or *semence* theory lingered through the eighteenth century. The two sexes were anatomically parallel as well in that male organs (such as testes and penis) were external versions of the female reproductive organs (ovaries and vagina) and were so represented in the illustrations of the day. Ovaries were, according to Friedrich Hoffmann, simply "female testes." Men's organs took external forms because the "hotter quality" of their bodies "drove" their organs outward. It is important to note here the purposefulness ascribed to human anatomy and physiology.

Although it is difficult to say exactly how many people accepted either of these two notions in their entirety, one can turn to the most widely published sex manual of the seventeenth and eighteenth centuries – *Aristotle's Masterpiece* – for some clues. The *Masterpiece* (not in fact authored by Aristotle) first appeared in the late seventeenth century and was repeatedly reissued through the eighteenth century in several formats and languages. The *Masterpiece* recognized that "lusts" and the pleasures of copulation existed in both men and women. The work stressed the significance of the clitoris and insisted that female sexual pleasure depended on adequate clitoral stimulation. Also prevalent was the belief that orgasm in the woman was the *sine qua non* of conception: no orgasm, no conception.

What happened after conception – that is, how the fetus developed – was more enigmatic. Two theories competed. One, the *epigenetic*, argued for the sequential development of the embryo: i.e., during growth, the fetus evolved from more primitive to more advanced forms. The other, the *preformationist*, maintained that minute life forms existed in the parent and that all that happened during gestation was that this tiny life grew larger. It is hard and perhaps even impossible to determine what was commonly believed about gestation, however, and this remains an area that scholars have not studied extensively partly because of the difficulties of sources.

Regimen referred to rules for the conduct of everyday life, especially in regard to the six non-naturals. (There were also special regimens for the sick, the elderly, infants, and convalescents.) Moderation in all things characterized early modern advice on regimen, and contemporaries took that advice to heart. The indefatigable civil servant and writer, Moser, observed that, because he avoided making unreasonable demands on either mind or body, neither had ever failed him. A good lifestyle served as the most practical way to maintain and restore health. Following a golden mean was the key. By modifying lifestyle, especially in the realm of diet, a person could hope to preserve health or regain it. People should avoid drafts, exhaustion, too much strong drink, and a sedentary life-style, as well as rich and fatty foods. On a trip from Delft to The Hague in 1641, John Evelyn was told, for example, that lepers "contract their dis-sease from their too much eating of fish."[7] A healthy regimen was predi-cated on observing the rules of nature, for every abuse of nature had to be requited and the sins of gluttony, intemperance, and lasciviousness brought with them bodily pains. Some writers on regimen attributed almost all illness (excluding accidents) to dietary indiscretions, while others joined disease to "hampered evacuations." Among the latter, the appropriate and regular expulsion of feces, sweat, and urine were most essential to health.

Common beliefs on health associated regimen with the idea of the bodily *constitution*. Each person possessed an individualized constitution that was more than the sum of bodily parts, humors, spirits, and habits together. Both popular and lay opinion saw a person's predisposition to certain afflictions and diseases as closely allied to his or her unique physi-cal nature. In Hippocratic and Galenic medicines, and throughout the early modern period, people strongly emphasized the importance of knowing an individual's constitutional idiosyncrasies if health was to be preserved or restored. Accordingly, cures must be highly individualized and snugly fitted to the person in question. Constitutional differences could also, however, explain why some individuals contracted a disease (and even ones generally viewed as highly contagious like plague and smallpox), while others living in close proximity, or even in intimate contact, remained unaffected. Constitutions were commonly character-ized as "strong," "weak," "robust," or "delicate." The frequent notations in parish registers on deaths of children "delicate since birth" (or some similar phrase) indicate how prevalent the concept of constitution was. Constitutions weak at birth were never right and could be blamed for deaths even in late adulthood. Yet even rugged constitutions could be ruined by bad habits, horrible accidents, or even frightening experiences that shattered the mind as they also wrecked the body. The "slings and arrows of outrageous fortune," like the terrors of wars and the insidious effects of years of overwork, imperiled all constitutions, no matter how inherently sound.

What went on inside the body was hard to discern and the ways people referred to bodily processes tended to be metaphoric. Their language of anatomy was always heavily laden with meanings. People thought about organs, to be sure, and especially about the heart, liver, brain, and womb, but more often they spoke of balances and sympathies, weighed the

[7] John Evelyn, *The Diary of John Evelyn*, ed. by William Bray (London, 1973), 16.

relationship of one humor to another, one organ to another, and related the entire human microcosm to the larger macrocosm of the universe.[8]

One way people had of knowing what went on inside the shell of humanity was to read the signs inscribed on the bodily exterior: on the skin, on the limbs, and especially in the face. Complexion, for example, showed on the features: the red or livid color of the sanguine personality or the yellow of the bilious one; likewise the "black looks" of the melancholic and the phlegmatic's "dull eye." According to the Elizabethan gentlewoman and practitioner, Lady Grace Mildmay, defects of countenance, like "foul pimples or warts," betokened "the stopping and inflammation of the liver."[9] Character traits, whether bad or good, also appeared on the face and the physiognomist's skill allowed laypeople and physicians to deduce the body's inner state from the external signs that also revealed a person's hidden intentions. Physicians closely noted characteristics of constitution and complexion, for such things were outward indicators of inner workings. Typical were the observations Dr. William Brownrigg set down in his casebook: for Mr. Carlisle Spedding, "robust and of keen wit and sanguine temperament"; for "the famous artist," Mr. Rhead, "thin and of a melancholic temperament, living a very temperate lifestyle, of a keen wit and utterly wrapped up in his work"; for Mrs. Holmes, "a widow . . . much given to hysterical affections, 45 years old with a spotty complexion, slow, and always suffering from some complaint or other"; and, finally, for Mr. Lamplugh Simpson "of an obese and leucophlegmatic disposition."[10]

Perceptions of physicality are historically determined, and it is difficult, as Barbara Duden observes, for us to transcend our own "medicalized" perceptions (that is, what physicians and the institutions of modern medicine have taught us to believe) and think back into our ancestors' minds and bodies. Duden's close examination of the casebooks that an early eighteenth-century physician, Johann Storch, kept on his female patients offers a fascinating glimpse into how people (and, in particular, women) sensed the workings of their bodies. Both Storch and his female patients accepted that the body was basically "opaque," that is, its interior was inaccessible. They tied "femaleness" to no particular organ, neither to womb nor to breasts. Rather, rhythms and periodicity – menstruation, for instance – defined the female. Patients spoke most frequently of osmotic

---

[8] Roy Porter and Dorothy Porter, *In Sickness and in Health: The British Experience 1650–1850* (Oxford, 1988), 46.
[9] Linda Pollock, *With Faith and Physic: The Life of a Tudor Gentlewoman, Lady Grace Mildmay, 1552–1620* (London, 1993), 125.
[10] *The Medical Casebook of William Brownrigg, M.D., F.R.S. (1712–1800) of the Town of Whitehaven in Cumberland*, ed. and trans. by Jean F. Ward and Joan Yell (London, 1993), 50, 53, 58–59.

and fluid processes, which they felt viscerally. For them the mental and physical permeated each other, and they viewed the body as easy prey to outside influences that could permanently alter it.

Understanding illness and seeking cures

Understanding contemporary views of health and illness allows us to grasp more easily the logic of cures that might at first appear ineffective or even silly. To recover health within the humoral system, it was necessary to regain a lost humoral balance. The reasoning behind taking a "spring cure" – a seasonal purging, sweating, or bloodletting – rested on just this premise. Oppositions such as hot/cold and wet/dry could both explain the occurrence of disease and point to a cure. The logic of sympathy, and sympathetic healing, worked in a similar manner. People sought to expel their diseases by transferring them to other objects. The principle of *transference* taught, for example, that if one rubbed a wart with the cut side of an onion and then buried the onion, the wart would shrivel as the onion rotted. As late as the eighteenth century, stories circulated about peasants who brought sheep into the bedroom of fever patients so as to transfer the fever from the human to the beast. Sympathy worked by both likes and opposites, especially in regard to herbal remedies. For example, yellow herbs – such as saffron, yellow broomseed, and radish – were good for curing jaundice as well as evoking strong diuretic reactions. Likewise, red plants and roots, such as bloodroot, dealt successfully with bloody discharges, much as the "red cure" (wearing red clothes, eating red foods, and drinking red wine) combated smallpox (a red rash). Shapes and textures also indicated proper applications: lungwort worked for all lung ailments; spotted and scaly plants for skin eruptions; and maidenhair for baldness.

For most early modern people – lay and academic alike – the road to health flowed through the bowels, bladder, skin, and veins. The stoppage or unnaturally meager or heavy flow of sweat, urine, stools, and blood (menstruation, hemorrhoidal flows, and nosebleeds) was sure to cause illness and, in severe cases, even death. John Evelyn prevented a recurrence of the piles (hemorrhoids) that had plagued him each spring by ensuring "greater evacuations" than normal. When such habitual evacuations failed and accumulated in the human body, their foulness was thought to attack the internal organs with predictably damaging, or even fatal, results. Accordingly a whole array of serious or mild diseases could emanate from the same "cause." Catarrh was, therefore, not merely the cough and cold we might think it to be, but a far more general condition where the watery and phlegmy humors thickened beyond their normal state and then clogged up the areas where they were usually found: the bowels, lungs, and nose. Such accumulations produced not only sniffles, but "wet coughs" and "slimy diarrheas," and the "whites" (a nonvenereal vaginal discharge). A very different affliction, stroke, resulted from abuses of the non-naturals: too cold, too warm, or too humid air; too sedentary a lifestyle; violent passions; gluttony; or the omission of a customary purging or bloodletting. Even using a strong sulfur salve to treat a skin eruption, like scabies (itself caused by corrupted humors), could "drive it back" into the body where it might work maleficently on the brain. Rheumatism came from an "obstructed perspiration." Even melancholy was caused by something going on not in the brain, but in the abdomen, the stomach, and the spleen.

Such perceptions also conditioned therapies. For William Lees, a blacksmith who suffered from rheumatism and a "pulmonary abscess," Dr. Brownrigg first prescribed a bleeding, getting "thick and inflammed" blood as well as "[a] large amount of whitish serum." He also tried a laxative, had blisters applied to neck and chest, and used poultices of bread, milk, and butter to try to open the hard swellings on Lees's sternum. Nothing worked, however, and after a month's treatment Lees was coughing up "whole pieces of lung mixed with blood." Two days later he died, "asphyxiated by purulent material."[11]

Beginning in the middle of the eighteenth century, a *new Hippocratism*, or what James Riley refers to as *environmentalism*, alloyed itself to these older beliefs, thus strengthening the effect climactic and environmental factors were believed to exert on human health. The new environmentalism did not necessarily downplay the workings of the humors, but maintained that factors of climate and environment, and especially weather patterns, water levels, and the presence or absence of "miasmas," greatly influenced the body, its solid and liquid parts.[12] One eighteenth-century authority argued that external factors, such as weather, could explain numerous afflictions, especially in persons whose constitutions were already predisposed or who were infirm or elderly:

External cold affects such people [strongly], making their pores contract [so much] that the discharge of harmful sera is inhibited. [This matter then] finds its way into the already weakened lungs, where its sharpness irritates them [and causes] a persistent cough and expectorations . . . and also strikes other parts, for example, the stomach, inducing vomiting, or the glandular parts of the head, resulting in a cold, of the bowels, provoking diarrhea.[13]

---

[11] *Medical Casebook of William Brownrigg*, 26–27.

[12] James C. Riley, *The Eighteenth-Century Campaign to Avoid Disease* (New York, 1987), x.

[13] Gottfried Samuel Bäumler, *Mitleidiger Arzt, welcher überhaupt Alles Arme Krancke . . . lehret/wie Sie mit Gemeinen Hauß-Mitteln und anderen nicht allzukostbaren Artzeneyen sich selbst curiren können* (3rd edn., Strasburg, 1743), 54–55.

1.1 Woman giving birth on a birthing stool with a horoscope being cast in the background.

Scholars generally accept that magic and astrology exerted a potent influence on the early modern mind (although one must be cautious not to draw divisions too sharply between "naturalistic" and "superstitious" cures). While much of this story belongs to a later chapter on healers, it is important here to understand how disease was cast in magical and astrological terms. Under magical healing, we understand a form of sympathetic magic that tries to obtain cures for diseases. It is not necessary that the disease itself be magically caused, although magical healing was often employed to combat magical harming. Those believed bewitched were sent to cunning-men or -women to have the curse lifted or "deafened." (For more on practitioners who employed magical means, see chapter 7.)

In astrological medicine, "man is said to be a Microcosm (or little World) and in him the Almighty has imprinted his own Image."[14] Sympathy worked because it accorded with the prevalent belief of that intimate microcosm/macrocosm association. Whereas magic and magical systems were made up of bits and pieces of folklore and customs, astrology in the sixteenth and seventeenth centuries drew on the *neoplatonist* tradition of the Renaissance (which regarded all nature as animate and alive) and on beliefs concerning the movements of the heavenly spheres. Put simply, astrology accepted that the heavenly bodies could and did influence the human body, could and did cause illness. During the sixteenth and seventeenth centuries, astrology was an intellectual pursuit that fascinated many of the best minds of the day and it had become a fad among socially superior groups, especially among princes and courtiers. Like the naturalistic means discussed above, astrological healing involved restoring the harmony between the macrocosm and the microcosm. While diagnosis depended on casting a horoscope, therapies often looked very much like those other practitioners employed: attempts were made to adjust a humoral derangement by purging, sweating, and bleeding.

Unfortunately, much of the evidence we have on magical and superstitious cures comes from hostile witnesses: from those who were interested in one way or another in the extirpation of magic and superstition or in propagandizing to their own advantage. Moreover, especially in the realm of magical practices, one must take special care to recognize change over time and the importance of religious differences. As Michael MacDonald has brilliantly demonstrated in his work on the healer, Richard Napier, faith in astrological and magical cures, with their affinities to religious enthusiasm in seventeenth-century England, lost their appeal because of their associations with religious fanaticism.[15]

Thus, by the eighteenth century, the tendency to resort to magical and astrological cures had probably waned significantly, although such practices often lived on in attenuated forms for much longer. The dog fat executioners rendered and sold, and that sufferers slathered on aching limbs, could continue to be prized while one only dimly remembered its thaumaturgic legacy. Overall, it appears that people in the eighteenth century were less willing than their ancestors to attribute their problems to spells, curses, or the evil eye, or were unwilling to do so publicly. Indeed, if they

---

[14] Quoted in Mary E. Fissell, *Patients, Power, and the Poor in Eighteenth-Century Bristol* (Cambridge, 1991), 22.

[15] Michael MacDonald, *Mystical Bedlam: Madness, Anxiety, and Healing in Seventeenth-Century England* (Cambridge, 1981), 229–31.

continued to consult magicians or cunning-men and -women (who were now much thinner on the ground because of significant changes in village structures and the increasing involvement of central governments in local affairs), they carefully avoided mentioning it. Silence acknowledged that such cures were no longer as familiar or as fashionable as they had once been and surely indicates at least some general diminution in beliefs in their efficacy. Sympathetic cures remained more popular, but the boundaries between the magical and the natural here are exceedingly difficult to discern.

What ailed people

The simple question "what ailed people in the past" is perhaps one of the trickiest the medical historian has to answer. Historians have exploited numerous documents in efforts to gauge rates of *mortality* (death) and *morbidity* (sickness): parish registers, funeral sermons, medical treatises, government compilations, diaries and memoirs, censuses, chronicles, and mortality tables (such as the famous London Bills of Mortality; see illustration 6.1, p. 185). All these furnish much information about health and illness in the past, but all of them present greater or lesser difficulties for the researcher. Parish records, for instance, are often patchy. Moreover, they note burials and baptisms rather than deaths and births. They are even sketchier on morbidity. Diaries and memoirs, while often affording the historian a colorful slice of life, generally relay information only about individuals and families, although journals kept during epidemics – such as that of the Barcelona tanner Miquel Parets – are often more informative, if not necessarily more "accurate." Daniel Defoe's wonderfully evocative, if fictional, account of plague in London, *Journal of the Plague Year*, conveys a picture of unmatched immediacy and vibrancy, but offers no help for those interested in mortality and morbidity rates. Yet Defoe increases significantly our understanding of what seventeenth-century people thought about plague.

Equally grave is the problem of diagnosing diseases in the past. Most medical historians remain very cautious in venturing opinions about what a disease "really" was. The task of *retrodiagnosis* is fraught with perils and often leads to serious (and sometimes laughable) misreadings. A large part of the historical predicament lies in how to interpret contemporary terms for disease. The disease names that early modern people used often seem incomprehensible to us. Even those we think we recognize, for example, dropsy, plague, or smallpox, do not invariably correspond to modern disease entities. Dropsy, for instance, in early modern times was seen as a disease; we would today understand the watery swellings of dropsy as a *symptom*, something like edema, caused, however, by a variety of ailments. The word "plague" as employed in early modern times cannot be facilely equated with bubonic plague; plague was rather a catch-all term for a number of ailments, quite different afflictions (and even nonmedical ones as the phrase "a plague of locusts" illustrates), or generally awful conditions. Under the rubric smallpox often lie concealed cases of measles, rubella, scarlatina, and scarlet fever. And early modern "syphilis" is probably better understood under its contemporary name "the great pox."

The convention of classifying diseases as disease entities, moreover, arose only in the seventeenth century when medical writers began proposing various *nosologies* (classifications of diseases). Because these nosologies depended on conceptions of cause that differed substantially from modern ones, however, we find it almost impossible to determine what early modern people meant by cynanche, dyspnea, phthisis or consumption (which was not necessarily pulmonary tuberculosis), catarrh, costiveness, marasmus, hypochondriasis, lethargy, and melancholy. Even such familiar-sounding ailments as vertigo, dyspepsia, dysentery, jaundice, or asthma were not the same as what we today understand under these names. In dealing with sources in languages other than English, the problems only become more obvious.

Must we then abandon all hope of determining what ailments afflicted people in the past? No, but we must proceed prudently. We can use the language of the times if we keep in mind the historical context and the contemporary diagnostic conventions. For instance, we must remember that the old woman listed as succumbing to jaundice in her parish's register may well have died from something else entirely. If we must be cautious in identifying and interpreting illnesses in the past, that circumspection does not mean that we can venture no analysis of what ailed and what slew our early modern ancestors.

Demographic studies have made it plain that the mortality curve for the early modern period differs significantly from that of modern times. Most striking are the enormous variations in rates of deaths during the first years of life. Today, infant death is considered highly unusual, even tragic, at least in the affluent areas of the world. One expects a tiny number of stillbirths and a very high survival rate from birth to age twenty. Today's children, of course, suffer many childhood diseases, such as measles, chickenpox, colds, and the like, but normally these prove more nuisance than threat. Typically, good health and vigor characterize the middle years of life and both persist well into the fifties and sixties. For women, intervals of childbearing (with an average of two to three births) usually produce only joy as deaths in childbed and from the complications of childbirth (trauma or childbed fever) are rare. Women approach menopause in their late forties and early fifties, and thereafter incidents of degenerative diseases – like heart disease, osteoporosis, arteriosclerosis, cancers, Parkinson's disease, and Alzheimer's – increase. Men, too, in their fifties and sixties begin to suffer the same degenerative diseases that plague women as well as a higher incidence of stroke, heart disease, lung cancer, and the uniquely male complaint of prostatitis. Nonetheless, many people enjoy relatively good health through their seventies, despite an increasing number of pesky chronic ailments – weakening eyesight, glaucoma and cataracts, deafness, poor digestion, arthritis, rheumatism, and memory loss, as well as an overall decline in vigor. Acute illnesses, such as pneumonia, influenza, other viral infections, and food poisoning, may strike at any time, but are usually fatal only to the very young, the elderly, or the frail. Automobile accidents and other forms of violence (in the United States, especially from handguns) claim a significant number of lives, although mostly among certain age groups (adolescents and young adults) and particular classes (the poor). The impact of deaths from infectious diseases of all kinds is generally not great, although AIDS is now the leading cause of death in the United States for people twenty-five to forty-four years old. Most people eventually die of heart disease or other degenerative ailments, such as the various cancers. Expanded life-spans and more years of old age have, of course, created problems of their own, psychological as well as social.

In early modern Europe, structures of mortality and morbidity diverged dramatically from this modern pattern. Infant mortality was high, and sometimes enormous. In general terms, and at least until the middle of the eighteenth century when infant/child mortality rates began to decline, the most dangerous age of life was infancy and early child-hood. One out of every four or five infants failed to survive the first year. Child mortality in the ages one to five also remained very high; about 50 percent of early modern mortality occurred before age ten. While overall infant mortality rates varied between 150 and 250 per 1,000 live births, large geographical and occupational variations were typical. In Geneva, for example, infant mortality for the upper and middle bourgeoisie stood at about 208/1,000 live births, while for the working classes it was 358/1,000. (Mortality statistics for other age cohorts are less reliable.)[16]

Childbirth could be fatal for infant and mother alike. Although many debate the safety or danger of early modern childbirth, they usually rely on few statistics about the incidence of normal or difficult births and the

---

[16] Michael W. Flinn, *The European Demographic System, 1500–1820* (Brighton, 1981), 17–18.

number of serious or fatal complications. In a careful study of midwifery and childbirth in late seventeenth- and eighteenth-century England, however, Adrian Wilson found that about 20 stillbirths occurred per 1,000 live births. Maternal mortality wavered between 1 and 2 percent. These rates were thus lower than many people believe. In fact, most births were normal and the majority of deliveries easy. Major complications – such as hemorrhage and *eclampsia* (convulsions that occur late in pregnancy) – were quite rare, although fatal unless an immediate delivery was effected. The incidence of *puerperal* or *childbed fever* seems to have increased greatly in the nineteenth century when more women began giving birth in hospitals. Once again it is hard to judge the incidence of childbed fever before the nineteenth century, because it was not until late in the eighteenth century that medicine recognized it as a hazard connected with childbirth. Minor complications – trauma, torn perinea, and post-parturient weakness – happened relatively infrequently; most women recovered from them rapidly.[17]

Wilson's study, of course, pertains only to England. It is possible that standards of living may well have been higher there than elsewhere in Europe and thus fewer deaths of either mother or child resulted from obstructed births. (Deformed or abnormally narrow pelvises were the commonest causes of fatally difficult pregnancies.) Still, in investigating mortality in eighteenth-century Belm (in the German territory of Osnabrück), Jürgen Schlumbohm found a maternal mortality of about 1 percent. In France before 1700, maternal mortality likewise hovered around 1 percent. A study of the case books of the Frisian midwife Catharina Schrader reveals that she lost only 14 mothers in 3,017 deliveries.

Not all scholars accept the favorable picture of early modern childbirth presented here. It was once typically argued that childbirth formed an extremely hazardous event in a woman's life, one which many women approached with great fear and trepidation. There can be no doubt that difficult deliveries – especially the abnormal in utero presentations that required the fetus to be "turned" before delivery was possible – could often be fatal to mother and child. The widespread introduction of forceps in the eighteenth century allowed some awkward presentations to be overcome safely and successfully, but, as these problems were themselves rare, such mechanical innovations probably contributed little to improving overall maternal and infant mortality rates.

What frequent childbirth and high infant mortality rates meant for individual lives and families can be easily portrayed. The seventeenth-

[17] Adrian Wilson, *The Making of Man-Midwifery: Childbirth in England, 1660–1770* (Cambridge, Mass., 1995).

Table 1.1 *Infant mortality, pre-1750*

	Number of deaths/1,000 live births
England	187
France	252
Germany	154
Scandinavia	224
Spain	281
Switzerland	283

Source: Michael W. Flinn, *The European Demographic System, 1500–1820* (Brighton, 1981), 16–17.

Table 1.2 *Survival rates, pre-1750*

	Number of survivors/1,000 live births at age			
	1	5	10	15
England	799	668	624	–
France	729	569	516	502
Switzerland	766	597	533	506

Source: As tab. 1.1.

century English couple, Ralph and Jane Josselin, had ten children, of whom five lived to marry (between the ages of about seventeen and thirty) and five died before they could wed. Of the five deaths, two children died in infancy, one at eight years of age, and two as adults of nineteen and twenty-nine. For Germany, Arthur Imhof used a computer-assisted program to construct a fascinating set of family histories that move from the demographic facts to a realization of what patterns of mortality, fertility, and nuptiality meant in real situations. One couple who married in 1680 had seven children of whom three were still alive when the wife was forty-five. But another couple who bore nine children saw none of them live beyond its seventh month. Theirs was hardly ever a family in the demographic sense of parents and children living together.

The years of childhood were not punctuated solely by nuisance ailments, but also by killing ones: smallpox, whooping cough, infantile diarrheas, and tuberculosis. A host of other diseases, like plague and typhus (which were not, of course, unique to infants), added to the mortality of this age cohort. Injuries suffered when young – such as fractures – often crippled children forever and rendered it impossible for them to participate fully in life thereafter. Worm infestations weakened young frames and made them more vulnerable to other illness. Eye infections often blinded children and the accidents of the farmyard, workshop, city street, and castle – falls, wounds, burns – terminated existences or maimed young bodies for life. Poor nutrition produced stunted physiques and twisted limbs, and glandular tuberculosis (known as *scrofula*) disfigured and deformed. Many children died while teething (which contemporaries attributed to the process of teething itself) and scurvy made gums bleed. Rotten teeth had to be extracted, but the incidence of tooth decay was probably less in early modern Europe (at least until the widespread introduction of sugar as a sweetener in the late eighteenth century) than in the nineteenth and twentieth centuries, although gum diseases, often nutritional in origin, were commonplace.

What we might roughly define as environmental factors – diet, housing, and war – played a major role in determining disease incidence. People of all ages suffered from insufficient or improper diets, as well as from the illnesses produced by consuming adulterated or rotten foods. Although diet varied greatly with time and place, a *subsistence crisis* – that is, famine – struck about one year in six almost everywhere in Europe at least until the middle of the eighteenth century. Inadequate amounts of food left people of all ages prey to various *pathogens* (any agent able to cause disease). Still, and although we know that some correlation between dietary deficiencies and causes of morbidity and mortality exists, the exact relationship has not been easy to assess. The poor in early modern Europe tended to consume too little protein and too few vitamins, while the rich might suffer from too much protein (accounting for the heightened incidence of gout among them) and too little fiber. Constipation and looseness (slight diarrhea) caused by eating too little or too much bulk were both common. Paradoxically, some diseases tended to bypass the weak or ill and seek out the strong (e.g., plague), which has something to do, apparently, with various immunological relations and reactions. Lepers, for example, appeared to enjoy a certain immunity to tuberculosis. Although it seems sensible to argue that poorly fed people suffer more disease than the well-nourished, the connection between nutrition and disease is less straightforward than one might expect. Moreover, although famines and epidemics are linked, for example, the relationship is not smoothly linear.

Certainly faulty sanitation facilitated the spread of intestinal ailments caused by bacilli, and poorly ventilated and overcrowded lodgings increased the rate of droplet infections (such as tuberculosis and influenza). Inadequate shelter and exposure to wind, rain, or cold reduced individual resistances and opened the body to more serious infections. Infrequently washed woolen clothing (wool was the commonest fabric until cotton became widely available in the eighteenth century) harbored body vermin that spread disease, as well as producing numerous skin ailments such as scabies, known in English as "the itch."

Dangers lurked everywhere in the environment of home and workplace. The caustic substances used in many trades – dyeing, bleaching, tanning, and etching, to mention only a few – were hazards to health, as were the molten metals of the silver and gold trades, the flames of the smithy, and the sharp knives of butchers. The open hearths and boiling cauldrons found in almost every home and kitchen proved especially dangerous for small children, but adults were hardly immune from scalds and burns. Close proximity to horses and cattle generated its share of broken limbs, contusions, and concussions, although falls from horseback and tumbles from coaches and carts must have been less hazardous than modern automobile smash-ups.

Wars, civil disorders, and revolts may also be viewed as "environmental conditions" having a profound influence on health. The wars and civil uproars of the sixteenth and seventeenth centuries (and, in particular, the Dutch Revolt and the Thirty Years War) tended to be more disruptive and more generalized in their violence than the conflicts of the eighteenth century. There were, of course, pronounced geographic differences. The Thirty Years War (1618–48) ravaged some areas of Germany while leaving others virtually untouched. English civilians, moreover, escaped the death and destruction of the religious wars of the sixteenth century and of the imperial conflicts of the eighteenth, but suffered grievously during the English civil war of the middle of the seventeenth century. Northern Italy was the battlefield of all Europe in the late Renaissance and declined accordingly, but then became less centrally involved at least until the outbreak of the revolutionary struggles of the late eighteenth century. Marauding soldiers destroyed crops and stole livestock. Occupation forces, whether friend or foe, quartered soldiers on the population. Overcrowding and makeshift sanitary facilities encouraged the spread of typhosoid fevers, dysentery, body vermin, and syphilis, to say nothing of the violence often done the populace in the form of rape and brawls. Every government – local or central – knew that troop movements meant a higher incidence of disease and necessitated more concern for public health. Epidemic diseases and food shortages due to war, however, always killed more combatants and civilians than did force of arms.

Things we today consider minor ailments – bladder infections, skin eruptions, and dental problems – were infirmities that became chronic for early modern people: kidney stones bothered Samuel Pepys, bad teeth tortured Queen Elizabeth I, and gout crippled Samuel Johnson, to name just a few famous patients. While it is commonly argued that early modern people lived lives of intermittent pain and thus tended to be more inured to it than we moderns are, we should accept these assertions carefully. Although early modern people were not healthier than we are today (the evidence to the contrary is overwhelming), one might consider that those who survived the perils of infancy and childhood were pretty hardy specimens whose immunological systems coped well with subsequent attacks of disease and infection. Furthermore, no good reason exists to assume that our ancestors stoically or fatalistically (depending on one's point of view) resigned themselves to lives of pain and suffering. They obviously recognized that the angel of death hovered about at all times, but they seldom nonchalantly accepted either pain or illness. Rather they did all they could – and that was considerable – to alleviate pain and banish their illnesses. Bodily ills were, for most people, evils to be vigorously combated and not preordained visitations to which one meekly submitted. Still, one must also take into account temporal and other displacements. A religious acceptance of pain or deformity as a mark of God's grace occurred more commonly in the sixteenth and seventeenth centuries than in the eighteenth, but individuals varied in their outlook as well. Not all sixteenth-century sufferers folded their hands and bowed to God's will gracefully, while some persons in the eighteenth century were necessarians who deemed attempts to combat illness and to use medicine, or to submit themselves or members of their families to inoculation and vaccination (both methods were introduced in the eighteenth century), as blasphemy and hubris. It is the shift in the proportions that is important. By the eighteenth century the acceptance of Providence or fate as an explanation for disease was receding in all groups, as God slowly became both a more distant and a more benevolent figure for most people.

Mental illness

We know less about the incidence of mental illness in the past than that of other afflictions. Mental illness is notoriously hard to define. Clearly behaviors that the contemporary western world describes as "mad" or "insane" were not always deemed such nor do all cultures judge them so today. Trance states that we see as symptomatic of mental distress or malfunction were, for example, common elements of religious expression in medieval and early modern Europe, as they remain in many parts of the contemporary world. In early modern Russia, for instance, the mad often fell into an undifferentiated group of "unfortunates" but could also be viewed as "blessed ones."[18]

Particularly since the provocative works of Michel Foucault began to appear in the 1960s, many historians have tended to speak about the "manufacture," or even the "myth," of mental illness. In its most extreme form, this line of argumentation insists that mental illness does not in truth exist (as does a somatic illness like leprosy or tuberculosis) and that definitions of madness and insanity developed historically as a form of social control: i.e., as another way to inculcate proper behaviors by defining more and more actions, once considered acceptable or merely odd, as radically unacceptable or "mad." Erik Midelfort, in his study of the *Mad Princes of Renaissance Germany*, observes that until well into the sixteenth century many behaviors fit easily within the range of the allowable and "one could be strange, eccentric, irresponsible, dangerous, willful, or just plain nutty without being judged crazy."[19] But this relative acceptance of difference would not prevail.

Foucault argued that, beginning in the middle of the seventeenth century, Europeans began the "great confinement": the wholesale incarceration of all those society defined as "deviant" – criminals, the poor, and the insane. It was particularly the wish to rehabilitate the prodigal and make the poor industrious that drove the great confinement. One of the "faults" the mad shared with the poor was their apparent refusal to work. In various institutions – the prison, the almshouse, and the insane asylum – the "mad, the bad, and the sad" could be better controlled and disciplined. Here, within four stout walls, desirable behaviors – and especially a bourgeois work ethic – could be implanted by force. Later, when freed from their chains (symbolically and theatrically by Philippe Pinel in Paris in the 1790s), the insane remained "moral prisoners" as the softer bonds of close supervision, moral suasion, guilt, and conscience replaced clanking irons.

According to these critics of psychiatry, the age of reason was thus a turning point in the treatment of the insane in Europe, and a disaster for them: stigmatized and shunned, they were ostracized, enclosed within asylums and madhouses, and, in Foucault's words, effectively "silenced." Whereas madmen and -women once roamed free, and were chained only if violent, and whereas the mad were previously seen as "voyagers both in reality and in imagination, fools whose hermetic wisdom signified to the sane the animality of the human and the humanity of vice,"[20] the mad were now banished and ridiculed. Whereas once the mad were often seen

---

[18] Kenneth S. Dix, "Madness in Russia, 1775–1864: Official Attitudes and Institutions for Its Care," Ph.D. diss. (UCLA, 1977), 8.

[19] H. C. Erik Midelfort, *Mad Princes of Renaissance Germany* (Charlottesville, 1994), 20.

[20] MacDonald, *Mystical Bedlam*, xi.

as sages who spoke hard truths (such as the fool in Shakespeare's *King Lear*), they were now transformed into the pathetic objects of a Sunday's entertainment at Bedlam (Bethlem Hospital in London).

The great strength of the Foucauldian interpretation is that it highlights the importance of historical context and historical change in the shaping of concepts of disease. Since Foucault, few doubt that definitions of madness and sanity are culturally and historically determined. Critics of the Foucauldian position, however, have pointed out its flaws. First, Foucault and his disciples insist that authorities – governmental and medical – defined madness and then foisted it on a populace that previously had no conception of madness and no fear of the mad. Second, they tend to deny that the mad themselves felt any pain or anxiety about their condition. In short, the mad did not know their affliction. Over the past twenty years, numerous studies suggest that neither of these premises is entirely valid. Ordinary people indeed possessed a conception of madness. As Michael MacDonald shows, English villagers of the seventeenth century feared the mad for what they could do. Onlookers deemed mad those who tore their clothing, disobeyed their natural masters (whether parents, employers, or social superiors), or wandered around unclothed. Similarly, *Mystical Bedlam*, MacDonald's examination of the casebooks of the Anglican divine and astrological physician, Richard Napier, clearly demonstrates that a goodly number of those who consulted him did so for mental problems that deeply disturbed them, their relatives, their friends, and their neighbors. While there is no denying that the confines of mad behavior have changed over time (and that the ways in which the definitions of madness evolved can tell us much about the values of a society), there seems little reason to embrace the view that the early modern world was somehow a heaven for the insane. They were defined as ill, sometimes shut away, sometimes beaten, sometimes treated, but their peculiarity was not unremarked and ignored. Finally, the timing of the great confinement seems all wrong; far more people were confined after 1800 than before.

How, then, did people know the mad and interpret the underlying causes of their affliction? People identified madness by the way the mad behaved. Madness could be read in the face, in rolling, unfocused eyes, twisted features, vacant stares, but also on the body more generally. Jerks and twitches, an impaired or unusual gait, strange motions of the body, or obsessive ones, such as a frantic and ceaseless wringing or washing of hands, could all mark the disturbed in mind. Doing bodily harm to one's self or others, threatening members of one's family (and especially one's own children), flouting authority, going naked or rending one's clothes, and the like were clear signs that all was not right. Sitting idle, sighing, showing no interest in one's surroundings were also indicators of a troubled mind. The seventeenth-century Dutch *burgemeester*, Koenraed Beuningen, first manifested his illness by offering a valuable set of porcelain to casual acquaintances at tea.

Almost everyone agreed that madness was fickle in its objects and protean in its manifestations. Popular and academic names for addled wits abounded and many terms described a vast array of mental disorders. One might speak, colloquially, of the mad, the lunatic, the distracted, the troubled in mind, the giddy, and the anxious, or, more learnedly, of those suffering from animi infirmitas, eroticos, petrified malice, and furor uterinus. Symptoms were equally prolix and ranged from childishness, confusion, and mopishness, to irrationality, wild behavior, hallucinations, and suicide. Academic practitioners and the laity alike took all these things, and many more besides, as evidence of mental distress.

For early modern people, the causes of madness were manifold: a crack on the head, a fever, a long illness, religious enthusiasm, disappointment in love, and childbirth. All emotional excesses, such as jealousy, hatred, and anger, could scramble the wits. And because the roots of madness were so multifarious and could be physical, intellectual, moral, or religious, mad-doctors came from many walks of life. Physicians enjoyed no monopoly over the right to diagnose and treat insanity or to care for the mad. Ministers, priests, divines, surgeons, family members, and all sorts of other people who did not necessarily have medical training were as likely to handle the mad as the university-trained physician. In the 1620s, the Dutch Calvinist minister, Henricus Alutarius, practiced corporal and moral "physick" in treating the mad and the melancholic. Moreover, and especially at the beginning of this period, madness was not always perceived as a curse; it could be as well a sign of special insight or a mark of Providence's favor. The fifteenth-century mystic, Margery Kempe, periodically saw visions and had hallucinations with religious overtones and even "rived the skin on her body against her heart with her nails spitefully" without being adjudged mad.[21]

In the sixteenth and seventeenth centuries (but not so often in the eighteenth), people accepted that a spirit or Satan himself could possess a person and drive him or her mad. Likewise the *maleficium* or harm a witch could do might cause loss of reason. Divine madness and religious melancholy were also acknowledged causes of troubled minds, and fears of a

---

[21] Willem Frijhoff, *Wegen van Evert Willemsz.: een Hollands weeskind op zoek naar zichzelf 1607–1647* (Nijmegen, 1995), 210; *The Book of Margery Kempe* (1436), quoted in Dale Peterson, ed., *A Mad People's History of Madness* (Pittsburgh, 1982), 9.

salvation lost or threatened, or a sin unshriven, could provoke a break-down. George Trosse described the religious fears that drove him mad:

> From this Perswasion, that I had been guilty of the Sin against the Holy-Ghost, I was fill'd with grievous Horrour and Anguish, with great Anxiety and sinking Despair; . . .
> I strongly fancy'd that GOD watch'd opportunities to destroy me; but I also pre-sum'd that GOD must get in by the Door, or he would not be able to come at me; and I foolishly conceited, that if I did but tie the Door with a particular sort of a Knot, He would be effectually shut out; which I attempted to do, that I might be secur'd from his Wrath.[22]

Throughout the early modern period there was a strong tendency to link afflictions of mind with bodily disturbances, such as a perturbed humoral balance or indigestion. The body moved mind as easily as the mind affected the body. Lady Mildmay felt that frenzy and madness to be "near of kin" and "proceed of the inflammation of the phlegms of the brain." The Württemberg pastor, Philipp Matthäus Hahn, linked a episode of melancholy to flatulence.[23]

Furious madness and madness connected with acts that seemed dangerous or criminal (suicide was a special case) led contemporaries to fetter or lock sufferers away to prevent them harming themselves or others. Society often decided that lunatics and the raving were too unpredictable and violent to be allowed to roam, although those who exhibited milder symptoms – melancholy, mopishness, light-headed-ness, anxiety, anguish, distraction, or despair – were far less likely to be incarcerated.

Melancholy is the form of madness with the most venerable pedigree. Today's definitions of melancholy – sadness or depression of the spirits, gloom, pensive reflection, or contemplation – by no means catch the wide array of characteristics subsumed under that label in early modern times. The term relates to black bile; melancholics were thought to suffer from an excess of that humor. Melancholy was notably changeable and could be characterized by a variety of attitudes and behaviors. The most famous work on melancholy, Robert Burton's *Anatomy of Melancholy* published in 1621, displays on the title page of the fourth edition the many visages of the affliction: "Jealousye," "Solitarinesse," "Inamorato," "Hypochondriacus," "Superstitious," and "Maniacus." Near the end of the sixteenth century, Philip Barrough wrote "Of Melancholie":

---

[22] Quoted in Richard Hunter and Ida Macalpine, *Three Hundred Years of Psychiatry, 1535–1860: A History Presented in Selected English Texts* (Hartsdale, N.Y., 1982), 155.

[23] Sabine Sander, "'. . . Gantz toll im Kopf und voller Blähungen . . .': Körper, Gesundheit und Krankheit in den Tagebüchern Philipp Matthäus Hahns," in *Philipp Matthäus Hahn 1739–1790: Aufsatzband* (Stuttgart, 1989), 104.

Melancholie is an alienation of the mind troubling reason, and waxing foolish, so that one is almost beside him self . . . The most common signes be fearfulness, sadnes, hatred, and also they that be melancholious, have straunge imaginations, for some think them selves brute beastes, & do counterfaite the voice and noise, some think themselves vessels of earth, or earthen pottes, therfore they withdrawe themselves from them that they meet, lest they should knocke together [and break]. Moreover they desire death, and do verie often behight and determine to kill them selves, and some feare that they should be killed. Many of them do alwayes laugh, and many do weep, some think them selves inspired with the holie Ghost, and do prophecy uppon thinges to come.[24]

Madness also wore a social face and bore political implications. Melancholy, already fashionable in Elizabethan England, became especially modish as a disease of courtiers after the appearance of Burton's work. Where nobles, princesses, and intellectuals sighed in melancholy's somber throes, their more common kinsmen and women were labeled "mopish" or distracted or giddy. And when rulers went mad, kingdoms trembled. Not that madness was probably any more frequent in royal, imperial, and noble families than elsewhere, but it was more remarked and became a matter of state. The daughter of Ferdinand of Aragon and Isabella of Castile and the mother of the emperor Charles V, Doña Juana, was quite mad and spent most of her life sequestered under lock and key; the behavior of the Holy Roman Emperor Rudolf II – he hallucinated, had paranoid delusions and suffered bouts of melancholy – led to the fear that he, too, had taken leave of his senses; and George III of England was beset with periodic bouts of madness (generally accepted as being caused by porphyria, a genetically transmitted metabolic disease) that led to a constitutional emergency and the eventual establishment of a regency in 1810. The dynastic crises and power vacuums that could result from the lunacy of rulers meant that the mad business could disrupt, or even immobilize, courts and governments.

In modern society, it appears that more women than men suffer from mental illness or at least women seek help more frequently. This overabundance of women seems to be true for the European past as well. Observers have often interpreted the disproportion as a result of the inferior status of women in almost all cultures and this subordination, of course, also pertained in the early modern period. Still, we know less about the madness of women than men because fewer writings – medical, biographical, or autobiographical – deal with them. Most autobiographical

[24] Philip Barrough, *The methode of physicke, conteyning the causes, signes, and cures of inward diseases in mans body from the head to the foote* (London, 1583), quoted in Hunter and Macalpine, *Three Hundred Years*, 27–28.

accounts of madness come from the pens of men (reflecting, of course, their greater literacy as well as their better access to the world of learning and publishing). And this is as true for queens as for scullery maids. Yet early modern peoples generally felt that women and men fell prey to the very same types of mental infirmities. As Erik Midelfort found for the Renaissance, the "medical language of melancholy and madness was not yet highly gendered, and except for hysteria . . . physicians expected to find roughly the same maladies among men and women."[25]

Nonetheless, the incidence of mental troubles (or at least those who sought assistance for their mental afflictions) among women in early modern times, working from the sparse evidence we have, seems to be greater than among men. The casebooks of Richard Napier, for example, listed substantially more women than men among his mentally distressed clients. Physical infirmities – menstrual difficulties, gynecological disorders, traumatic childbirth, and infertility – could also ravage the mind. The disasters of normal life – miscarriages, the death of children or close relatives, infertility, pressures to receive undesired suitors (or being forbidden to marry a preferred lover), or marital infidelities (the woman's or that of her husband) – all sent women (and men, too, although in smaller numbers) to Napier.

Certainly, many felt that women were more predisposed to such disturbances than men (although there was also a countercurrent which argued that women's periodic "cleansings" – their menstrual cycles – made them healthier, both mentally and physically, than men). At the beginning of the seventeenth century, Edward Jordan observed that "the passive condition of womankind is subject unto more diseases and of other sortes and natures than men are" and he especially identified the womb and its afflictions – such as the "suffocation of the mother" or hysteria – as principally responsible.[26]

Occasionally historians have argued that women indicted as witches, or those who felt themselves bewitched, were in fact mentally ill. Some early modern writers agreed. The French skeptic philosopher, Pierre Bayle, felt that "an imagination that is alarmed by the fear of a witch's spell can overthrow the animal constitutions, and produce . . . extravagant symptoms." He also thought it "very possible for a woman to persuade herself that someone has put the Devil into her body," causing her to believe herself possessed and act so as well by screaming and convulsing, for example.[27]

---

[25] Midelfort, *Mad Princes*, 17.

[26] Edward Jordan, *A Brief Discourse of a Disease Called the Suffocation of the Mother* (London, 1603), quoted in Hunter and Macalpine, *Three Hundred Years*, 71.

[27] Pierre Bayle, "Superstition and Imagination" (1703), in Alan C. Kors and Edward Peters, eds., *Witchcraft in Europe, 1100–1700: A Documentary History* (Philadelphia, 1972), 361.

Certainly the attempt to historicize disease must be applauded, but one wonders whether these are quite the correct conclusions. It may be more than just a little simplistic to apply modern, "scientific" explanations to cultural phenomena of great complexity, like witchcraft persecutions. Likewise, other instances or manifestations of "insanity" in women in early modern Europe must be dissected with equal caution. There is, no doubt, a temptation to believe that women who fled marriage and then suffered hallucinations and sexual fantasies – such as Margery Kempe – were sexually repressed. In a close examination of many of the female saints of the late medieval and early modern period, Rudolph Bell concluded that such women were in truth anorectic and were anorectic for many of the same reasons that twentieth-century pubescent women are: sexual frustrations or confusions. However, as Caroline Bynum has demonstrated for the retrodiagnosis of *anorexia nervosa*, this labeling often proves quite inappropriate. The reasons for such seemingly pathological behaviors were deeply religious and neither sexual nor medical. By the late seventeenth century, authors described severe inanition in terms coupling mind and body. Richard Morton felt that the "immediate cause of this Distemper . . . to be in the System of the Nerves proceeding from a Preternatural state of the Animal Spirits, and the destruction of the Tone of the Nerves," and he, like others, noted its greater frequency among women.[28] Since then anorexia nervosa has been variously diagnosed and explanations have ranged from the physical to the psychosocial to the cultural.

About the mental illness of children, we know next to nothing. Napier treated very few children under the age of twenty; even fewer younger than ten. Families in early modern Europe (at least until about the eighteenth century and the rise of what Lawrence Stone has called the "affectionate family") did not revolve around children. Moreover, common beliefs about children regarded them as little more than animals, if often happy ones, basically not yet capable of reasoning. Thus, there was little heed paid to their mental health or distress. Children who did not walk or talk at the appropriate age might be considered "slow," or, worse, idiots, but one rarely sought assistance of any kind for them. Children who exhibited more aberrant or bizarre behaviors might be diagnosed as bewitched or possessed and perhaps be exorcised.

Old age, on the other hand, was generally believed especially prone to melancholy (Burton viewed old age as one of the most frequent causes of melancholy), as well as of forgetfulness and childishness. But again, how

---

[28] Richard Morton, *Phthisiologia; or, a Treatise of Consumptions* (London, 1694), quoted in Hunter and Macalpine, *Three Hundred Years*, 231.

much of this behavior was attributed to mental disorder and not simply considered part of the final stage of life is in truth very difficult to ascertain. Unquestionably, contemporaries joined the physical infirmities of age to crabbiness and misanthropy, as the old man or woman contemplated death, family woes, and declining powers. Such grumpiness was not necessarily thought tantamount to mental illness. Here, too, there was little hope or need of treatment. Death would make a natural end of the problem.

In sum, it is clear that early modern peoples perceived sickness and health, understood the workings of their bodies, and anticipated their mortality in ways that diverged meaningfully from our own. And yet if these people differ from us, they were not unconcerned with health nor were they stoically inured to pain and suffering. If they fought disease and afflictions differently than we do today, they fought them no less fiercely, as the following chapters will show.

2   Epidemics and infectious diseases

In the same year [1348] there were immense upheavals in many parts of the world, as the result of a cruel pestilence which first broke out in countries across the sea and killed everyone in various horrifying ways. First, through the malignant influence of the planets and the corruption of the air, men and animals in those countries were struck motionless while going about their business, as if turned to stone. Then, in the countries where ginger comes from, a deadly rain fell, mixed with serpents and all sorts of pestilential works, and instantly killed everyone it touched. Not far from that country dreadful fire descended from heaven and consumed everything in its path . . . The smoke which arose was so contagious that merchants watching from a long way off were immediately infected and several died on the spot. Those who escaped carried the pestilence with them, and infected all the places to which they brought their merchandise . . . and the neighboring regions through which they traveled.[1]

[Smallpox] extended over all parts of their bodies. Over the forehead, head, chest . . . Many died of it. They could no longer walk, they could do no more than lie down, stretched out on their beds. They couldn't bestir their bodies, neither to lie face down, nor on their backs, nor to turn from one side to the other. And when they did move, they cried out. In death, many [bodies] were like sticky, compacted, hard grain . . . many [of the survivors] were pockmarked . . . some were blind . . . this pestilence lasted sixty days, sixty lamentable days.

(Fray Toribio Montolinia, 1541)[2]

In recent times I have seen scourges, horrible sicknesses, and many infirmities afflict mankind from all corners of the earth. Amongst them has crept in, from the western shores of Gaul, a disease [syphilis] which is so cruel, so distressing, so appalling that until now nothing so horrifying, nothing more terrible or disgusting, has ever been known on this earth.

(Joseph Grünpeck, 1503)[3]

---

[1] From "Continuatio Novimontensis," quoted in *The Black Death*, ed. by Rosemary Horrox (Manchester, 1994), 55.

[2] Fray Toribio Montolinia, *History of the Indians of New Spain* (1541), quoted in Donald R. Hopkins, *Princes and Peasants: Smallpox in History* (Chicago, 1983), 206.

[3] *Libellus Josephi Grunpeckii de mentalagra, alias morbo gallico* (1503), quoted in Claude Quétel, *History of Syphilis*, trans. by Judith Braddock and Brian Pike (Baltimore, 1990), 17.

As a science, epidemiology – the branch of medicine that investigates the causes and control of epidemics – is only about 150 years old, but the human experience of epidemics is ancient. Yet, explaining what an epidemic is proves less easy than one might imagine, although the following definition is a good place to start: "An epidemic in the popular sense of the word is merely a prevalence of a particular type of infection which appears to be highly concentrated in time and space."[4] Whatever the definition, epidemics and diseases have long histories.

A short natural history of disease

Paleolithic humans were hunters and gatherers who lived in small groups of fewer than one hundred. The mobility and the very low density of population in Paleolithic times (c. 2,000,000 B.C. to c. 10,000 B.C.) prevented much exposure to infectious diseases, or at least to those diseases which no other animals carried. The earliest humans enjoyed relative security from epidemics, therefore, and to a large extent were also spared infectious diseases and parasitic infestations. All this changed with the first, or Neolithic, agricultural revolution (c. 8,000 B.C. to c. 3,500 B.C.).

Quite simply, the settling down of populations and, in particular, the introduction of irrigated agriculture created the preconditions for the rise of infectious diseases. Such diseases require a pool of susceptible victims that only a population of sufficient density can generate. With the domestication of plants, and especially animals, some animal diseases or *zoonoses* passed to humans. For example, it is now thought that measles originally came from dogs, syphilis from monkeys, and leprosy from water buffaloes. Thus the growing density of population that agriculture demanded also nurtured the poorer hygienic conditions that accompanied population aggregations, and the close proximity to domesticated animals made the rapid spread of infectious diseases possible. From that point, and until well into the twentieth century, infectious diseases produced most human mortality.

Before considering the subject for early modern Europe, it is useful to review briefly the biology and ecology of infectious diseases in order to realize how multifarious disease-causing mechanisms are. While *macroparasites* like worms can bring about illness, *microparasites* – that is, either bacteria, protozoa, or viruses – cause most human diseases and these diseases are then propagated in several ways: through the air, by water or food, and through nonhuman vectors, such as mosquitoes, ticks, fleas, and lice (the *arboviruses*, or those spread by arthropods). For the early modern period, the most important infectious diseases were plague

---

[4] Macfarlane Burnet and David O. White, *Natural History of Infectious Disease* (4th edn., Cambridge, 1982), 127.

(caused by a bacillus; bacilli are rod-shaped bacteria); dysentery (bacillus); influenza (virus); smallpox (virus); measles (virus); tuberculosis (bacillus); typhus (bacterium); syphilis (bacterium); and malaria (protozoan parasites). Genetic predispositions and nutritional factors, of course, influence individual susceptibility. There seems to be a correlation between famine or malnutrition and disease, although it is not a simple one. A *Malthusian theory* postulating that pronounced and rapid population increases intensified the effects of crop failures in the early fourteenth century (when the weather was unusually cold) and accounted, in some part at least, for the virulence of plague has been shown to be not very satisfactory. In other words, while famines sometimes precede epidemics, they by no means inevitably do so, and there is no direct causal connection because the disease cannot develop in the absence of the responsible microorganism. Malnutrition indeed reduces resistance to disease or at least to some diseases. However, well-nourished people, who have a fairly high standard of living, do not enjoy complete protection from infections; especially in the case of airborne viral diseases, such as smallpox, they are susceptible (as long, of course, as they have not had a previous case of smallpox or have not been inoculated). Moreover, because the plague bacillus requires a certain level of iron to multiply in the human body, people with anemia are poor hosts.

During early modern times, four diseases assumed particular weight: plague, smallpox (and measles), influenza, and tuberculosis. Leprosy, an affliction of great consequence during the twelfth and thirteenth centuries, was already disappearing by the middle of the fourteenth century, although it remained a problem in some isolated spots, such as Iceland, until much later.

Plague

The mortality in Siena began in May . . . it is impossible for the human tongue to recount the awful truth. Indeed, one who did not see such horribleness can be called blessed. And the victims died almost immediately. They would swell beneath the armpits and in their groins, and fall over while talking. Father abandoned child, wife husband, one brother another; for this illness seemed to strike through breath and sight. And so they died. And none could be found to bury the dead for money or friendship. Members of a household brought their dead to a ditch as best they could, without priest, without divine offices. Nor did the death bell sound. And in many places in Siena great pits were dug and piled deep with the multitude of dead. And they died by the hundreds, both day and night, and all were thrown in those ditches and covered with earth. And as soon as those ditches were filled, more were dug . . . And so many died that all believed it was the end of the world.[5]

---

[5] Chronicle of Agnolo di Tura, quoted in *The Black Death*, ed. by William Bowsky (New York, 1971), 13–14.

So did Agnolo di Tura, citizen of Siena, describe a disease that first despoiled Europe in the middle of the fourteenth century and which then frequently reappeared, with greater or lesser killing force, until it rather mysteriously vanished from the European continent almost 400 years later. The last major epidemic in western Europe stormed through Marseilles in 1721, although Moscow was severely struck as late as 1770–72. Most historians now accept that this disease was probably a mixture of *bubonic* and *pneumonic* plagues. (A third form of plague, known as *septicemic* and which is exceptionally virulent, invariably fatal, and frighteningly rapid in its progress, appears not to have been of great importance in early modern times.) The most popular name for the epidemic of 1348–50 is the Black Death, although this is a modern name that was not current at the time; people then generally spoke of pestilence. Not until the epidemic of 1893–94 in China did researchers discover the bacillus, *Yersina pestis* (sometimes known by the older name, *Pasturella pestis*) responsible for plague, while subsequent work uncovered the mode of transmission. Basically, the story is one of an *epizootic* (an epidemic of animal populations): in this case a disease of the European black rat (*Rattus rattus*) transferred to humans by the bite of the rat flea (*Xenopsylla cheopis*). When the flea's preferred host (the rat) dies, the flea seeks a new home, often biting a human and transmitting the disease to him or her. For the disease to become epidemic, a suitable environment must exist to support this transferal mechanism. Fleas, rats, and humans must live in close proximity and the populations of each must be dense enough to sustain the epidemic.

Once infected, a person develops alarming symptoms within about six days. A very high temperature of 103 to 104 °F (39.5 to 40 °C) soon follows initial feelings of discomfort, nausea, and pains in the limbs and lower back. *Buboes*, or swellings in the lymph nodes, often appear in groin or armpit, and are extremely painful. Individual *case mortality* (that is, the chance an infected individual has of dying from the disease without treatment) is about 60 percent. A more severe form of plague evolves when plague bacilli settle in the lungs and then are expelled with every cough. Plague spread by this sort of droplet infection is called pneumonic plague and it is virtually always lethal.

Even without being able to say exactly if early modern plague was bubonic (or pneumonic) plague or not, one can unhesitatingly discuss the impact this disease had on early modern society and the reactions of early modern people to a event which, in the great plague of 1348–50, wiped out anywhere from 30 to 50 percent of the European population. Urban mortality rates varied, reaching about 40 percent in large cities and in some smaller cities, such as Siena, as high as 60 percent.

Table 2.1 *Plague mortality in some Italian cities*

	City	Pre-plague population	Deaths	Deaths/ % population
1576–77	Venice	180,000	50,000	28
1630–31	Bologna	62,000	15,000	24
	Cremona	37,000	17,000	46
	Florence	76,000	9,000	12
	Milan	130,000	60,000	46
	Padua	32,000	19,000	59
	Pistoia	8,000	1,200	15
	Venice	140,000	46,000	33
	Verona	54,000	33,000	61
1656–57	Genoa	75,000	45,000	60
	Naples	300,000	150,000	50
	Rome	123,000	23,000	19

Source: Carlo Cipolla, *Fighting the Plague in Seventeenth-Century Italy* (Madison, Wisc., 1976), 64.

The fourteenth-century *pandemic* (an epidemic spread over a wide geographical area) of plague began in China and moved along the trade routes to Tashkent, Astrakhan, and cities in southern Russia. By 1346, it had reached the Crimean peninsula and spread to Genoese merchants in Caffa then under siege by the Mongol army. The fleeing merchants (or rather the rats that accompanied them) conveyed the plague throughout the Mediterranean littoral, to the islands of Sicily, Sardinia, and Corsica, to Spain, to Italy, and to north Africa. Plague then edged its way up the Rhône River into France, through Italy to central Europe, and into southern Germany. By 1348, France, Sweden, the south of England, Germany, Switzerland, and Poland had all been affected. By 1351 plague had reached northern Russia. Plague's initial attack was curiously uneven; some areas, such as Italy, suffered cruelly, while other parts of Europe, especially the Low Countries and Bohemia, escaped virtually unscathed. Thereafter, plague recurred in almost every generation from 1350 to 1720. Later plagues, however, were more scattered and, while they could be quite disruptive and lethal, such as in Florence and Pisa in 1631, in Barcelona in 1651, and in London in 1665, these flare-ups seem to have involved other diseases as well as forms of plague. For instance, in the United Provinces from 1450 through 1668 (a period of 219 years), plague appeared in one or more places in 107 years. The longest reprieve lasted from 1539 to 1550. Major epidemics in several places at once occurred in 1557–58, 1573–74, 1595–1605,

1624–25, 1635–37, 1652–57, and, finally, 1664–67, whereafter plague disappeared from the Low Countries. In addition, after 1557–58, and especially after 1599, plague tended to affect larger areas with each subsequent incursion.[6]

Historians have made a veritable industry out of plague – both the Black Death and subsequent recurrences. For generations, scholars rated plague, along with the Renaissance, the Reformation, the Thirty Years War, and the Enlightenment, as a major factor in the subsequent development of Europe. In the past fifteen to twenty years, however, skepticism has grown as to whether the Black Death truly represented a "turning point" in European history. While it seems counterintuitive to argue that an epidemic that caused so much death might not be as disruptive as once asserted, the progressive dismantling of the "plague-as-crisis" theory has produced a considerable body of new scholarship that downplays the global dimensions of plague's effect, while stressing the unique social and cultural implications of plague on specific places and groups. The assessment of plague's impact is neither easy nor self-evident. Many of the things we thought we knew about plague, products of a consensus that developed in the 1940s and 1950s, have shown themselves to be less convincing under more rigorous questioning and under the impact of recent biological knowledge about the workings of the pathogen involved.

The modern medical and biological evidence on plague, concerning cause and transmission, for instance, has proven very difficult to integrate smoothly with the historical record. Almost every point in the simple, rather elegantly constructed story of rats and fleas related above has come under fire. Historians and epidemiologists have raised doubts about the suitability of various vectors to spread the disease in the manner described, about the requisite density of fleas and rodents, and indeed about whether the disease we today "diagnose" as bubonic/pneumonic plague was the "plague" of the fourteenth and subsequent centuries. These problems have no easy answers and raise crucial issues about how we deal with diseases in the past. As we have seen, medical historians are wary of retrodiagnosis. Moreover, some have come to question whether the epidemics of early modern times that we have facilely labeled "plague" were bubonic plague, pointing out that many of the facts do not seem to correspond well to the modern manifestations of the disease. Critics have argued that perhaps another disease entirely was responsible (one scholar has, for example, suggested anthrax), while others wonder if

[6] L. Noordegraaf and G. Valk, *De gave gods: de pest in Holland vanaf de late Middeleeuwen* (Bergen, 1988), 225–28.

perhaps the "plague" did not combine several diseases, including small-pox, typhus, and dysentery.

Epidemic diseases in the past often elude identification. A classic example here is the sweating sickness or English sweat (*sudor anglicus*). Victims showed sudden high fevers accompanied by profuse sweating, falling into comas and dying within one to two days. The first outbreak probably befell London in 1485 or 1486, and the disease reappeared several times in the first half of the sixteenth century. It has never been identified; it was almost certainly not influenza. It may have been a totally new and lethal virus that struck and then disappeared, perhaps because it killed so effectively and thus rapidly depleted the pool of sus-ceptibles.

We are also now much less sure about the economic consequences of plague than we once were. Did real wages climb in response to a shortage of workers? Did areas recover quickly or only belatedly from the Black Death? Did plague contribute to the rise or decline of serfdom? None of these questions has received a fully satisfactory answer, and historians have found it extremely difficult to disentangle the effects of plague from other factors that made the 1300s so "disastrous." We must remember that the century was a period of endemic warfare, famine, and declining population even before the plague hit. Moreover, aggregate economic and population data are simply too crude to allow us to draw sustainable con-clusions except for very specific areas, occupational groups, or isolated religious communities.

In short, although there is no reason to deny that the plague was a great blow for Europeans, it is no longer obvious exactly how to measure and appraise its effect. Still, there are some points upon which most historians agree. One of these involves the relationship of the Black Death and subsequent plagues to the genesis, or at least the intensification, of early public health measures. The methods of preven-tion and control of plague, of course, depended heavily on contempo-rary understanding of its causes. Many interpreted the occurrence of plague as a mark of divine disfavor, as a punishment for wickedness, or as a sign of approaching armageddon. Under such circumstances the reactions to plague involved attempts to expiate sin or placate God's wrath. The "remedy" prescribed by the priest Dom Theophilus of Milan for plague advised that

Whenever anyone is struck down by the plague they should immediately provide themselves with a medicine like this. First let him gather as much as he can of bitter loathing towards the sins committed by him, and the same quantity of true contrition of heart, and mix the two into an ointment with the water of tears. Then let him make a vomit of frank and honest confession, by which he shall be purged of the pestilential poison of sin, and the boil of his vice shall be totally liquefied and melt away. Then the spirit, formerly weighed down by the plague of sin, will be left all light and full of blessed joy.[7]

Cities often organized processions and religious services in hopes of curbing the spread of plague. Catholics and Protestants alike prayed and fasted either to prevent or to alleviate plague. In Protestant England, for instance, in 1636, the government ordered copies of *A Forme of Common Prayer, Together with an Order of Fasting: For the Averting of God's heavie Visitation upon many Places of this Kingdome* printed and distributed, and four years later proclaimed "a generall fast to be kept thorowout the realm." In Amsterdam in 1655, the Reformed church council, after a week when 750 people died, held a prayer meeting each Wednesday evening. More extreme religious treatments included flagellation and the scapegoating of Jews for purportedly poisoning wells.

Unquestionably two systems of belief worked jointly. Many ordinary people and many in positions of authority (secular and ecclesiastical alike) did not reject the idea that plague could have natural *and* supernatural origins. Thus, both faith and reason conditioned responses, and the solutions chosen did not always prove antagonistic to one another. And even if most people accepted the ultimate divine origin of plague, they also acknowledged the role of other factors, including odd weather patterns (scorchingly hot summers or viciously cold winters), famines, wars and troop movements, "fetid miasmas," stagnant pools of water, prodigies, monstrous births, and premonitions. Guillaume de Nangis observed a "great star" which "sent out many separate beams of light," which he felt "presaged the incredible pestilence which soon followed."[8]

Acknowledging the divine fount of all disease did not prevent people from seeking assistance from mortal healers nor cities from enacting public health ordinances, however. Besides the religious restoratives of penance, prayer, and submission, one deployed natural remedies and dietary prescriptives. Writing during the plague of 1631 in Pistoia, Dr. Stefano Arrighi advised patients to take "meals of good meat and eggs," apply "cupping glasses morning and evening," and swallow a daily dose of eight drops of *olio contravelem* (anti-venomous oil).[9] Prevention and control mixed old rules and more recently evolved practices. For example, the most common reaction (and one testified to in the *Decameron* of Giovanni Boccaccio) was flight, which physicians, munici-

---

[7] Quoted in *The Black Death* (ed. by Horrox), 55.   [8] Ibid.
[9] Carlo Cipolla, *Fighting the Plague in Seventeenth-Century Italy* (Madison, Wisc., 1976), 64.

2.1 Scenes from the plague at Rome, 1656: (a) disinfecting a house by burning its contents.

1. Carrozza dell'Ecc.^{mi}Sig.Pnpi D.Mario, suo figliolo, e Nipote, Che uanno à uisitar le Porte 2. Porta del Pop.co sue Cancellate,e guardie, conforme sono in tutte l'altre di Roma.

2.2 Scenes from the plague at Rome, 1656: (b) the transportation of the dead and dying.

pal officials, and religious authorities all sanctioned. Martin Luther, for example, vindicated magistrates who fled their jurisdictions in times of plague as long as they appointed appropriate substitutes to carry out essential duties in their absence. Failure to take flight could constitute a mortal sin as a form of suicide. During the plague of 1651 in Barcelona, the tanner Miquel Parets remarked that

it is quite right to flee in order not to suffer from this disease, for it is most cruel, but it is just as right to flee in order not to witness the travails and misfortunes and privations that are suffered wherever the plague is found, which are more than any person can stand.[10]

During the Great Plague in London, Pepys remarked, "But Lord, how empty the streets are, and melancholy."

Cities set up quarantines, arranged for the fumigation of goods and persons, forbade public assemblies (and often church-going), established plague hospitals for the isolation of victims, ordered houses closed, provided medical and nursing care to sufferers, and hired more grave-diggers. Although these measures were more or less ubiquitous, the larger cities enforced them more rigorously than smaller towns and villages. After the invention of printing, numerous municipalities and territories issued short pamphlets dealing with "preservation and cure" that advised rules of diet and regimen and proposed treatments such as lancing buboes and then cauterizing the wounds. A virtual flood of such advice poured off the presses in the seventeenth and eighteenth centuries and, over the years, gradually came to address not only plague (which was by then waning), but also other sorts of "folk diseases" such as dysentery.

In fact, many historians have seen in the plague epidemic of 1347–48 the initial stimulus for humankind's first effective disease-preventing intervention into the environment. Others are more skeptical, suggesting that many public health practices were much older or derived from other sources and concerns. More recently it has been argued that it was the *repeated* experience with several epidemics that generated the first real public health measures which took shape in the late fifteenth rather than in the middle of the fourteenth century. Factors other than disease also appear to have played a concomitant role. Ann Carmichael, for example, concludes that plague legislation had more to do with longterm shifts in attitudes toward the poor rather than with any immediate experience of plague. Brian Pullan points out that some people hoped to assuage the anger of God by directing acts of charity toward the poor, although the endowment and building of plague hospitals could be motivated by practical considerations as much as by religious and charitable motives.

Pestilence, whether we mean bubonic plague or a confluence of afflictions conveniently gathered under the umbrella term "plague," was the reigning epidemic disease of the fourteenth through the middle of the seventeenth centuries. Then its grip on Europe began to loosen, and fell away entirely (at least for western Europe) by 1721 when the last major epidemic vanished from Marseilles. Plague had by the sixteenth century ceased to cause major reversals in a general population growth, despite

---

[10] James S. Amelang, trans. and ed., *A Journal of the Plague Year: The Diary of the Barcelona Tailor Miquel Parets 1651* (New York, 1991), 59.

the two great waves of plague that broke over Europe in 1630–31 and 1665–70. The question that continues to perplex historians is why.

The mystery surrounding the end of plague in Europe has defied the combined efforts of historians, epidemiologists, and demographers to dispel it. Whereas once it was thought that the replacement of the black rat by the brown rat was responsible, few today accept this as a convincing explanation. Current thinking on the disappearance of plague is likely to turn in one of two directions. Some insist that, quite simply, quarantine worked. Because rats (and rat fleas) moved with people, by interdicting human travel early modern public health measures contributed substantially to the disappearance of plague from the European landscape. One problem with this interpretation is that it is by no means clear that states and cities carried out quarantines rigorously; much anecdotal evidence testifies to the opposite. Moreover, the network of public health arrangements typical of early modern Europe – including rules about quarantines, the founding of pesthouses, and measures of sanitary reform – developed as regular parts of urban policies only later, and, even in large cities, often not until the middle of the sixteenth century or later. In a world in which effective policing units were unknown, it is perhaps not very likely that quarantines could effect such a change. Furthermore, this argument depends on the idea that plague was always imported into Europe and that no foci of infection existed there. It now seems clear that reservoirs of both bubonic and pneumonic plague had developed in Europe and the Middle East by the sixteenth century. Others have suggested that shifts in the Eurasian trade routes disrupted the movement of the disease from east to west. Another possible explanation is that climatic shifts influenced the decline of plague with the last great plague epidemics in northern and southern Europe (respectively in the 1660s and in 1720) corresponding to the phases of what historians of climate call "the mini ice age" when mean temperatures averaged lower than usual, resulting in reduced crop yields and subsequent economic dislocation. New forms of housing and sanitation could have played a role as well, but it is difficult to document what these were and when or if they took hold. Also possible is that the bacillus responsible for plague mutated to a less virulent strain as other microparasites are known to do in a biologically "seasoned" population.

Even though plague vanished, its memory remained vivid and the word fell into the daily vocabulary as a synonym for misery and evil. Plague had a profound effect on the consciousness of Europeans and on their art, even if one can no longer accept that plague alone produced some great tidal change in European mentalities. The famous Dutch historian, Johan Huizinga, set the tone in 1924 for many of the subsequent assertions about the impact of plague on European culture. In *The Waning of the Middle Ages*, he argued that the disasters of the fourteenth century, and especially plague, marked the end of the flourishing culture of the high middle ages and ushered in a period of despair, decay, and lack of innovation. Art became "morbid" and people were less creative; the rich learning of the high middle ages evaporated and was replaced by an arid and unimaginative scholasticism. More recently scholars have come to suspect this picture of unmitigated gloom and doom. Clearly the plague influenced art and literature – Boccaccio's magnificent *Decameron* is a celebrated example. We now realize, however, that many of the themes, topics, religious practices, and attitudes that seem to have emerged from the horrors of the Black Death were actually in place well before the disease entered Europe. Still, the Black Death undoubtedly shaped the trajectory of Italian painting, even if it may have only accelerated tendencies already underway. The general popularity of themes associated with death was not new in the middle of the fourteenth century, but they were more common, as were the motifs of *memento mori* and the various Dances of Death. More recently, Samuel Cohen has argued that plague stimulated an artistic revival. Its survivors did not slip into religious pessimism and civic inactivity, but rather became more vigorous patrons of the arts than before.

Plague could also serve political purposes. Consider, for example, the canonization of Domenica Nardini da Paradiso during the plague outbreak of 1630–31 in Florence. In a close study of events, Giulia Calvi shows how the ecclesiastical proceedings that began at the very height of the epidemic formed a kind of "political theater" in which the Medici rulers of the city used "the drama of votive masses, of the exhumed body and relics [of Domenica] . . . [as] a deliberate attempt to proclaim the legitimacy of the embattled regime through an appeal to 'its' plague saint."[11]

Smallpox

In 1715 the 26-year-old Lady Mary Wortley Montagu (1689–1762) was a great beauty. Then she got smallpox. Although she survived, she was badly scarred. "How I am changed!," she lamented in verse, "alas! how I am grown / A frightful spectre to myself unknown!"[12] Nonetheless, she was lucky – she lived. One-quarter of those who contracted smallpox in

---

[11] Giulia Calvi, *Histories of a Plague Year: The Social and the Imaginary in Baroque Florence* (Berkeley and Los Angeles, 1989), xiii–xiv.

[12] Quoted in J. R. Smith, *The Speckled Monster: Smallpox in England, 1670–1970, with Particular Reference to Essex* (Chelmsford, 1987), 19.

early modern Europe were less fortunate. Many more were, like Lady Mary, severely disfigured or even blinded by the diseases. Millions of Europeans and millions more in the New World were affected.

Smallpox today is no longer an active infection. Beginning in 1967, the World Health Organization embarked on a campaign to eradicate smallpox that finally succeeded ten years later. Today, the smallpox virus exists only in laboratories. Because smallpox afflicted only human beings (other mammals have their own forms of the disease: cowpox and monkeypox, for example), the disease could not hide away in animal reservoirs (as plague does in rodent populations) to reactivate later. Smallpox was an acute viral infection transmitted by droplet infection. There were two important types, *variola major*, which exhibited a mortality rate of about 25–30 percent and a less virulent form, *variola minor*, with far milder symptoms and a death rate of no more than 1 percent. Variola minor seems to have appeared in Europe only in the nineteenth century and thus it was the far more deadly variola major that was common in early modern times.

The first symptoms often did not seem alarming. However, high fever, severe pains in limbs and back, splitting headaches, and sometimes convulsions soon succeeded the vague aches and soreness that heralded the start of the infection. The typical red rash manifested itself within two to five days and could be mild, with just a few, discrete pustules on face, hands, or legs; or more severe, with the pox covering hands, face, legs, and trunk, and producing scarring, blindness, or impotence (in men); or confluent, which caused the skin of victims to peel away in large chunks and frequently resulted in death when the virus attacked major internal organs such as the liver, lungs, or intestines. Populations previously unexposed to the virus, such as the indigenous peoples of north and south America, suffered terribly. A Portuguese man in Bahia, Brazil, described the 1563 outbreak there:

> This was a form of smallpox or pox so loathsome and evil-smelling that none could stand the great stench that emerged from [the victims]. For this reason many died untended, consumed by the worms that grew in the wounds of the pox and were engendered in their bodies in such abundance and of such great size that they caused horror and shock to any who saw them.[13]

Surviving an attack, however, conferred a perfect lifelong immunity.

Smallpox is a very old disease that probably beset even the aggregating Neolithic populations. Many epidemics ravaged the ancient world and perhaps it was smallpox that was responsible for the famous "plague of Antoninus" which struck the Roman Empire in the second century A.D.

---

[13] Quoted in Hopkins, *Princes and Peasants*, 214.

Smallpox probably became permanently established in western Europe by the twelfth century, although it did not have a major impact on European populations until the sixteenth and seventeenth centuries when it became, in the words of the nineteenth-century historian Thomas Macaulay, "the most terrible of all the ministers of death." At the beginning of the 1520s, smallpox had crossed the Atlantic Ocean to strike the unseasoned and disease-inexperienced populations of the New World, which it decimated. Most of the Amerindians, and especially the Arawaks and Incas who perished during the first century of contact, died from the biological weapons the Europeans unwittingly deployed. Mortality was fearful, and smallpox, far more than the swords and arquebuses of the conquistadors, vanquished the great Aztec and Inca empires.

By the sixteenth century in Europe, however, smallpox was becoming a disease of childhood with young children in urban areas especially at risk. Historical epidemiologists have frequently noted the tendency of diseases to strike with fearful results at both adults and children during their first incursion. (Consider for example the extensive mortality among adults and children when measles first reached the Hawaiian islands in 1848.) Gradually, however, as populations become "seasoned," diseases tend to become less virulent and more selective. Over time, adults are no longer susceptible because of exposure in their youth, and children become the most frequent sufferers. This is apparently what happened with smallpox. In early modern Europe, smallpox was almost the obligatory rite of passage from childhood to adulthood. It was the "river that all must cross." Smallpox accounted for about 10–15 percent of all deaths, and most of its victims (up to 80 percent) had not yet reached the age of ten.

By the sixteenth century, smallpox had made itself at home throughout Europe and had been carried across the seas where, in addition to its depredations among the Amerindians, it also wrought fearful losses on the population of Iceland and literally exterminated the Greenland colony. Smallpox assumed increasing demographic importance in Europe in the sixteenth and seventeenth centuries and continued to be one of the chief biological killers of the eighteenth. Epidemics were common throughout these centuries and often had calamitous histories. Northern Italy was hit hard in the 1560s and 1570s, smallpox raged Europe-wide in 1614, and England suffered frightfully in the second half of the seventeenth century with major epidemics in 1667 and 1668. The eighteenth century brought little respite: in 1707 an epidemic in Iceland affected almost every one of the 50,000 inhabitants of the island and major outbreaks were recorded in the great European cities – in London in 1719, 1723, 1725, 1736, and 1746; in Rome in 1746 and 1754; in Paris in 1734–35; and in Geneva in 1750. Smallpox was no respecter of person and struck rich and poor alike. Numerous members of several royal lines – the English/Scottish Stuarts in the seventeenth century, the Austrian Habsburgs, the Spanish Bourbons, and the Russian Romanovs in the eighteenth century – died of smallpox. Willem II, Stadtholder of the United Provinces, perished at the zenith of his political career (and at just twenty-four years old) in 1650; the promising young king of Spain, Luis Ferdinand, succumbed to small-pox in 1724 just eight months after ascending the throne; and the old monarch Louis XV of France died a horrible rotting death in May 1774.

Once a person contracted smallpox, survival depended on whether one had been infected with a mild or severe form of the disease and upon the strength of one's own body. No one understood just how the disease cir-culated, but smallpox, like plague, was widely deemed contagious. People dreaded the disease not only because of its lethality, but also because of its ability to maim and disfigure. Treatments had little positive effect. Healers often tried bleeding, heat (or sweat) regimens, and the "red cure" on smallpox victims. Bleeding from a vein was supposed to drain off the impurities causing the disease. Physicians and surgeons might prescribe purgatives for the same purpose. The sweat therapy became known in Europe through the writings of the Muslim physician Rhazes (850–925) who in his *Treatise on the Small-pox and Measles* recommended that patients be wrapped up and kept as warm as possible to induce a copious perspiration that would cleanse the body of the corrupted humors causing the disease. This therapy, along with the "red treatment" (which had patients dress in red clothing, sleep in a bed hung with red curtains, and even drink red liquids), was a fairly common procedure and both together were the normal ways of dealing with smallpox patients at least until the seventeenth century. Then the English physician, Thomas Sydenham (1624–89), proposed a radical new way to handle smallpox cases. Instead of enclosing patients in hot, stuffy rooms, Sydenham rec-ommended the "cooling treatment." Patients were to be confined in airy bedrooms, covered only by light blankets, kept clean, and given chilled drinks.

In the eighteenth century, Europeans began an experiment that focused on prevention, not cure, and that innovation is known as *inocula-tion*. To inoculate a person, the inoculator made small, rather deep inci-sions in the flesh of the arm (usually), inserted a scab and some pustulous matter from an active smallpox case into the gash, and then bound the wound. The inoculee would develop a true case of smallpox, although usually a far milder one than he or she might have contracted "naturally." In the eighteenth century no one knew why less dangerous cases resulted from inoculation, although inoculators tried to select donors with few pustules and mild symptoms. The process of "ingrafting" described above – that is, introducing the virus through the skin rather than inhaling it into the lungs (the normal means of transmission) – might itself have been most responsible for the attenuation of the disease in inoculees.

Legend has it that inoculation was introduced into Europe by the activities of Lady Montagu who learned of it while in Turkey with her husband, the British ambassador. Writing to a friend in England, she spoke of a practice which rendered smallpox "entirely harmless." "There is," she continued, "a set of old women [here], who make it their business to perform the operation, every autumn . . . when the great heat is abated . . . thousands undergo this operation . . . [and there] is no example of anyone that has died in it."[14] After returning to England, Lady Montagu had her daughter inoculated in 1721. Inoculations among the royal family followed and soon thereafter smallpox inoculation had become firmly established in England. Similarly, after Catharine the Great of Russia had herself and her son, the future Tsar Paul, inoculated in 1768, support for inoculation grew among medical practitioners in Russia, while a similar decision of the duc d'Orléans in 1756 helped turn the tide in France. While there is certainly some truth to this legend and good reason to note the important roles Lady Montagu and the royal family played, there are other factors to evaluate as well. First, "buying the pox" seems to have been a folk practice in several parts of Europe (as elsewhere) long before 1721. Healthy children would be sent to play with those who had mild manifestations of smallpox in order to catch a less deadly form of the disease. Second, the introduction and eventual success of smallpox inoculation in England must be attributed to a concatenation of factors, of which Lady Montagu and royal example were only two. Important and influential men, such as the physician Hans Sloane (1660–1753) and the surgeon Charles Maitland (1668–1748; who had inoculated Lady Montagu's daughter), worked to popularize inoculation and to improve its technique. The realization slowly took hold that one had a better chance of surviving inoculation than "natural" smallpox and this became a more compelling argument over time as a general statistical sense began to permeate more levels of the European population. Finally, famous propagandists for smallpox inoculation, such as Voltaire, sought to elucidate the process by simple explanations. Voltaire, in his *Lettres philosophiques ou lettres anglaises* (Philosophical or English letters, 1734), compared the action of inoculation to the ferment of yeast in dough, thus simultaneously familiarizing and taming the process.

Smallpox inoculation, of course, provoked opposition. Religious concerns about whether inoculation represented an arrogant interference in

---

[14] Ibid., 47–48.

God's will and sheer pigheaded superstition have often been highlighted as primary reasons for popular antipathy to the practice. Voltaire was quick to pillory parents who sacrificed their children to smallpox because of foolish and anachronistic beliefs. Yet such presumed foolhardiness was perhaps not the most important factor in explaining resistance to inoculation. Increasingly we realize that other objections (hardly irrational ones) to the procedure might have borne as much or even more weight. In fact, inoculation was *not* a totally safe process. The inoculee developed a real case of smallpox and could, if not isolated, infect others, perhaps even triggering an epidemic among the unprotected. Moreover, medical opinion divided on the benefits and dangers of the operation. While some medical men fervently advocated inoculation, others, just as learned and respectable, worried about disseminating smallpox or spreading other diseases, and doubted whether the immunity accorded by inoculation was permanent (it was). Inoculation did result in a certain, if small, number of deaths, and complications, including serious infections and unsightly scarring, occurred more frequently. In any case, inoculation tended to take hold fairly rapidly in England during the late 1720s and 1730s, if more slowly on the continent where medical faculties tended to be more conservative. In France, the opposition to inoculation was strong – despite the best efforts of Voltaire and the mathematician de la Condamine to promote the process – and it was not until the mid-1750s that isolated inoculations began. In the 1740s, 1750s, and 1760s, inoculation, however, dispersed throughout the continent and by 1770 had become a common, if not quite routine, and still often contested, method of combating smallpox.

The continued fury of smallpox, especially during the middle decades of the eighteenth century, surely accounted for popular acceptance of inoculation, but other elements weighed in to help promote the method. Most significant of these were substantial improvements in inoculation techniques and meaningful reductions in expense. In the 1760s, an English family of physicians and inoculators introduced the "Suttonian method" that reduced the long preparatory phase (thus cutting costs). The Suttons (Robert and Daniel) also instructed inoculators to make superficial, rather than deep, incisions. The last practice reduced the number of complications and minimized scarring. About the same time, smallpox came to be recognized as a specific disease transmitted by contact (that is, it was contagious), and thus inoculation, rather than quarantine, was increasingly perceived as the best way of handling it.

In fact, however, inoculation proved a short-lived medical phenomenon. Early in the nineteenth century, the far safer technique of *vaccination* supplanted it. In 1796, the English naturalist, physician, and inoculator,

Edward Jenner (1749–1823), inoculated a young boy, James Phipps, with lymph taken from a pustule of cowpox on the hand of a milkmaid. When Jenner subsequently inoculated the boy with smallpox, there was no reaction, leading him to conclude that inoculation with cowpox bestowed immunity against smallpox. Over the next few years, Jenner repeatedly experimented with his newfangled process (which he called vaccination, from *variolae vaccinae* or "smallpox of the cow"), finally publishing his results in a 1798 pamphlet, *An Inquiry into the Causes and Effects of Variolae Vaccinae, a Disease, Discovered in some of the Western Counties of England, particularly Gloucestershire, and known by the Name of Cow Pox.* Although objections to smallpox inoculation had been fairly widespread, if by no means universal, people rapidly and easily came to allow vaccination, and evinced only little of the opposition that had greeted the older process. Vaccination indeed conferred protection against smallpox, although that security was not lifelong, as was later discovered. A program of regular revaccinations at specific intervals solved this problem. Vaccination was safer and less expensive than inoculation; those vaccinated could not spread true smallpox and thus did not have to be isolated at some trouble and expense.

Jenner was not the only person who had noticed that people who caught cowpox did not fall prey to smallpox; that fact was well known in dairy areas. Jenner did, however, demonstrate that cowpox could be transferred from human to human without the intermediary of the cow. As vaccination gained favor, governments began to forbid inoculation as a dangerous practice. Still, the earlier experiences gained in introducing inoculation, and its eventual acceptance among many, smoothed the path to a widespread and (relatively) swift adoption of vaccination.

With the introduction of inoculation and vaccination, Europeans had at their disposal for the first time effective prophylaxes against a murderous disease. Both procedures – inoculation and vaccination – can be seen as initial steps in the process of the worldwide eradication of smallpox achieved in the second half of the twentieth century. Moreover, it may well be, as Peter Razzell has argued, that smallpox inoculation (and later vaccination) had a significant and positive effect on population growth in the eighteenth century, both in terms of reducing deaths from the disease and in preventing male impotence (a frequent complication of smallpox in adults).

Syphilis, tuberculosis, and influenza

The histories of syphilis, tuberculosis, and influenza in early modern Europe differ from those of plague and smallpox. With the exception of syphilis, no one counted any of these among the "true" epidemics, although their impact was in many ways as noteworthy as that of plague and smallpox. Moreover, whereas scholars have written prodigiously on plague, smallpox, and syphilis, tuberculosis and influenza (and also dysentery, malaria, diphtheria, and ergotism) have received much less attention.

Syphilis is a communicable disease, caused by the spirochete *Treponema pallidum* (a bacterium). Although primarily transmitted sexually, syphilis can also spread through contact with lesions, blood, and over the placenta from an infected mother to her child. The demographic impact of syphilis in early modern times, unlike that of smallpox or plague, remained slight. Nonetheless, the disease profoundly affected the mentality of Europeans.

During the French king's Italian campaign of 1494–95, a frightful and previously unknown disease with horrifying symptoms broke out among Venetian troops. The physician attached to the army observed

several men-at-arms or footsoldiers who, owing to the ferment of the humours, had "pustules" on their faces and all over their bodies. These looked rather like grains of millet, and usually appeared on the outer surface of the foreskin, or on the glans, accompanied by a mild pruritus [itching]. Sometimes the first sign would be a single "pustule" looking like a painless cyst, but the scratching provoked by the pruritus subsequently produced a gnawing ulceration. Some days later, the sufferers were driven to distraction by the pains they experienced in their arms, legs, and feet, and by an eruption of large "pustules" [which] lasted . . . for a year or more, if left untreated.[15]

This was one of the first clinical depictions of the "great pox" or the "French disease" (the names contemporaries used rather than syphilis), a malady that would within a decade sweep over Europe and subsequently destroy the bodies and haunt the imagination of Europeans for centuries.

Most eyewitnesses regarded the great pox as a terrifying new disease, for syphilis (if the great pox was in truth the same disease as modern syphilis) in the sixteenth century assumed a uniquely virulent form. Today we know syphilis as a chronic disease, contracted almost exclusively by venereal infection, and that normally exhibits several long periods of asymptomatic latency. Even untreated, two-thirds of the people infected will suffer little or no impairment, although more severe symptoms – such as motion dysfunctions, paresis (muscular weakness caused by disease of the nervous system), and serious cardiovascular problems – appear in the rest. "Syphilis" in the sixteenth century had another disease profile altogether. That epidemic was especially malignant, and the early modern

---

[15] Quoted in Quétel, *History of Syphilis*, 10.

disease – atypically for modern chronic syphilis – often killed in its initial stages. Girolamo Fracastoro (c. 1478–1553), whose lengthy poem on syphilis gave the disease its familiar name (but one which was not used commonly until two hundred years later), reported disgusting pustules filled with purulent matter, and even "joints stripped of their very flesh, bones rotting, and foully gaping mouths gnawed away." Syphilis devoured noses and genitals, and twisted limbs. Joseph Grünpeck, whose infection dated from 1498, narrated how "the disease loosed its first arrow into my Priapic glans which, on account of the wound, became so swollen that both hands could scarcely circle it."[16] Even casual contact seemed enough to pass the malady on to others.

The novelty of the disease in the sixteenth century led to the speculation that syphilis had arrived with Columbus's sailors returning from the recently discovered New World. If this is true (and there are, as we shall see, dissenting views), then syphilis excellently illustrates the consequences of "contact" between two worlds that had for millennia been isolated from each other. (We have already observed the destruction smallpox wrought on the native American populations.) The establishment of colonial empires, the new regularity of traffic between Europe and America, and a burgeoning triangular commerce which also touched the west coast of Africa, transported disease pathogens across oceanic expanses, and altered the world's biological and demographic history forever. Malaria, long present in Europe, may have become more prevalent due to reinfection from the Americas and Africa. Yellow fever was probably carried from Africa to America in the sixteenth century, where it had dealt a devastating blow to colonial settlements, and then from America to Europe where appalling (if ultimately very limited) outbreaks occurred in the seventeenth and eighteenth centuries.

But *did* syphilis come from the New World? Many early modern observers firmly believed in what is now known as the *Columbian theory* of the origin of syphilis which Roderigo de Isla first broached in his *A Treatise on the Serpentine Malady* (1539). According to this idea, syphilis was a New World disease brought back to Europe in the explorers' bodies. The timing, of course, seems about right, especially if we consider that syphilis in its initial fury apparently moved through venereal and nonvenereal pathways alike. Thus we do not have to assume the sexual hyperactivity of a handful of sailors. Paleopathologists have compared Old World and New World bones for hundreds of years before the 1493

---

[16] Girolamo Fracastoro, *Syphilis sive morbus Gallicus* (1546), quoted in Roderick E. McGrew, *Encyclopedia of Medical History* (New York, 1985), 331; Joseph Grünpeck, *Libellus Josephi*, quoted in Quétel, *History of Syphilis*, 17.

return of Columbus's flotilla and have spotted evidence of syphilitic-like lesions in skeletons from the New World, but not from the Old. The bone evidence, however, offers no unequivocal proof, as other diseases produce similar pathological traces. Another, more recent hypothesis argues for the *unitarian theory*. According to this point of view, syphilis had always been present in the Old World in the form of milder diseases like contemporary *bejel* (endemic syphilis), a nonvenereal form whose causative microorganisms are similar to syphilis. Bejel and similar diseases, like *yaws* and *pinta*, are found in hot, dry climates, and the unitarian theory further postulates that, in temperate and wetter climates, like Europe, the spirochetes recede deeper into the body, finding a congenial habitat in the human genitals. To explain the violence of the sixteenth-century epidemic, the unitarian theory turns to sociomilitary factors, especially those accompanying the almost constant warfare of the sixteenth century. (Early modern armies drew along in their wake hordes of prostitutes, women, children, and hangers-on in numbers that far outstripped the actual size of the combatant forces.) There has been much heated debate over the origins of syphilis and neither theory is totally convincing.

To treat syphilis in the sixteenth century, physicians and surgeons first turned to a long-favored therapy: bleeding. Other remedies quickly became popular. One of these was *guaiac*, a decoction of bark from the guaiac tree imported from Hispaniola (the island that Haiti and the Dominican Republic today share). The treatment that soon gained the upper hand, however, and one that appears to have had some effect against syphilis, was mercury. The saying "a night with Venus, a lifetime with Mercury" described a sad reality for the syphilis sufferer. In the sixteenth century, mercury was applied externally, as a salve, ointment, plaster, or rub; it was later taken internally. According to many who underwent mercury treatments, the cure proved as bad as the ailment. Mercury corroded the membranes of the mouth, loosened teeth in their sockets, and even ate away the jawbone, often turning the mouth and throat into one large stinking ulcer. Patients salivated profusely. By the eighteenth century, the preferred substance for the treatment of venereal diseases was sublimate of mercury (known as "Van Swieten's liquor" after its most famous physician-proponent). Not until the twentieth century did more effective and safer medicines (first *salvarsan* and then *penicillin*) become available. In addition, because of the fearsomeness of both the disease and its cure, and because of the venereal nature of its transmission, there arose a huge market for alternative treatments and for ways to be treated discreetly. In the eighteenth century, newspapers printed numerous advertisements for proprietary remedies for syphilis, often sold under euphemistic names such as Kennedy's Lisbon Diet Drink.

Less upsetting and less rich in literary allusions, but far more porten-
tous in terms of their demographic outcome, were tuberculosis,
influenza, and dysentery. Whereas tuberculosis has enjoyed a good deal of
scholarly attention for the nineteenth century, historians have – rather
curiously – almost ignored it for earlier periods. Tuberculosis seems to be
of ancient origin and exists worldwide attacking both humans and
animals. Especially important for its effects on human health is bovine
tuberculosis, which can be communicated to people via infected milk. A
bacillus, *Mycobacterium tuberculosis*, causes tuberculosis, a disease most
commonly transferred by droplet infection. Tuberculosis usually roots
first in the lungs, although it can settle in almost any part of the body. The
disease progresses slowly, and people typically suffer debilitation for
months and years before finally dying.

In the early modern period (and, for that matter, even later) pulmonary
tuberculosis was generally known as *phthisis* or consumption because the
disease appeared to "consume" its victims leaving wasted husks behind.
Tubercular infections of the lymph nodes of the neck, producing a disease
known as *scrofula*, were also quite familiar in early modern times.
Tuberculosis was apparently very common in sixteenth- and seventeenth-
century Europe and accounted for a substantial percentage (perhaps 20
percent) of all deaths. Unquestionably the accelerating urbanization of
European populations in the sixteenth century contributed in no little
measure to the increasing incidence of tuberculosis, but it was not until
the eighteenth century that "the world's greatest epidemic of tuberculosis" began and then continued well into the late nineteenth or even the
early twentieth century. Indeed, it is now believed that almost everyone in
major cities such as London and Paris had at one time or another developed some type of tuberculosis. Unlike the terror connected with both
plague and smallpox, however, almost no fear or hysteria accompanied
tuberculosis, nor did it evoke many public health measures. Instead, it
was treated as a disease of individuals and a matter for the patient's physician and not for municipal governments.

The cultural impact of tuberculosis, however, was more pronounced.
Two topics should be mentioned here: the romanticization of the tubercular patient and the linkage of the disease to genius (a story which,
however, properly belongs to the nineteenth century), and the practice of
the "royal touch." From the twelfth to end of the seventeenth century, the
monarchs of France and England "touched for the scrofula." The sacral-
ity of royalty was believed to make the mere stroke of a monarch's hand
enough to banish disease. Thousands with scrofula, including the young
Samuel Johnson, went through an elaborate ceremony that included the
"touch" itself followed by the presentation of a medal or "cramp-ring" to

2.3 Henry IV of France, touching for scrofula, early seventeenth century.

the sufferer. Subjects high and low might, in fact, judge the legitimacy of monarchs by their ability to work such miracles. Moreover, the faith in such cures proved quite tenacious. Marc Bloch in his pioneering work on the royal touch suggests that a complex set of effects that he calls "the psychology of the miraculous" explains the persistence of this ritual. Because scrofula often goes into remission by itself, the "touch" might appear to cure. Moreover, the whole legacy of a sacred royalty was ancient and was consistently strengthened by monarchs needing to raise their prestige and assert their legitimacy, and by publicists and politicians who at least half believed in the ritual themselves.

Much as in the case of tuberculosis, few scholars have turned their attention to the incidence of influenza in the early modern period. The only outbreak of influenza that has received much scholarly interest at all is the famous pandemic of "Spanish" influenza after World War I that probably killed as many as fifteen million people worldwide by 1920. Partly this neglect arises from the problem of identifying influenza in historical records. Because influenza can assume many forms, information on morbidity and mortality is notoriously fragmentary and unreliable. Influenza is an acute viral disease that is transferred from person to person through the respiratory route. Influenza has long been a disease of the three Old World continents – Europe, Asia, and Africa – but was probably introduced into the Americas only in the sixteenth century. It seems that flu first became epidemic in Europe toward the end of the fourteenth century. Thereafter the disease recurred in large epidemics (or perhaps even pandemics) several times in the sixteenth century, including a truly vicious manifestation in 1557–59 in England. The incidence of influenza seems to have declined somewhat in the seventeenth century, but during the eighteenth century at least three influenza pandemics occurred: in 1729–30, 1732–22, and 1781–82, and these were flanked by another ten or so major epidemics. In most cases, influenza caused many people to fall sick, but relatively few to die, and these deaths – as today – were scattered mostly among the elderly, the already ill, or the malnourished. Influenza epidemics and pandemics followed the routes of commerce, and one can track the progress of the disease from city to city, and from town to countryside.

Other diseases

Plague, smallpox, syphilis, influenza, and tuberculosis were the most significant infectious diseases of early modern times. They were, of course, not the only ones. Occasioning both morbidity and mortality, if often on a more limited geographical scale and within more confined chronological boundaries, were dysentery, diphtheria, and malaria. Of the other historically important infectious diseases, scarlet fever, known variously as *rossolia, purpurea epidemica maligna,* or *febris miliaria rubra,* can be identified as early as the middle of the sixteenth century in Europe, although its epidemic incidence was sporadic and its impact on overall mortality negligible. At the end of the eighteenth century, however, parts of northern Europe experienced virulent outbreaks. Measles was apparently also common among children in early modern Europe. Because the disease is so easily confused with other rashes and rash-diseases, especially smallpox, it has been difficult for historians to gauge its significance. (Through clinical observations, Thomas Sydenham differentiated effectively between measles and smallpox in the 1670s.) Measles probably did not result in much mortality, although it surely brought about considerable morbidity among children. Ergot poisoning, which might have on occasion been epidemic in its reach, was not infectious. Spread by consuming bread baked from rye contaminated with mold, the disease could cause serious illness characterized by hallucinations, peculiar neuromuscular impairments (St. Vitus's dance), or gangrene of the extremities (St. Anthony's fire).

Bacillary dysentery was also known as the bloody flux, or simply as diarrhea (although diarrhea could also indicate a milder, temporary, or innocuous condition). Once plague no longer mattered in Europe, dysentery and smallpox came to define epidemics in the minds of most people and their governments. Dysentery was a harrowing, and some-times fatal, disease. Patients perished from massive dehydration and progressive debilitation, although mortality was generally light (about 10 percent) especially among young, strong adults. Very small children and the elderly frequently succumbed. Dysentery often surfaced in the late summer and early fall, and seemed connected to the fullness of the harvest season. Popular and learned opinion blamed overeating, or consuming too much fruit, especially that not fully ripe, for the onset of the disease. Thus to control the incidence of dysentery, physicians and governments issued instructions about proper eating habits, warning people to avoid certain foodstuffs and general gluttony.

A disease peculiarly lethal to children was that known as *angina maligna* and, in Spain, colloquially, as *garrotilla* (from garrote, a method of execution using an iron collar to strangle the prisoner). A very severe sore throat, combined with flows of pus and blood from nose and throat, characterized the disease. Its victims died of slow suffocation. This terrible killer of children was probably *diphtheria*, a disease caused by a rod-shaped bacterium and transmitted by droplet infection. While diphtheria, like tuberculosis, is probably an age-old disease, it first made its presence known in Europe in the middle ages; however, not until the seventeenth and eighteenth centuries did physicians begin to depict the disease explicitly as an epidemic. In the seventeenth century, the most serious outbreaks took place in Spain, Portugal, and Italy; the disease then reached other parts of Europe in the eighteenth century. Not until the middle of the nineteenth century did diphtheria became a demographic factor with high mortality rates being recorded throughout the world. Once again, the victims were almost exclusively children.

Today immunization provides effective protection against diphtheria; antibiotics have no effect on the disease organism itself. In the early modern period, although healers tried a variety of remedies – bleeding, purging, leeching, and the use of caustic substances to clear the throat – nothing worked very well except tracheotomies which were, perhaps sur-prisingly, successfully performed in some places although obviously on a limited scale.

Malaria may be thought to be a disease of the tropics, but in fact it was quite prevalent in Europe during ancient, medieval, and early modern times, and even in temperate climates. Protozoan parasites of the genus *Plasmodium* provoke the disease and the bite of the female *Anopheles* mosquito transmits malaria from human to human. Characteristic of malaria are periodic fevers, chills, and sweating which recur at specific intervals. The name derived from the Italian "mala" and "aria" (for "bad air") because people thought that miasmas arising from marshy and swampy areas bred the disease. People clearly associated malaria with specific places and seasons. Ludovico Castelvetro warned a friend in 1552 that "Pisa is not a place you should stay in May if you value your life."[17] Incidence was greatest in such areas and at such moments. Malaria was probably an important disease during Roman times; it then receded, only to resurge in the seventeenth and eighteenth centuries. In those years, malaria occurred as far north as southern Scandinavia, Poland, and Russia.

The real burden of malaria, however, bore upon Europeans living in Africa and the Americas. Malaria-carrying mosquitoes had probably traveled with ships sailing from Africa to the Americas since "contact." The disease then moved inward from coastal areas to affect large sections of north, central, and south America. The Mississippi River valley as far as modern St. Louis and Illinois, for example, formed reservoirs of malarial infestations and proved death traps for early settlers. The first effective treatment for malaria – Peruvian bark or *cinchona*, which contained *quinine* – also came from the New World, and healers dosed patients liberally with these "Jesuit powders."

Epidemics and history

Epidemics, like diseases in general, are in and of themselves empty of meaning. Any disease, any epidemic "only acquires meaning and significance from its human context, from the ways in which it infiltrates the lives of the people, from the reactions it provokes, and from the manner in which it gives expression to cultural and political values."[18] Giving relevance to epidemics has long occupied the historian in two major ways: in discussing how people in the past understood these diseases and in evaluating (as I have done here to some degree) their attendant social, economic, demographic, and cultural consequences.

When looking back on the early modern period, historians have often identified two principal means of explaining the occurrence of epidemics.

---

[17] Quoted in Carlo Cipolla, *Miasmas and Disease: Public Health and the Environment in the Pre-Industrial Age* (New Haven, Conn., 1992), 79.
[18] David Arnold, "Cholera and Colonialism in British India," *Past and Present* 113 (1986): 151.

In short, we can speak of two general ideas about how diseases, and especially epidemic diseases, spread: either diseases are communicated from
person to person (or from animal to person) directly or indirectly (i.e.,
contagion) or diseases arise and are transmitted through environmental
factors such as air and water (i.e., anti-contagion). These two explanations are frequently labeled *contagionist* and *anti-contagionist*. Concurrent
ideas about individual predispositions and contingent causes helped
account for why some people remain unaffected even during the most virulent of epidemics and for why the same environmental circumstances
sometimes did and sometimes did not precipitate outbreaks.

The idea of contagion played little role in either Hippocratic or Galenic
medicines. Hippocrates's famous *Airs, Waters, and Places* postulated that
environmental factors bred and fed disease. The Bible, however, offers
more support for the idea of contagion, especially, for example, in respect
to leprosy. In 1546, Fracastoro formulated the classic contagionist tract,
On Contagion, in which he argued that "seeds" or "fomites" propagated
diseases. Thus, rigorously enforced quarantines, fumigation, and isolation of individual cases could impede or check the transmission of
disease. The microscopic work of Athanasius Kircher (1602–80) and
Antonj van Leeuwenhoek (1632–1723) in the seventeenth century bol-
stered the contagionist position: both men observed *animalcules* through
their primitive instruments.

Still, many people believed that epidemics arose from various factors
that can be roughly categorized as environmental. The environmental
ingredients frequently involved impropitious meteorological and cosmic
events, such as severe heat or a peculiar conjunction of the heavenly
bodies, miasmas or "bad air," and dietary flaws. Medical historians
usually attribute the heyday of such thinking to the late eighteenth and
early nineteenth centuries and link its rise, in particular, to the yellow
fever epidemics of the 1790s (especially that of 1793 in Philadelphia) and
to the waves of cholera that periodically swept over Europe in the middle
of the nineteenth century. In fact, however, both notions coexisted in
early modern Europe and both ideas conditioned responses to epidemics.
Indeed, as the eminent medical historian Charles Rosenberg observes,
"much of epidemiological thought between classical antiquity and the
present can be usefully understood as a series of shifting rearrangements
of these thematic building blocks. In the great majority of instances, both
styles of explanation were employed in combination, with one element or
another figuring more prominently."[19]

[19] Charles Rosenberg, *Explaining Epidemics and Other Studies in the History of Medicine*
(Cambridge, 1992), 295.

Thus, medical and lay thinking on causes of epidemics demonstrates far greater complexities than the simple dichotomy of "contagionist/anti-contagionist" implies. Responses to epidemics over the early modern period mixed precautions derived from both theories, although, admittedly, governments and physicians usually favored quarantine and isolation as the most effective means of handling biological emergencies. Still, it was not the sanitarians of the nineteenth century who first attempted to combat environmental ills in order to stave off or curtail the ravages of epidemic disease. Early modern cities in the grip of plague sought to purify the air by shooting off cannon or building fires and to fumigate the corrupt atmosphere of diseased houses with essences of vinegar or other aromatic oils. Large-scale projects to drain swamps (that were begun quite early in the middle ages) sought on the one hand to win more arable land, but, on the other, to eradicate dangerous disease-laden miasmas. Efforts to deal with dysentery also focused primarily on undertakings we might today view as forms of behavior modification: advice to adjust diet and to avoid drafts and chills. Thus, even in the sixteenth and seventeenth centuries, when anti-contagionist theories seemed to hold the upper hand among the learned, contagionist-conditioned responses to disease always formed part of the answer to fighting epidemics. Of course, religious and pious endeavors, such as prayers and processions, were also important weapons in any city's armory against disease. Yet most people apparently persisted in viewing epidemic disease as somehow or other "contagious."

Certainly all the scholarly puzzles raised by the historical study of epidemics have by no means been solved, and many of the guiding verities of the past fifty years have started to crumble under the relentless pursuit of new perspectives on health and illness. But epidemics remain inherently fascinating, even mesmerizing, to historians, and the flood of books and articles dealing with them shows no sign of ebbing. Increasingly, the history of epidemics has flowed into the historical mainstream to enrich our understanding of the past.

This chapter cannot close without noting that epidemics have almost monopolized scholarly attention. The epidemic experience is, however, by definition highly unusual. Epidemics have been so frequently and fruitfully studied because they threw up mountains of archival material and excited contemporary commentary. These sources have proven invaluable. Strains within communities are laid bare by the terror of the times; hidden realities of power bubble to the surface and become observable; and attitudes and prejudices seem more transparent. The sheer weight of documentation discloses the details of everyday life that so often remain obscured from the historian's gaze. Still, while epidemics reveal, they also distort. People's experiences of illness did not begin and end with epidemics. Any quick perusal of poor relief rolls or parish registers, for instance, produces a long list of diseases ranging from irritating to incapacitating to killing. These diseases and afflictions as much as, and perhaps even more than, the odd if admittedly horrifying epidemic deeply affected lives. Some of these diseases plague us today, while others have become far less common or have disappeared entirely with time. A list of them is virtually unending. Skin ailments like "scald" or "the itch," circulatory impairments like "running sores" and ulcerated varicose veins, persistent complaints like "weepy eyes" or "wry-neck" were common then and far less so today. The cancers and other degenerative diseases that slay us slew our forbears as well.

3   Learned medicine

[Medicine is] the most obscure of all [the arts].   (Laurent Joubert, 1578)[1]

Like all of nature, medicine must be mechanical.
(Friedrich Hoffmann, 1695)[2]

Open up a few corpses: you will dissipate at once the darkness that observation alone could not dispel.   (Xavier Bichat, 1802)[3]

Western learned medicine inherited its theoretical framework from Greco-Roman antiquity. *Galenism*, as subsequently elaborated in the middle ages and modified by Arabic writings, dominated theory and therapeutics until the seventeenth century and remained resilient for at least a hundred years thereafter.

The decline of Galenism and the "rise of modern medicine" have often been linked to scientific innovation. According to this line of argumentation, momentous breakthroughs produced medical progress. One often pointed, for example, to advances in anatomy as well as the discovery of the circulation of the blood by William Harvey in the early seventeenth century. Such innovators supposedly corrected the misconceptions bequeathed by ancient and medieval medicines. A medicine based on experiential knowledge, observation, and experimentation thus came to replace a medicine of texts. Accordingly, the Flemish anatomist Andreas Vesalius, the Englishman Harvey, or even poor Michael Servetus who was burned in Geneva for his heretical teachings were seen as scientific pioneers, leading the way toward a brave new world where science rather than theology reigned supreme.

The truth of the matter is, however, rather different, less simple, and far

---

[1] Quoted in Laurence Brockliss and Colin Jones, *The Medical World of Early Modern France* (Oxford, 1997), 115.

[2] Friedrich Hoffmann, *Fundamenta medicinae*, trans. and ed. by Lester S. King (London, 1971), 6.

[3] Quoted in Irvine Loudon, "Medical Education and Medical Reform," in Vivian Nutton and Roy Porter, eds., *The History of Medical Education in Britain* (Amsterdam and Atlanta, 1995), 232.

more intriguing. The story presented here will, of course, take into account the events of what is generally known as the *scientific revolution* of the seventeenth century, but will stress that by no means all of the men who have been celebrated as the heroes of that movement themselves categorically accepted its projects or methods. Harvey, for instance, expressly distanced himself from what some have called the "new science." Others, like Isaac Newton (once referred to as the last of the *magi*), remained deeply influenced by older magical and alchemical traditions. Recent work in the history of science has tended to dispel the mystique of scientific progress and to argue instead that "'science' is what 'scientists' do, not an abstract body of knowledge separate from those who create it, use it, and pass it on to others."[4]

It is also important to bear in mind that in many ways "science" itself (as we today understand it) did not exist in the early modern world, or at least not until the very end of our period. In some respects, it makes more sense in the context of the times to speak of *natural philosophy* rather than science. Natural philosophy was a far broader intellectual endeavor that reached well back into antiquity. *Natural philosophers* sought to read the "book of nature" and they accepted occult or secret ways of knowing that seem at odds with what we term science. Most of those people lazily and incorrectly termed "scientists" in the early modern period were rather natural philosophers and saw themselves as such.

Moreover, medicine and medical theory did not change through an uncomplicated process of uncovering errors and rectifying them. Scholars today generally stress the broader intellectual contexts in which medical ideas were embedded and seek to understand older medical systems and explanations on their own terms rather than just rejecting them as wrong. To avoid such value judgments, we must attempt to think our way into the mental worlds of premodern people. This thought experiment permits us to develop more sophisticated ways of discussing and comprehending these metamorphoses rather than merely relying on the simplistic mechanism of "correcting errors."

Medicine in the Galenic mold

During the middle ages, Arabic sources transmitted the writings of the second-century Greek physician, Galen, to the west. By the thirteenth century, a corpus of Galenic beliefs and teachings lay at the heart of medical learning and practice. Many of those involved in the project of

---

[4] Susan C. Lawrence, *Charitable Knowledge: Hospital Pupils and Practitioners in Eighteenth-Century London* (Cambridge, 1996), 20.

translating Greek medical texts were enamored of Galen. John Caius (1506–73), for instance, remarked that "Except in trivial matters, nothing was overlooked by [Galen]."[5] Galenism or *school medicine*, in fact, proved extremely durable and persisted in shaping medical theories until the middle of the seventeenth century. "Indeed," as one medievalist astutely observes, "certain basic physiological concepts and associated therapeutic methods – notably humoral theory and the practice of bloodletting to get rid of bad humors – had a continuous life extending from Greek antiquity into the nineteenth century."[6]

Galenism endured because it was pliant. Far from being a rigid and immutable system, it proved especially adaptable; over the centuries it responded to challenges and even absorbed them. Thus the "decline" of Galenism in academic medicine was a long, slow process that was just barely completed by 1800. There is some good evidence to suggest, moreover, that many of its canons, such as humoralism, persisted much longer in widely dispersed if attenuated forms.

What was Galenism and why was it such a hardy intellectual construct? "Galenism" must be distinguished from the teachings and writings of Galen the man. Galen of Pergamum (A.D. 129–200) was a prolific author and the middle ages did not possess his complete oeuvre, the most important of which were *On the Use of the Parts* and *Anatomical Procedures*. The materials on anatomy, for example, were missing from the medieval corpus and what medieval Europeans knew about Galen had also been filtered through Arabic sources. Galenism was, therefore, a melange of concepts and to speak of a Galenic "system" is somewhat forced. Nonetheless the learned medicine of the middle ages accepted a series of fairly standard physiological concepts that we can, without exaggeration, term Galenic. (This is not to suggest that such ideas were the sole property of professors and learned physicians; the overlap between learned and lay medicine was quite extensive and many of these physiological ideas were quite widespread.)

Galen, like all Greco-Roman physicians, was interested in medical practice and believed in natural causes of disease and nonsupernatural cures. Galenic medicine was in addition rational and learned. (Nonetheless, Galen also believed in a purposeful anatomy and physiology that were *theistic* [divine] in character.) Galen had stressed in equal measures the detailed knowledge of the human body and a love of philosophy as the basic prerequisites for a good physician. His belief that the

[5] Quoted in Charles D. O'Malley, "Medical Education During the Renaissance," in O'Malley, ed., *The History of Medical Education* (Berkeley and Los Angeles, 1970), 93.
[6] Nancy Siraisi, *Medieval and Early Renaissance Medicine: An Introduction to Knowledge and Practice* (Chicago, 1990), 70–71, 97 (quote).

"best doctor is also a philosopher" led to the continued linkage of medicine with philosophy and especially with natural philosophy in the early modern world.

The Galenic system worked on the basis of the *non-naturals* (which we already encountered in chapter 1; see p. 10); the *contra-naturals*, which were pathological conditions or disease; and the *naturals*. It is the last of these – the naturals – that we need to explore in greater depth. The naturals comprised seven things: (1) the four classical *elements* of earth, air, fire, and water; (2) the four *humors* (phlegm, blood, black, and yellow or red bile); (3) the *complexions* or *temperaments*, which reflected the unique blend of hot, cold, wet, and dry in specific bodies; (4) *parts of the body*, including organs such as the liver, heart, and brain; (5) the *spiritus*, which was a sort of air or *pneuma*, produced in the heart and carried throughout the body by the arteries; (6) the *virtues*, which were the activities of systems; and (7) the *operations*, which were the functions of individual organs. While this may seem tremendously complicated and extremely peculiar (at least to modern eyes), all the workings of the human body could be conveniently and logically explained by combining these seven qualities.

In the Galenic system there were three important organs (often called *principal members*): heart, liver, and brain. Each of these governed a specific bodily system, although the Galenic understanding of system differs from what we mean when we speak, for instance, of the circulatory system or the reproductive system or the central nervous system. (The modern meaning of system in anatomy is a group of organs and tissues associated with a particular physiological function.) The heart, the liver, and the brain, in Galenic anatomy, governed – or held the highest hierarchical position in – a group of organs with discrete functions. The heart, for instance, was the principal member of the organs of the chest and the arteries, known as *spiritual members* because they distributed a mixture of blood and spiritus (air) throughout the body. The brain was the principal member of a collection of organs that also included the spinal cord and the nerves. This system controlled thought, motion, and sensation: the *animal virtues*. The liver was responsible for the *natural virtues*, or nutrition, growth, and reproduction. Other organs in this group included those associated with digestion, such as the stomach, but also the veins, which carried blood (i.e., nourishment) to all parts of the body. Food taken into the stomach was transformed into *chyle* and was then conveyed to the liver through the vena cava. The liver *concocted* (a process something like cooking or blending) chyle, which formed into the four humors: blood, phlegm, and the two biles. Chyle was the *ur*-liquid of life. According to Friedrich Hoffmann, writing at the end of the seventeenth century, chyle "poured into the blood, by whose motion it is broken up and rendered finer, passes in part into the blood itself, . . . partly into nutritive juice, . . . partly into serum, and . . . partly into lymph." A certain part of blood was further concocted into semen, but the vast majority of blood coursed through the veins carrying nutriments to all parts of the body. Galenic physicians tended to regard the liver as the source of health "by making the good blood which nourishes all parts."[7]

This breakdown into groups of organs ordered the body and its functions in ways that accounted for most bodily processes in a coherent manner. It is useful, perhaps, to concentrate for a moment on the disparities between the Galenic systems and our own on the basis of what we call the circulatory (or cardiovascular) system. Twentieth-century definitions of the cardiovascular system typically include "the heart and two sets of blood vessels – the systemic circulation and the pulmonary circulation." The cardiovascular system, then, "effects the circulation of blood around the body, which brings about transport of nutrients and oxygen to the tissues and the removal of waste products."

The Galenic system was strikingly different. First, there were two systems, not one. The arterial system, carrying spiritus and blood, did not connect at all with the venous system, except when blood seeped through small, invisible (in fact, nonexistent) pores in the septum of the heart to allow the blood to mix with spiritus. Blood was not pumped through the body by the heart, but rather ebbed and flowed and was attracted to different organs by their need for nourishment. What the Galenic system lacked was the notion of the *circulation* of blood, i.e., that blood moved in a circuit through the body. If the Galenic systems were "wrong," they were nonetheless rational and logical. Long before William Harvey demonstrated the circulation of the blood in 1628, others had begun to observe flaws or quirks in the system.

Such Galenic concepts proved quite resilient. Beginning in the Renaissance, however, a series of challenges began gradually, almost imperceptibly, to undermine the old order. The collapse of Galenism was a slow deflation rather than a sudden implosion, and real breaks with the Galenic system took literally centuries to occur. These confrontations came in several waves: the sixteenth-century anatomical "revolution"; the Paracelsian attack on medical orthodoxy; the impact of the new science of the seventeenth century; and the rise of iatromechanical and iatrochemical medicines.

---

[7] Hoffmann, *Fundamenta medicinae*, 21; François du Port, *The Decade of Medicine or the Physician of the Rich and the Poor in which all the Signs, Causes and Remedies of Disease Are Clearly Expounded* (reprint edn., Berlin, 1988; original, 1694, in French).

The sixteenth century: Renaissance anatomy and Paracelsus

One of the oldest misconceptions in the history of medicine is that no one dissected human beings in the middle ages. Dissection had, it is true, fallen into desuetude since Hellenistic times, but the dissection of animals then revived at Salerno in the twelfth century and human dissection in the next century. Still, anatomy failed to develop as an important part of the medical curriculum at medieval universities. In the early sixteenth century, however, with the rediscovery of Galen's texts on anatomy and the teaching of the Flemish physician Andreas Vesalius (1514–64) at Padua in the 1530s, anatomy became increasingly central to medicine.

The impact of the Renaissance and the Reformation on medicine was oblique, but nonetheless profound. During the closing decades of the fifteenth and the opening years of the sixteenth century, humanist scholars were busily engaged in the "revival of classical learning" that, at this point, consisted of the rediscovery of ancient Greek texts and their publication or translation into Latin. For the first time, medical professors had the anatomical texts of Galen available to them. At the same time, Renaissance artists studied anatomy in order to portray better the form and motion of the human body. Of these artist-anatomists, Michelangelo Buonarroti (1475–1564) and Leonardo da Vinci (1452–1519) were the most famous, but almost all the great artists of the time familiarized themselves with human anatomy. Influence flowed the other way as well. Drawings assumed greater importance in anatomical texts and their quality improved. The most famous anatomical text (probably of all time) is Vesalius's magnificent *De humani corporis fabrica* (On the fabric of the human body, 1543) and it is as renowned for its splendid prints as for its text. Peter Paul Rubens made equally beautiful anatomical studies at the beginning of the seventeenth century (the *Théorie de la figure humaine* was not published, however, until 1773).

It is too easy, however, to cast Vesalius in the mold of the intrepid trailblazer who broke with Galenic and medieval anatomy and led medicine into a new age of "seeing is believing," i.e., of observation as the key to knowledge. Older medical scholarship has tended to bifurcate the history of anatomy into "pre-Vesalian" and "post-Vesalian," implying that the pre-Vesalians were decidedly inferior to Vesalius. In fact, a whole series of able anatomists, dedicated to the idea of "autopsia" (i.e., literally seeing for one's self) paved the way for Vesalius. Berengario da Carpi, for example, some twenty years before Vesalius published the *Fabrica*, had produced a dissection-based commentary on anatomy. Likewise the old saw that pre-Vesalian professors lectured at their students while assistants (or surgeons) performed the actual dissections will not stand up to serious investigation. Nonetheless, Vesalius had available much more human material for dissection than anyone before him and thus could conduct methodical and detailed investigations into the substance of the human body.

Vesalius saw himself as righting many of Galen's errors, but he still operated very much within the Galenic tradition and Galenic precepts often shaped his perceptions. Galen had believed that observation was crucial to anatomy and thus provided the basis for others to undercut his own teachings on anatomical particulars. What Vesalius did, in part, was to carry out Galen's own anatomical program and in so doing he demonstrated some Galenic mistakes. For example, he found that the *rete mirabile*, that "marvelous network" of blood vessels found at the base of the brain in animals, did not exist in humans. Ergo, it seemed clear that Galen had dissected animals and composed his human anatomy by analogy. In the *Fabrica*, Vesalius disagreed with many details of the Galenic system. For instance, he showed that the human liver was not five-lobed as Galen had maintained and that the human breastbone had not seven but three segments. Furthermore, he cast doubt upon the existence of Galen's invisible pores in the septum of the heart. Even if the careful anatomical method executed by Vesalius corrected some errors, it was not enough to observe. Prior beliefs could cause people to "see what they believed" rather than vice versa. Whereas Vesalius challenged Galen on points of anatomy, he never moved out of the penumbra of Galenic physiology and believed as firmly as any in the central tenets of that system.

Vesalius paved the way for further anatomical studies by his careful plan of dissections and by his success in raising the status of anatomy. Anatomy became the "queen of the medical sciences" in the sixteenth and seventeenth centuries. Many of the post-Vesalian anatomists amended Vesalius in the same way that he had rectified Galen. After Vesalius, other anatomies of the entire human body appeared which criticized Vesalius: for example, that of the Spaniard Joán de Valverde de Hamusco (c. 1525–88; *Historia de la Composción del Cuero Humano* [The account of the composition of the human body]) in 1556 and that of Gabriele Fallopia (c. 1523–62; *Observationes Anatomicae* [Anatomical observations]) in 1561. Other researchers concentrated on parts of the body, such as Bartolomeo Eustachio (c. 1500–74) who worked on the kidney, the ear, and the venous systems. Still others, such as the Dutchman Volcher Coiter (1534–1600?), pioneered comparative anatomy. The noted comparativist, Hieronymus Fabricius ab Aquapendente (1533–1619), became as interested in how organs worked as in how they were structured. It was Fabricius's writings on the "little doors" (the valves of the veins) that proved valuable to Harvey's discovery of the circulation of the blood.

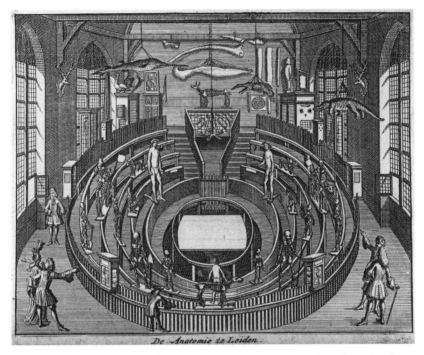

3.1 Anatomy theater in Leiden. (Note skeletons and stuffed animals hanging from ceiling.)

When William Harvey (1578–1657) published *De Motu Cordis* (On the motion of the heart, 1628), he was in fact completing the anatomical revolution of the Renaissance. Harvey had been trained in medicine and anatomy at Padua and was, like Vesalius, one of the new anatomy's brightest stars. In demonstrating the circulation of the blood through the body, Harvey thought critically about the Galenic model and used the methods of Renaissance anatomy as well as that of experimentation. He also made an inspired guess about circulation. "I meditated," Harvey says,

on the amount, i.e., of transmitted blood, and the very short time it took for its transfer, and I also noticed that the juice of the ingested food could not supply this amount without our having the veins, on the one hand, completely emptied and the arteries, on the other hand, brought to bursting through excessive inthrust of blood, unless the blood somehow flowed back again from the arteries into the veins and returned to the right ventricle of the heart; I then began to wonder whether it had a movement, as it were, in a circle.[8]

[8] William Harvey, *The Circulation of the Blood and Other Writings*, trans. by Kenneth J. Franklin and with intro. by Andrew Wear (London, 1990), 45–46.

He dissected not only human corpses, but also vivisected cold-blooded animals to observe the less rapid actions of their hearts. He noted that if one sliced into veins and arteries one found blood in both but no air or spiritus in the arteries at all as, according to Galen, there should have been. A whole series of other quantitative experiments were involved in his great "discovery" (such as calculating the quantity of blood in the human body), as well as a very famous experiment to show the direct linkage between the veins and the arteries, and thus between the two circulatory systems Galenic teachings had held separate. Taking a cord (*ligature*), Harvey tied it very tightly about a man's arm to prevent arterial blood moving down the limb. The veins below the band remained normal in appearance. Harvey then loosened the tourniquet somewhat, allowing arterial blood to flow down the arm, which caused the veins to swell because venous blood could not move past the ligature. (Pressure in the arteries is stronger than in the veins.) Thus, Harvey demonstrated the attachment between arteries and veins and postulated that blood must pass through tiny connections from the arterial system to the venous system, although he could not see the joining vessels. (The existence of capillaries, literally the missing link in the circulatory system, was proven by Marcello Malpighi [1628–94] who, using a microscope, identified these minute blood vessels in the lung tissue of a frog. Almost as important was his discovery that the trachea terminated in bronchial filaments.) Blood, therefore, streamed through the body in a great circle, or rather two circles: one systemic and the other pulmonary. Likewise, Harvey demonstrated that blood moved through the lungs (although others, including the anatomist Realdo Columbo [c. 1510–59], Servetus in the middle of the sixteenth century, and the Arab Ibn al-Nafis in the *thirteenth* century, had advanced the same idea).

Was Harvey's discovery then the last gasp of an old system or the first breath of a new one? Harvey's use of experimentation and observation seems to set him squarely in the mold of a "new man of science," but he consistently distanced himself from those later tagged "new scientists." Like Aristotle, he believed in design, and thought the soul responsible for the workings of the body. When he spoke of the pulmonary circulation, he argued that: "When . . . Nature wished the blood to be filtered through lungs, she was forced to make the extra provision of a right ventricle." Harvey saw the body much as the Galenists did, as a vessel filled with vital forces. Unlike those who later would conceive of the body as a machine, Harvey did not regard it as primarily mechanical. Blood moved through the body purposefully. Moreover, neither Vesalius nor Harvey codified a single anatomical agenda. After closely examining the work of other anatomists, Andrew Cunningham concluded that there was not just one strand, or one program, of Renaissance anatomy, but several.

If Vesalian anatomy and even Harvey's discovery made few cracks in the Galenic system, was the radical and idiosyncratic Paracelsus more successful in splitting the Galenic mold? If the story of Vesalian anatomy cannot be told apart from that of the wider history of the Renaissance, it is even less tenable to discuss Paracelsus without the Reformation. Paracelsus, or rather Philip Bombastus von Hohenheim, was born in Einsiedeln (in today's Switzerland) in 1493. His place in the history of medicine has been the subject of much debate during his life and since his death. Charles Singer and E. A. Underwood's well-known *A Short History of Medicine* (2nd edn., 1962) concluded that "it is not easy to assess the importance of Paracelsus to medicine. Some of his ideas were in advance of his time, but their expression is so clouded in mystical language that it is hard to separate the gold from the dross."[9]

Paracelsus lived a restless life, filled with controversy. He possibly studied medicine at a university, but probably never took a doctorate. He became city doctor in Basel in 1527 and feuded with the medical faculty there. Partly this was because of his own cranky and "bombastic" personality, but, more to the point, it was because he explicitly rejected school medicine and because he vehemently attacked the whole university system.

Paracelsus proposed a novel way of looking at physiology, and he rejected anatomy as "dead knowledge." He argued that "there are three substances which give every single thing its body. The names of these three things are Sulphur, Mercury, and Salt." An *archeus*, that is some-thing external to the human body, caused disease. Infections originated in "star-born" poisons "concealed beneath the goodness in everything." One immediately notices how fundamentally Paracelsian concepts diverged from Galenic ones. Whereas in the Galenic system, disease was caused by an imbalance of humors within the body and therefore was unique to each individual, Paracelsus taught that diseases were specific. He offered the basis for an *ontological* understanding of disease (i.e., each disease was a real entity with an independent existence). If this appears to our eyes a "more modern" concept of disease than that of the Galenists, then our eyes deceive us, for Paracelsus endowed his archeus with a spiri-tual essence. Paracelsus perceived a world full of occult energies and other parts of his teaching reflected this bent toward mystical and magical explanations. For example, he believed firmly in the relationship between

[9] This discussion of Paracelsus draws heavily on the work of Walter Pagel, *Paracelsus* (Basel, 1958), and Charles Webster, *From Paracelsus to Newton: Magic and the Making of Modern Science* (Cambridge, 1982); quote from Charles Singer and E. Ashworth Underwood, *A Short History of Medicine* (2nd edn., Oxford, 1962), 100.

the macrocosm and the microcosm and the influence of the celestial
bodies on the human form: "The stars compel and cause the animal man,
so that where they lead he must follow." He accepted the doctrine of sig-
natures that "like cures like," i.e., objects with shapes or colors similar to
particular organs could cure them, such as maidenhair for baldness or
lungwort for lung diseases. (Much later, and admittedly in a different
form, the idea that "like cures like" would be revived by Samuel
Hahnemann [1755–1843] and forged into a homeopathic system that
continues to attract adherents to this day.) On the other hand, he also
advocated chemical remedies and these were slowly accepted in the late
sixteenth and early seventeenth centuries.[10]

Obviously, Paracelsus was in many ways an iconoclast, but in other
ways he reflected the times in which he lived. Paracelsus, although he
remained a Catholic (at least nominally), followed in medicine many of
the developments that had occurred in religion and intellectual life.
Luther's insistence on the sole authority of scripture and his call for a
priesthood of all believers (i.e., the claim that priests were unnecessary
and perhaps even counterproductive to salvation) paralleled Paracelsus's
pronouncement that anyone could practice medicine by reading the book
of nature and that one should turn to the folk – to artisans and ordinary
people – to learn about healing. The reformers were prolific pamphleteers
who wrote in the vernacular (Luther, of course, translated the Bible into
German), and Paracelsus first made his name with a pamphlet of
Prophecy for the Next Twenty-Four Years in 1536. He delivered his teaching
and wrote books in German in a very different style from the usual
medical teaching aids of consilia, compendia, and practica bequeathed by
the medieval universities. While academic medicine was fixated on the
scholastic dissection of texts, Paracelsus consulted the people and read
the book of nature.

The teachings of Paracelsus attracted few members of medical faculties
or academically trained physicians. His violent assaults on the theory and
practice of Galenic medicine did little to endear him to the medical establishment. When denounced by his opponents, he responded with characteristic fervor and insolence:

You are serpents and I expect poison from you. With what scorn have you proclaimed that I am a heretic. I am Theophratus . . . and a monarch of physicians as
well, and can prove what you are not able to prove.[11]

He offered little room for compromise. Nor did his equally vitriolic anti-
clericalism and social revolutionism delight others. Yet he did attract fol-

[10] Quotations are taken from *Paracelsus: Essential Readings*, selected and trans. by Nicholas
    Goodrick-Clarke (Wellingborough, 1990), 51, 78, 185.   [11] Ibid., 73.

lowers and disciples. His populist message appealed to the common folk. Court circles lionized him. Many Renaissance courtiers and princes (both those who remained Catholic and those who converted to Protestantism) were strongly influenced by *neoplatonism* (a doctrine which held that the world was alive and filled with spirits) and were fascinated by alchemical and astrological projects. Paracelsus's brand of medicine appealed to these men and women. The Holy Roman Emperor Rudolf II supported a whole crew of Paracelsian doctors, alchemists, and astrologers at his court in Prague. Moritz of Hesse conducted chemical experiments and established a *Collegium chymicum* in Marburg in 1609. Royal and princely patronage of Paracelsian physicians was ample and generous in the sixteenth and early seventeenth centuries. No less a personage than Henry IV of France employed several Paracelsian physicians.

Not too surprisingly, Catholic universities excoriated Paracelsus and Paracelsianism. Yet, whereas few practitioners embraced the whole of Paracelsian beliefs, academic medicine did absorb some elements. The endorsement of chemical remedies (which were not, of course, solely Paracelsian in origin) proceeded rapidly and these soon found their way into the standard medical armamentaria. If one surveys the pharmacopeias published after the late sixteenth century, most included chemical compounds in the form of minerals, salts, and metals. The second edition of the *Pharmacopoeia Londinensis* (1618) listed 122 chemical preparations, including mercuric sulfate, calomel, and several amalgams of antimony. By the middle of the seventeenth century, men who accepted parts of Paracelsus's teachings, and even those who identified themselves more closely with him, could be found throughout Europe. Perhaps the greatest influence of Paracelsus was on the evolution of iatrochemistry and iatromechanics in the seventeenth century.

The new science and the iatromedicines

Not long ago, one still spoke quite self-confidently about the "Scientific Revolution," carefully capitalizing the initial letters to stress the importance of the event. The most influential writer on the subject, Herbert Butterfield, saw the Scientific Revolution as "the real origin both of the modern world and of the modern mentality."[12] Since these words appeared in print more than fifty years ago, however, most historians of science and medicine have adopted another perspective. They are now far more likely to speak of the "so-called" or "purported" scientific revolution, disavow its

---

[12] Herbert Butterfield, *The Origins of Modern Science, 1300–1800* (London, 1957; original, 1949), viii.

cohesion as a program, or deny its existence entirely. Likewise, scientists themselves have become skeptical about the reality of a scientific method in the sense of "a coherent, universal, and efficacious set of procedures for making scientific knowledge" that arose in the seventeenth century and which was then passed on to succeeding generations.

Popular writers on science, however, still often project images of the victory of truth over obscurantism and experiment over belief to characterize medical "progress." For example, a recent "Facts on File" publication, despite pointing out that "few scientists pretend anymore" that they are strictly "detached" and "objective," insists that Vesalius "threw down the gauntlet . . . to challenge the intellectual hold of the ancients" and describes Harvey's work as "the last major blow to Galen and the stranglehold that the ancients held upon medicine."[13] Men such as Harvey and Vesalius are portrayed as far-sighted individuals, who struggled alone, and often against huge odds, to shine the light of truth into the darkness of error. Vesalius, we learn, was a precocious genius who dissected animals on his mother's kitchen table; the seventeenth century was "the age of individual scientific endeavor," which spawned the fathers or founders of this, that, or the other, such as Malpighi as the founder of *histology* (the study of tissues by microscopy) or Wilhelm Fabricius (1560–1634) as "the father of German surgery."

We must be careful, however, in venturing such judgments. The affinity of Vesalius for Galen (despite correcting his errors) and Harvey for Aristotelian philosophy prevents us from setting them up as right-thinking moderns against wrong-thinking ancients. There was, to be sure, a conflict between those who venerated classical learning and the moderns who believed that the teachings of the past were flawed and must be jettisoned to facilitate the quest for knowledge. Yet the line dividing the ancients and the moderns often tends to blur in complex ways; ancients often seem curiously modern, and people like Harvey often explicitly separated themselves from those later viewed as early avatars of science and modernity. Indeed, it often seems best to see "the Modern projects" as "attempts to give new birth (re-naissance) to the Ancient projects, not to reject them." One must nevertheless admit that many of these men (and women) did believe that they were engaged in something distinctly novel.[14]

[13] Ray Spangenburg and Diana K. Moser, *The History of Science: From the Ancient Greeks to the Scientific Revolution* (New York, 1993), viii, 81, 84, 89, 110.

[14] Andrew Cunningham, *The Anatomical Renaissance: The Resurrection of the Anatomical Projects of the Ancients* (Aldershot, 1997), 7; more generally on the "ancients" and the "moderns," see Joseph Levine, *Dr. Woodward's Shield: History, Science, and Satire in Augustan England* (Berkeley, 1977).

So what were these people about? Can we speak about a "new science" at all? Instead of a "single coherent cultural entity called 'science,'" Steven Shapin sees "a diverse array of cultural practices aimed at understanding, explaining, and controlling the natural world, each with different characteristics and each experiencing different modes of change."[15] And it is also wise to keep in mind that even if these men (and some women) did believe that they were involved in change, their ideas of how that transition would occur and of what constituted method often diverged from one another and from our contemporary ideas of "doing science." Nowhere were these differences in perception more evident than in the consideration of what life was and how the body functioned.

The prefix *iatro-* denotes either "medicine" or "doctors." For example, an iatrogenic condition is one resulting from medical treatment. As a prefix with chemistry and mechanics, iatro- denotes systems of medical explanation and practice that arose in the seventeenth century and that contested Galenic physiology. Such *system building* distinguished the 1600s.

Iatrochemistry can, of course, be traced back to Paracelsus. While few people listed under the rubric of iatrochemistry took up the whole program of Paracelsianism, many accepted portions of it. Iatrochemists stressed the processes of *effervescence, fermentation,* and *putrefaction* as the bases of all physiology. An early iatrochemist, Joan Baptista van Helmont (1579–1644), argued that physiologic processes such as digestion and respiration were essentially chemical in nature, and a special ferment or gas caused each. Van Helmont also believed that chemical analysis was the passkey to understanding God and nature. Whereas Paracelsus had spoken of a "religion of medicine," van Helmont proposed a "Christian philosophy" that rejected the teachings of the ancient non-Christians, including Galen. Thus, a strong thread of reformism ran through iatrochemistry as it had through Paracelsianism. Iatrochemistry gained a reputation as a charitable and accessible form of medicine in distinction to the grasping avarice purportedly typical of academic physicians and Galenists in general. Contributing greatly to the popularity of iatrochemical physicians was the creation of a *bureau d'adresse* in Paris by Théophraste Renaudot (1584–1653) in 1630. The bureau provided a labor exchange and a facility for treating the sick-poor free. The physicians who worked for the bureau were chemical physicians.

Van Helmont's ideas were, initially, about as unpalatable to the university faculties as Paracelsus's had been, although with time, the faculties – and the Galenic system – found ways to assimilate iatrochemical notions.

---

[15] Stephen Shapin, *The Scientific Revolution* (Chicago and London, 1996), 3.

Galenism changed by accepting parts of iatrochemistry, and in doing so extended its lifespan by decades. Some historians find that Galenism was "in tatters" by the 1600s (and especially by the end of that century); others see a Galenism modified by the iatrochemists (and later iatrome-chanists) that still retained a certain vitality and a certain ability to adapt, at least until the 1680s.

Iatrochemistry in the guise of a Christian philosophy as preached (liter-ally) by van Helmont was not what conquered the medical faculties; rather it was iatrochemistry in the form that developed in the early seventeenth century in France, England, and Italy that won the day. Franciscus Sylvius de la Boë (1614–72) rejected the philosophical and theological parts of van Helmont's system, and he and others constructed a theory more con-genial to academic medicine and more compatible with Galenism.

The iatrochemists offered what seemed sensible explanations for several bodily functions. La Boë, for instance, viewed digestion as a chem-ical process, i.e., as a result of a acid–alkali fermentation taking place in the stomach. He also recognized the importance of saliva and pancreatic secretions for digestion. Neither idea seemed fundamentally incompat-ible, however, with older humoral doctrines.

Respiration was as enigmatic as digestion. Renaissance and Harveian investigations had revealed the precise structure of the organs of respira-tion, but gross anatomy registered little success in explaining their func-tions. Samuel Pepys observed "that it is not to this day known or concluded among physicians . . . how the action [of respiration] is managed by nature, or for what use it is."[16] Galen had believed that the lungs were organic fans which "cool[ed] the fiery heart." Only in the seventeenth and early eighteenth centuries, did investigations into air solve the riddle of respiration. Using a vacuum-jar, Robert Boyle (1627–91) demonstrated in 1660 that animals could not live without air nor could flames be sustained, thus implying a link between combustion and respiration. Seven years later the microscopist Robert Hooke (1635–1703) kept a dog alive by using bellows to pump air through its opened trachea, suggesting that some chemical change in blood, involv-ing air, allowed life to continue. Both Hooke and another Englishman, Richard Lower (1631–91), were then able to explain what the difference was between bright red blood in arteries and darker venous blood; the first was full of air. They noted that blood going to the lungs was bluish (i.e., venous), but when it returned it was scarlet, having been "trans-formed" in the lungs. Later researchers, such as the Frenchmen Antoine

---

[16] Quoted in Fielding Garrison, *An Introduction to the History of Medicine* (4th edn., Philadelphia and London, 1929), 267 n. 4.

3.2 Respiration experiment conducted by Lavoisier.

Lavoisier (1743–94) and the Englishman Joseph Priestley (1733–1809), discovered that atmospheric oxygen supported life and that the oxygenation of the blood was the vital respiratory process.

Early physiologists were equally puzzled by reproductive processes. As we saw in chapter 1, opinion divided almost equally between ovists and spermists. The iatromechanist Hoffmann understood fertilization and early embryology growth in terms of *vital motion*:

For reproduction, the ovum must be suitable for fertilization. This is accomplished by the extremely subtle spirituous effluvia of the masculine seed, introducing a new internal vital motion into the fluid parts contained within the egg.

Despite the importance of the "male seed," it was the "female ovule" that contained "the material principle of the offspring." Hoffmann's physiology offered no idea of how the fetus matured after fertilization.[17] Major advances in the study of reproduction had to wait until nineteenth-century work in *embryology* and for the discovery of *hormones* at the very beginning of the twentieth century.

---

[17] Hoffmann, *Fundamenta medicinae*, 35.

One should also mention here early attempts to understand human *metabolism* (i.e., the sum of all the chemical and physical changes that take place with the body and enable its continued growth and functioning). The invention of tools for making more accurate measurements greatly advanced the study of metabolism. The Paduan professor Sanctorius Sanctorius (1561–1636) collected data on what he called "insensible perspiration." Sanctorius devised a chair-balance to weigh himself to determine the exact mathematical relationship between food intake and excretions. He was also the first to describe a clinical thermometer and a pulse-clock (a pulse-watch was introduced by John Floyer [1649–1734] in 1707).

The work of the early *microscopists* exposed many of the unseen secrets of life. Both the microscope and the telescope rendered visible what the naked eye was unable to discern. The polymath Jesuit priest, Athanasius Kircher (1602–80), examined all sorts of putrefying matter as well as the blood of plague patients in which he identified "little worms." Robert Hooke used his microscope to scrutinize as much of the living world as would fit between its plates. His *Micrographia*, published in 1665, portrayed a range of life, plant and animal, including what he referred to as "little boxes, or cells." Jan Swammerdam (1637–80), who had studied medicine, was fascinated by zoology and, like Hooke, published bewitching prints of the tiniest sections of animal anatomy. Particularly relevant for medicine were his observations of red corpuscles, which the great Dutch microscopist, Antonj van Leeuwenhoek (1632–1723), fully depicted some years later. Leeuwenhoek also observed spermatozoa, as well as grinding fine lenses for improved microscopes. And we have already seen how important the microscopic work of Malpighi was for completing Harvey's work on circulation by revealing the capillaries that coupled the arterial and venous systems.

The mathematical and mechanical nature of the work of Sanctorius and, to some extent as well, the microscopists leads to another strand of medical explanation: *iatromechanics*. Iatromechanists argued that body processes obeyed the same laws of physics as did the larger terrestrial and celestial bodies, such as the planets and the stars. The human body, like the heavens, followed precise mathematical rules. For the Italian physician Giorgio Baglivi (1668–1707), the human edifice "operate[d] by number, weight, and measure." For instance, whereas an iatrochemist would explain digestion in terms of a process of fermentation taking place in the stomach, iatromechanists would see digestion as a result of the grinding and churning action of the stomach.

The estimable parent of iatromechanism was the French mathematician and philosopher, René Descartes (1596–1650). In his *Traité de l'homme* (Treatise of man, 1662), Descartes distinguished between the *soul*, which he viewed as incorporeal, immortal, and infinite, and the *body*, which was corporeal, mortal, and measurable. For Descartes, matter in motion explained all nature including humankind. As nature was a giant clock set into motion by the Creator, so, too, was the human body a mechanism. This way of thinking, of course, seemed to negate the purposefulness that Galen and Aristotle, but also Harvey, had imputed to nature.

The great Dutch physician and teacher, Herman Boerhaave (1668–1738), applied Cartesianism to human physiology. Students flocked to Leiden, where Boerhaave taught, and then disseminated iatromechanical theories throughout Europe. Boerhaave proposed a hydraulic model of the human body, which was composed of "membranous pipes or vessels." He compared the parts of the body to mechanical structures and tools like pillars, wedges, levers, pulleys, and bellows. He, too, saw health as a balancing act, but one of maintaining a proper fluid pressure in the human receptacles.

By 1700, iatromechanism was in the ascendance. The German physician and author, Friedrich Hoffmann (1660–1742), offered a thoroughly mechanized physiology in his *Fundamenta medicinae* (Fundamentals of medicine, 1695): "Medicine is the art of properly utilizing physicomechanical principles, in order to conserve the health of man or to restore it if lost."[18] Both Boerhaave and Hoffmann avoided the ascription of purpose (which they denigrated as "occultism") to specific organs or processes within the body that underlay Galenism.

One of Boerhaave's students was Albrecht von Haller (1708–77), a Swiss physician who garnered fame at the new university at Göttingen in Hanover (founded in 1737). In 1757, Haller supervised 567 experiments, which demonstrated the difference between nerve impulse (which he termed *sensibility*) and muscular contraction (*irritability*). By dividing bodily tissues into sensible and irritable parts, he laid the foundation for the subsequent theories of William Cullen (1710–90) and Johann Blumenbach (1752–1840). Boerhaave viewed the body as a hydraulic machine, while Cullen placed greater emphasis on the nervous system. Cullen thought that all disease was rooted in a pathological action or "spasm" of the nervous system. To treat fevers, Cullen recommended: removing the source of irritation; sedation with opiates; bloodletting; and bedrest. From here it was but a step to the theories of John Brown

---

[18] Quoted in Thomas H. Broman, "The Medical Sciences," in David C. Lindberg and Ronald L. Numbers, *The Cambridge History of Science*, vol. IV, *The Eighteenth Century*, ed. by Roy Porter (Cambridge, forthcoming).

(1735–88) that maintained life was only a result of the action of external stimuli, or *excitement*. Brown then divided diseases into two groups, either *sthenic*, those arising from too much systemic stimulation, or *asthenic*, of too little. Brown's theories were also linked to quantification: he suggested that excitement could be mathematically calibrated on a scale like a thermometer. Brown's system, called *Brunonianism*, was never very popular in France or England, but gained a large number of converts in Italy, Germany (including Johann Peter Frank), and in the infant United States where one of his disciples was Benjamin Rush (1745–1808), a signer of the Declaration of Independence and the most famous physician of his day.

Not everyone subscribed to iatrochemistry or iatromechanism. For some, like Thomas Sydenham (1624–89), theory was irrelevant or even harmful. For others, neither the iatrochemists nor the iatromechanists could adequately explain "life" and both seemed to deny what the Galenists had always found imperative: purpose. Those classified as *vitalists* or *animists* argued that neither chemistry nor physics could account sensibly for physiologic purposes.

The Halle professor of medicine, Georg Stahl (1657–1734) remained unconvinced by the iatrotheories, and offered a different version: animism. For Stahl, the God-created soul or *anima* assured the functioning of the body. For Stahl, the body was neither machine nor chemical cooker, but a God-driven and soul-directed organism. The Montpellier professor, François Boissier de Sauvages (1706–67), postulated something similar: each organ had a unique vital force that maintained it and ensured its proper functioning. By the end of the eighteenth century, vital phenomena attracted many people interested in natural philosophy, including Luigi Galvani (1737–98; best known for his experiments with electricity and frogs' legs); Antoine Lavoisier (famous for his work on oxygen); and the German natural historian and traveler, Alexander von Humboldt (1769–1859). All these theories had political as well as philosophical implications. "Iatromechanism could be represented as very much an 'absolutist' medical theory, where the body was largely controlled by a single centre, the brain; vitalism was the more 'democratic' ideology in that the bodily parts governed themselves." This interpretation offers only one example of the analogy between the body social (or political) and the body human.[19]

While today Johann Friedrich Blumenbach is most famous (or perhaps infamous) for his work on craniology and is often considered one of the founders of physical anthropology, his identification of a life-force driving toward regeneration was akin to the ideas of the animists and vitalists. Similarly, the renowned surgeon and anatomist, John Hunter (1728–93) postulated the presence of a *life-principle* to distinguish between living and nonliving things. At the same time, however, Julien La Mettrie (1709–51) declared in his *L'Homme machine* (Man a machine, 1747) that even thought and soul were products of organized matter. This basically materialist position, while never dominant, attracted some enlightened thinkers and medical men.

Historians stick out their necks when they construct such theoretical schools and try to shoehorn major figures into one category or another. For the iatrochemists, -mechanists, and vitalists/animists, we at least are using many of the terms that contemporaries employed to describe themselves, their disciples, and their enemies. Still, none of these schools or programs was rigidly constructed. No unique set of beliefs glued them together. There was no iatrochemical bible, for instance, that all iatrochemists swore on nor a rulebook which determined their actions. There were, however, places where one philosophy or the other flourished. Montpellier medicine, for instance, was by the 1680s completely in the grip of iatromechanical theories.

When we look at individuals, however, the lines separating the iatrochemists from the iatromechanists from the vitalists often smudge. Hoffmann has most frequently been characterized as an important iatromechanist, but this label may pigeonhole him too neatly. Hoffmann also employed the language of chemistry in speaking, for example, of blood as "volatile, fixed, alkali, or sulfurous." Thus, Hoffmann and others might best be identified as eclectics. One must further bear in mind that these categories have no real life of their own and systems were always less than fully systematic.[20]

Medicine and the Enlightenment

The medical science of the eighteenth century was devoted to explaining the complexity of life, debating whether life was purely mechanistic (or chemical) or, in eighteenth-century terms, *material*, or whether there was something else going on – such as the vitalism addressed above – that made the body and human life add up to more than the sum of either mechanical parts or chemical equations. The discussions of Stahl, Haller, Cullen, and Brown above have already moved us well into the eighteenth century. Here, however, the focus will be on the relationship between medicine and the broader cultural movement generally referred to as the Enlightenment.

[20] Broman, "Medical Sciences."

What does Enlightenment mean in regard to medicine? Traditional medical historiography tended to represent most of the eighteenth century (the Enlightenment included) as a lull before the clinical storm of the 1790s broke. Certainly no single item or belief typifies the Enlightenment in medicine (or medicine in the Enlightenment). Yet, as Roy Porter has pointed out, the eighteenth century "produced extensive and innovative medical discourses," and, just as importantly, "medical images . . . were central to the sociopolitical visions of the *philosophes*."[21] The second of these can be touched on only briefly in a volume of this size, but changes in medical theory and in how that theory was distributed (for instance, in a vastly expanded medical press) over the eighteenth century were of critical moment.

Defining what enlightenment meant is not easy. This question bedeviled those in the eighteenth century who thought that they lived not in an *enlightened* age perhaps, but definitely in an age of *enlightenment*. They all believed that human beings could build a better world. The *philosophes* (the French word for those who promoted enlightenment) sought improvements and argued that rational planning and an unceasing vigilance against obscurantism and folly could perfect man and society. Most of these men (and women) accepted that state action was essential to realize significant, beneficial changes. In this sense, the Enlightenment was not revolutionary. In fact, the ideas of the Enlightenment dovetailed neatly with mercantilist schemes to augment the productivity of the state through meticulous planning. In many places governments and their bureaucrats eagerly advocated enlightenment under the rubrics of betterment and efficiency. Most philosophes (or *Aufklärer* in German) retained a belief in God, although not all remained orthodox Christians. Only a handful – such as Jean-Adrien Helvétius (c. 1661–1727), Paul Henri Thiry, baron d'Holbach (1723–89), and La Mettrie – chucked God out and embraced fully materialist explanations. In the end, however, the orientation of the philosophes was to this world and not to the next, and thus they promoted "a radically different conception of health, which was now figured as the key to terrestrial happiness."[22] This profound transformation in mentality was, however, best reflected in attempts to correct deficiencies in environmental conditions, to augment the size of populations (*populationism*), and to cultivate the better health of the people. (For more on public health, the state, and medicine, see chapter 6.)

In many ways, anatomy had progressed steadily from the time of Vesalius through the eighteenth century. A more abundant supply of

[21] Roy Porter, "Introduction," to Porter, ed., *Medicine in the Enlightenment* (Amsterdam and Atlanta, 1995), 3.   [22] Brockliss and Jones, *Medical World*, 378.

corpses, as governments delivered the bodies of criminals, lunatics, and paupers to the dissection table, fostered anatomical investigations. At the same time, protests against anatomizing, as well as against the vivisection of animals, swelled. Everyone feared the "resurrection men" (body-snatchers) who robbed graves, or even (purportedly) murdered the unsuspecting and sold the corpses to those starved for dead flesh. Not only ghouls and shady characters plied the trade. Fully respectable men, like the Hunter brothers, John and William, often purchased their anatomical raw material.

Alongside the continued investigation into normal bodies and normal organs in order to ascertain form and function, one can document a keener interest in *morbid anatomy*. The rise of morbid anatomy made anatomy more immediately relevant to medical theory and practice. Giovanni Battista Morgagni (1682–1771) sought signs in specific organs that he believed were the seats of disease. Morgagni, for instance, first noted lesions of tuberculosis in the kidney and identified the clinical features of pneumonia. Distinguished successors to Morgagni were the Scot Matthew Baillie (1761–1823) and the Frenchman Xavier Bichat (1771–1802). Baillie first accurately described cirrhosis of the liver. Bichat shifted the focus of morbid anatomy to the tissues that make up organs rather than the organs themselves. All three men moved toward thinking in the opposed categories of normal and abnormal, and all believed with Bichat that opening corpses would supply solutions to medical puzzles.

The focus of morbid anatomy shifted spatially as well, from the anatomy theater to hospital wards. According to many scholars, the hospital was the fountainhead of "Paris medicine" and "the clinic." There, for the first time, medicine would become truly "objective," that is, based on quantifiable results. This reorientation and the elaboration of pathological anatomy would also ultimately achieve the reunification of surgery with medicine. (*Pathological anatomy* focuses on opening dead bodies to investigate and locate the causes of disease. *Clinical pathology* is the application of the knowledge thus attained to treatment. The second step took much longer to accomplish than the first.) The serried rows of patients in hospital beds supplied the raw material for case histories that could be approached numerically for the first time. Case histories were not newly initiated on the wards of the Paris hospital, of course. Earlier records, however, were generally highly individualized and idiosyncratic; that is, they had focused on very unusual cases, were narrative, and not easily quantified or compared. On the Paris wards, however, case-taking was standardized. Much of this story, however, belongs to that of medical education (see the next chapter) and to the development of hospitals (see chapter 5).

Therapeutics, systems, and empirics

The short-term purpose of the clinico-anatomical method was to locate the site of disease in the body; the longer-range goal was, having once identified the "true cause" of disease, to generate a more knowledgeable basis for curing, i.e., to develop a clinical pathology. One needs to inquire to what extent, if at all, the discoveries in anatomy, physiology, and pathology traced above contributed to *therapeutics* (i.e., methods of treatment). Throughout early modern times, therapeutics had remained overwhelmingly Galenic. Few of the theoretical changes introduced, even the Paracelsian ones, made much difference in how illnesses were treated and none, by itself, contributed to cures. Rather, it was the discovery and introduction of some previously unknown substances – many coming from the New World – that offered the first real advances in drug therapies.

Galenic therapeutics was highly individualized. Because disease was the product of a particular and peculiar imbalance of humors in each human being, Galenic physicians had to exercise great skill in selecting a proper therapy. Galenic therapeutics was *allopathic* (i.e., allopathy is defined as the system of medicine in which the use of drugs is directed to producing effects in the body that will directly oppose and so alleviate the symptoms of disease). The French seventeenth-century country doctor, François du Port, succinctly noted that "every disease is expelled by its opposite" and then continued in rather florid Baroque prose (and originally, in Latin verse),

Etna's heat is nullified by glacial cold, dryness and moisture interact, fire absorbs fluid and renders dry, the thin sunders the thick, hard iron resists what is soft, the rough opposes the smooth, the porous the solid, what is closed or joined is contrary to the open, the sticky to the polished.

In more concrete terms, this meant that, "when a purple humor distends the vessels, opening a vein is helpful," while in fever "a healing draught will cool and water give relief, countering the body's drought." Galenic therapeutics also relied on *polypharmacy*, i.e., a combination of many different ingredients, carefully picked, blended, and refined to fit each individual's singular condition, body type, complexion, and humoral imbalance. Du Port, for instance, would first tap a vein in a case of diarrhea accompanied by "fever and flow of bile" and then order that

three sandelwoods and rhubarb be swallowed: or infuse these with water of barberry, endive, plantain, drunk with liquour of pomegranate, myrtle or rose.

Prepare an enema of roses and red dragon's blood [a plant], Armenian bole with scalded milk. And let the diet be light . . . [and] the water drunk should contain iron, and one part of wine diluted with two parts of water.[23]

Herbal remedies and a generally conservative approach to therapeutics were fairly benign. But if they did little harm, they also could not affect responsible pathogens. Some herbal remedies certainly worked to alleviate symptoms. Willow-bark tea, for instance, is a good *febrifuge*, i.e., it reduces fever. In the nineteenth century, willow bark was discovered to contain *salicylates*, the active ingredients in aspirin.

Paracelsian remedies were predicated to a large extent on the idea that a specific external agent caused disease. Chemical physicians, therefore, prescribed particular drugs for particular afflictions. Many chemical remedies, especially mercury, antimony, and calomel, had dramatic and severe effects. Mercury when used for treating syphilis seems to have been somewhat successful, but also produced distressing salivation, loosened teeth, and progressively poisoned the patient. Calomel was an effective, but harsh, purgative. Still, with the few exceptions noted above, Paracelsian remedies did not offer much more hope for cure or even palliation of ailments than traditional Galenic ones did.

A number of useful drugs in the medical pharmacopeia were "new" in early modern times. The pain-stilling effects of wine, opium, hemlock, and mandragora were all known to the ancients. By the middle ages, belladonna was being used to still cramps and ergot was known to cause abortions, although it could also be administered to induce labor or expel a retained afterbirth. Peruvian or Jesuits' bark (*cinchona*) came from the New World in the 1630s; it contained quinine and was effective against intermittent fevers (malaria). *Ipecacuanha*, another New World plant, was an emetic (vomitive) that also helped loosen thick congestion in the chest. Other colonial products – cacao and tobacco from the western hemisphere and tea and coffee from the east Indies – were originally lauded and promoted for their health benefits. Hoffmann recommended that "the smoking of tobacco should be permitted more as a medicine than for pleasure." Such remedies were widely advertised in the columns of the continent's new newspapers. One could find, for example, advertisements for "health-chocolate" (*Gesundheits-Schokolade*) in German papers early in the eighteenth century. All of these soon became more popular as beverages or forms of enjoyment than medicines, however. The diuretic properties of foxglove (digitalis) and its usefulness in cases of dropsy and heart failure were first discovered in the late eighteenth century.

---

[23] Du Port, *Decade of Medicine*, 84–85, 159, 204–05.

During the late seventeenth and eighteenth centuries, skepticism about existing drug therapies took two forms: one argued against the polypharmacy of Galen and the other against systems in general. Cullen and Brown reduced a broad spectrum of diseases to one or two. Brown's schema of sthenic and asthenic diseases allowed for extreme reductionism in medications and therapies. For Brown, drugs need do only one of two things: stimulate if the disease was asthenic and calm if the disease was sthenic. He turned especially to opiates and alcohol, therefore. Sometimes simplification was even more radical. The French physician, François Joseph Victor Broussais (1772–1838), believed that disturbances (he called them "irritations") in the gut caused disease, and thus mild blood-letting cured all illness. An American disciple of John Brown, Benjamin Rush, was more bloodthirsty and recommended massive bloodletting, combined with extreme purgation, as the panacea for almost everything, including madness. During the yellow fever epidemic of 1793 in Philadelphia, Rush and his students were inundated with patients whom they took into the front yard of his house and bled until the ground was literally caked. Rush recommended depleting up to 80 percent of the body's blood. Such one-shot sure-cures were the property of extremely respectable physicians (such as Rush), but also made the fortunes of others who speculated in the medical marketplace. Jean Ailhaud (1684–1756) and his son built up a commercial empire on the sale of their "purgative powders" which worked on the simple theory that all disease arose from retained feces and thus all diseases could be corrected by a thorough purging.

At the same time, many – such as Thomas Sydenham – came to doubt the purpose of medical theorizing altogether. Such medical *empiricism* cast a jaundiced eye on heroic intervention, the complex and often bizarre polypharmacy of the Galenists, and the harsh therapies of the systematizers alike.

Sydenham has often been dubbed the "English Hippocrates," an appellation that reflects his emphasis on empiricism and a more general revival of interest in the Greek "father of medicine" with the decline of Galen's influence. Sydenham valued Hippocrates for his clinical (i.e., bedside) observations and for his stress on the physician's duty to "do no harm." Sydenham's therapeutics, although not radically different from those of his contemporaries, was more restrained. He believed in the use of cinchona, vegetable simples, and "cooling treatments." Although he also turned to phlebotomy, he preferred to let a little blood often rather than much once. Sydenham had little patience for the sophistry of elaborate systems and medical hypothesizing, but rather emphasized close, clinical observation and the gradual assemblage of meticulous case-histories. Sydenham believed that such investigations could be used to classify diseases like plants. "It is necessary," he wrote, "that all diseases be reduced to definite and certain species." He held that diseases were real things, and thus was moving toward an ontological view of disease. His own descriptions of diseases exhibited clinical genius; and he is best known for his masterpiece on gout (1683). (Sydenham was also important for his commentary on epidemic diseases, which he connected to climatic conditions in speaking of "epidemic constitutions.")

Sydenham became a hero to eighteenth-century physicians who prided themselves on their empiricism. "Empiricism" was a word academic physicians had once used to denigrate those who were not university-trained. In the eighteenth century, however, empiricism gained a positive meaning of being "based on experience and observation." Eighteenth-century physicians became less interventionist in practice. They repeatedly invoked the healing powers of nature and thought it better to do nothing than to act too vigorously. (There was, of course, another side to the coin, as we have seen above, especially among the adherents of Brown and Cullen.) In some cases doubt led to *therapeutic nihilism*, the idea that no extant medicines or therapies worked. Using a system of early clinical trials, Pierre Louis (1787–1872) tested the efficacy of bloodletting in treating pneumonia and found that it did no good whatsoever.

During the last half of the eighteenth century, many physicians expressed a similar caution about a range of medications. The vitalist Paul-Joseph Barthez (1734–1806) at Montpellier taught that no one was able to explain how drugs worked in the human body, so the only solution was to proceed cautiously. Only after thousands of cases had been successfully collated *might* it be possible to (re)establish therapeutics on a sound basis. The French *Encyclopédie* was much blunter: what physicians had written about medications was sheer babble and completely devoid of meaning or merit.

As the eighteenth century drew to a close, physicians throughout most of Europe had shed the successive skins of Galenism, iatrochemistry, and iatromechanism. The vitalists, in some form or another, were still around, but the dominant "theory" of the day was an empiricism that stressed observation and experience, and which was moving toward a more restrained use of drugs and treatments and a renewed emphasis on regimen and hygiene (see chapter 6). Such changes, as we shall see in the next chapter, could not help but influence medical education as well.

4   Medical education

I admit that not everything [I have written] adheres to the rules of academic style . . . Where I have erred, I will be thankful to him who corrects me with good reasons.   (Justina Siegemund, 1690)[1]

[N]othing is more certain than demonstration from experience.
(Herman Boerhaave, 1739)[2]

[Hospitals are] the principal pillars of a rational system of instruction in the healing art.   (William Blizzard, 1796)[3]

Multiple roads led to the practice of "physic" in early modern Europe: apprenticeship, academic study, experience, and self-tutelage. This chapter will, to some extent, discuss all of these, but it focuses on the first two. More will be said later about the less structured manner of education – both experiential and self-attained – in chapter 7. The decision to concentrate on formal education here is not intended to imply that those trained formally were either better or more popular than the others.

The education of physicians (and to some extent surgeons as well) took root in the universities of twelfth- and thirteenth-century Italy. Universities remained at the heart of medical education until the early eighteenth century, when private schools and bedside teaching began to alter traditional forms of instruction.

Medical education: the medieval background

The middle ages suffers a bad press. Even the term "middle" suggests that what happened before – antiquity – and what came after – renaissance – were more meaningful. This misconception is unfortunate

[1] *Die Chur-Brandenburgische Hoff-Wehe-Mutter* (1690), quoted in Waltraud Pulz, *"Nicht alles nach der Gelahrten Sinn geschrieben": das Hebammenanleitungsbuch von Justina Siegemund* (Munich, 1994), 65.

[2] Quoted in Lawrence I. Conrad, Michael Neve, Vivian Nutton, Roy Porter, and Andrew Wear, *The Western Medical Tradition 800 B.C. to A.D. 1800* (Cambridge, 1995), 361.

[3] William Blizard, *Suggestions for the Improvement of Hospitals and Other Charitable Institutions* (London, 1796), 34.

because many of the institutions of early modern (and modern) life can be traced to their medieval antecedents. Nowhere is this truer than with universities. Medieval medical education has gained a particularly bad reputation as "scholastic," text-based, and altogether unmodern.[4] The overwhelming emphasis on textual analysis, it has been argued, stultified medical education long after the middle ages had passed. Accordingly, medical education remained "untouched" by the Renaissance and lay "like some antiquated fossil buried beneath layers of tradition and an inert mass of indifference."[5]

Universities produced the academically trained physicians of Europe. Many people, of course, practiced with little or no formal training (and were accepted as doctors); others gained knowledge through apprenticeship (such as surgeons, midwives, and many "practical physicians") or even self-education. Here, however, I want to tell the story of medical education as it evolved from the late middle ages until the eighteenth century when nonuniversity institutions – such as private schools and hospital wards – supplemented (and sometimes almost replaced) universities.

The oldest universities in Europe appeared in Italy, France, England, and on the Iberian peninsula in the twelfth and thirteenth centuries, to be followed by a second wave of foundings in central Europe, beginning in 1348 when the Holy Roman Emperor Charles IV chartered the university at Prague. This second surge lasted through the sixteenth century; Martin Luther's Wittenberg was a new university in the sixteenth century. Surgery and the teaching of surgery had, as we shall see, only very tenuous connections to the universities at this point except in southern Europe. One major center of medical learning was Salerno (as early as the tenth century); its prestige, however, had waned considerably by the thirteenth century. It was replaced by Bologna, Montpellier, and Paris, and, in the fifteenth century, by Padua (which remained important through the eighteenth century) and Ferrara (which soon declined). Areas on the periphery, such as Russia, had no universities at all in the middle ages. The first Russian university opened in 1755 and a medical faculty was set up in 1764, but it did not receive the right to award doctorates until 1791. The number of physicians in Russia was low (in 1690–1730, somewhere between 125 and 150 and perhaps only as many

---

[4] My discussion of medieval medical education relies heavily on the excellent account by Nancy Siraisi, *Medieval and Early Renaissance Medicine: An Introduction to Knowledge and Practice* (Chicago, 1990), and on the relevant material in C. D. O'Malley, ed., *The History of Medical Education* (Berkeley and Los Angeles, 1970).

[5] C. H. Talbot, "Medical Education in the Middle Ages," in O'Malley, *History of Medical Education*, 85.

as 236 in 1800) and, until late in the eighteenth century, all were foreign-ers. Most were recruited from Germany. Medical education in the Americas began with the establishment of chairs of medicine at, for example, the Royal and Pontifical University of Mexico in 1578 and with the endowment of two medical professorships at the University of San Marcos in Lima in 1571. Full-blown medical curricula took longer to develop but were well in place throughout the colonies by the beginning of the nineteenth century.

By the thirteenth century, medical education in the medieval university rested on ancient knowledge filtered through Arabic texts and Latin translations. The full corpus of Greek learning was not available until the fifteenth century at the earliest. In a pre-print age, the number of medical manuscripts was very limited and most professors knew only a small portion of the medical literature that existed. How, then, were medieval students taught? Professors spent a good deal of time orally explicating topics such as regimen, therapeutics, diseases, and symptoms. Professors also lectured from the major texts available (and some students must have had their own copies): the *articella*, the *commentaries*, and the *consilia*.

The articella was the most important and long-lived of these texts; the last version appeared in 1534. A compendium created at Salerno in the thirteenth century, the articella laid out the basics of Hippocratic and Galenic teachings. The commentaries, first presented verbally, but some-times subsequently written down, conveyed the professors' own inter-pretations or explanations of standard works. The consilia described individual cases. Texts were studied *scholastically*, which meant that "questions on which opinions differed were isolated, the views of author-ities were listed and distinguished, objections to each were raised and solved in turn."[6]

Lecturing made up only part, if admittedly a major part, of medieval medical education. Before students attained their doctorate, they were supposed to spend time practicing under the supervisory eye of an experi-enced mentor. Students also attended public dissections (begun in Bologna in 1316). Thus, many of the "evils" and "insufficiencies" attrib-uted to medieval medical education at universities, and, for that matter, to its early modern successors, prove less damning than its critics would have us believe. Still, one cannot deny that "the centerpiece of medical education remained the spoken and written word."[7] If one compares "typical" curricula from the middle ages and the eighteenth century, one

---

[6] Siraisi, *Medieval and Early Renaissance Medicine*, 76.
[7] Thomas H. Broman, *The Transformation of German Academic Medicine, 1750–1820* (Cambridge, 1996), 30.

immediately notices a considerable degree of overlap, although the texts presented and the character of the knowledge conveyed differed (i.e., to reflect, for example, either iatrochemistry or iatromechanism in seventeenth and eighteenth centuries and the relative decline of Galenism).

In the middle ages, medical students mastered a precise body of material. Information was delivered by lecture, although dialectical teaching and illustrations enriched that format. Learning was primarily a matter of listening. Texts were few and expensive, and students were expected to memorize extensively. The structure of the texts and of the curriculum assisted the process of assimilation and recollection. Students were taught to apply the subtle tools of scholastic inquiry and to think analytically. Texts were often composed like catechisms, in question-and-answer form. The professor would query: "What is phlebotomy?" or "What is an aphorism?" The student was expected to supply the authoritative answer (in Latin, of course).

Lectures, too, emphasized repetition. At Bologna, for instance, four lectures took place each day. The two in the morning went over theory; the other two, in the afternoon, discussed practice. Lectures presented the practical side of medicine as well as the theoretical. The spoken word was frequently supplemented by a series of pictures which were intended less to act as accurate representations of, for instance, anatomical structures or as guides to the proper sites for letting blood than to function as mnemonic devices. In addition, the lecturing style was often highly ritualized. As rhetoric in the terms of spoken words had its rules, so, too, did body language and gestures. Mannered movements of the professor's body, and especially his hands, emphasized particular items, indicated avowal or disapproval, and generally signposted points of importance.[8]

Over four years students would hear several reiterations of important subjects, for example, explanations of Hippocrates's *Aphorisms*, Galen's work on critical days, and the like. During the second year, afternoon lectures introduced no additional materials, but merely repeated and amplified the first year's courses. Moreover, the entire fourth year recapitulated what had already been offered in the previous three. At the end of this sequence, the student would defend his thesis on a medical topic publicly, and at such *disputations* professors set questions and raised objections. The student's *rhetorical* skill in responding to inquiries and exceptions determined whether or not he would be awarded a baccalaureate. The more advanced degrees of licentiate and doctorate were

[8] Cornelis O'Boyle, "A Marginal Existence: The Role of Visual Representation in Late Medieval Medical Education," presented at a Work in Progress seminar, Wellcome Institute for the History of Medicine (London), 2 June 1998.

received after further study and the presentation of additional theses. The universities themselves provided no clinical teaching.

Medical education, 1500–1800: change and continuity

Universities remained the locus of academic teaching for the next several centuries. Continuity was marked, yet change was inevitable. If we compare, for example, medieval curricula to those followed at early modern universities, we note a large number of similarities in the character of education as well as several modifications in substance. The curriculum indicated for preparation for the baccalaureate in Paris in the early seventeenth century differed in content if not form from medieval precedents. Students now learned physiology, pathology, hygiene, obstetrics, anatomy, surgery, and pharmacy. The lesson plan, however, continued to rely on the repetition of topics to inculcate knowledge.

The most striking feature of post-fifteenth century medical education was the presence of medical texts for students. With the advent of printing and with the subsequent decline in the cost of books, medical students no longer had to depend exclusively (or almost so) on the spoken word. They also had increasing access to more elaborate and detailed anatomical prints. The earliest of these, known as "fugitive sheets," first appeared during the Renaissance as guides to dissections and were run off especially for students. The effects of printing were, of course, hardly limited to medical education or even to education alone. Suffice it to say that by the seventeenth and eighteenth century students owned medical books. Physicians had been assembling libraries ever since printing came into fashion and, even in the sixteenth century, bibliophilic collections could be quite extensive. John Hatcher (d. 1587) of Cambridge owned 575 titles, of which 350–400 were medical, and Thomas Lorkyn (d. 1591), also of Cambridge, had 588 of which about 400 were medical texts.[9]

In early eighteenth-century Germany, for example, the textbook was central to instruction. Professors read passages from texts and then offered supplementary information in the form of explanations and extended commentaries. Two widely used texts were the *Fundamenta medicinae* (Fundamentals of medicine, 1695) of Friedrich Hoffmann and the *Institutiones medicae* (Institutions of medicine, 1708) of Herman Boerhaave. Such courses in the "institutes of medicine" (a concept dating at least to the middle ages) included five subjects: physiology, pathology,

---

[9] Peter Murray Jones, "Reading Medicine in Tudor Cambridge," in Vivian Nutton and Roy Porter, eds., *The History of Medical Education in Britain* (Amsterdam and Atlanta, 1995), 163.

semiotics, therapeutics, and dietetics (and Hoffmann, like others, divided his book into chapters with these titles). Medical education might last either three or four years and was expanded in the eighteenth century by topics first added in the sixteenth and seventeenth: botany (as a result of the Greek revival of the Renaissance), anatomy (also a Renaissance/sixteenth-century addendum), and chemistry (from the seventeenth century). This "lesson plan," however, is only a sketch and individual medical faculties varied it. No instruction was practical in the sense we would understand. Even anatomy remained theoretical because of a general shortage of cadavers. Before we criticize the "obvious insufficiencies" of such abstract training and book-learning, however, we must remember that the definition of the physician turned on his erudition as much (and perhaps more) as it did on his performance at the bedside. It was, however, the increasing emphasis on "medicine at the bedside" that was already modifying the structure of medical education and would continue to transform it throughout the eighteenth century.[10]

The picture presented above suggests slow and perhaps barely perceptible shifts in the character of medical education. One might, therefore, argue that alterations in medical education were less apparent than overall continuities. The picture was not one of stagnation, however, even before the widespread introduction of clinical teaching (bedside teaching) in the eighteenth century.

Clinics and clinical instruction

A vast sea of ink has been spilled in arguing about when and where clinical teaching became dominant and when and where it transformed medical education and, indeed, medicine as a whole. One can maintain that the "birth of the clinic" was a sudden shift that occurred in France in the 1790s (or even more precisely, on the wards of the Paris hospitals in 1794–95). Antoine Fourcroy's report to the French revolutionary government in 1794 pointed out that "that which up to now has been lacking in schools of medicine, the practice of the art and observation at the patient's beside, would become one of the main parts of teaching." Bluntly overstated: "The modern period began in 1795 [with the opening of the new school of health]. The long hibernation that had prevailed since the middle ages gave place to a sudden and radical change."[11] One

[10] Thomas H. Broman, "The Medical Sciences," in David C. Lindberg and Ronald L. Numbers, *The Cambridge History of Science*, vol. IV, *The Eighteenth Century*, ed. by Roy Porter (Cambridge, forthcoming).

[11] Quoted in Dora Weiner, *The Citizen-Patient in Revolutionary and Imperial Paris* (Baltimore and London, 1993), 30–31, 92–99, 127–29; Charles Coury, "The Teaching of Medicine in France from the Beginning of the Seventeenth Century," in O'Malley, *History of Medical Education*, 168.

might, however, insist that the "birth" of the clinic was far less precipitous and, for that matter, less conclusive than has been suggested. Let us examine each of these possibilities in turn, beginning with the "birth of the clinic."

This story can be briefly summarized. The "birth of the clinic" and the concomitant rise of "hospital medicine" was "the critical epoch" in modern medical history and marked the watershed from premodern to modern medical science and medical education:

[The clinic's] consequences for medical knowledge unified medicine and surgery, taught doctors to think in terms of local lesions, to use the techniques of careful, systematic physical diagnosis, to correlate whenever possible the signs and symptoms observed during the patient's life with the changes in his body discoverable at post-mortem examination, and to make use of the large medical experience available through hospitals in more accurate disease descriptions and more careful therapeutic evaluations.[12]

Those who speak of the birth of the clinic recognize that it had its precursors in what have been termed *protoclinics*. The question for them is to what extent the protoclinics differed from the clinic of the 1790s.

One can construct a line of continuity running from the elementary protoclinics of the middle of the seventeenth century to the full-blown clinics of the late eighteenth. While it is, of course, impossible to identify all the professors who might have taken one or more favored students out with them on their rounds of patients, one can imagine that the numbers were probably not trifling. Organized bedside or clinical teaching, however, apparently began in Padua in 1540s with Giambatista da Monte (1498?–1551) who used the Hospital of St. Francis to teach practical medicine. One of these Paduan students, the Dutchman Jan van Heurne (1543–1601), carried these ideas with him to Leiden, where he became professor of medicine. Although it is not clear that Jan van Heurne did anything more to inaugurate bedside teaching in Leiden than propose it, his son Otto (1577–1652) actually instituted such instruction. In 1636 the university set up the *collegium medico-practicum*: a three-month course of systematic practical training in the Caecilia Hospital. Eventually two special wards of six beds each were designated for the collegium's use.

Yet clinical instruction at Leiden – generally regarded as the mecca of bedside teaching – was probably only sporadic throughout the seventeenth and eighteenth centuries. Franciscus Sylvius de la Boë, professor of medicine from 1658 in Leiden, taught at the bedside, but it was

---

[12] W. F. Bynum, "Physicians, Hospitals and Career Structures in Eighteenth-Century London," in Bynum and Roy Porter, eds., *William Hunter and the Eighteenth-Century Medical World* (Cambridge, 1985), 107.

Herman Boerhaave (1668–1738) whose name has been most frequently associated with the reform of medical education. Boerhaave became known as the "teacher of all Europe." For twenty-five years, he conducted clinical teaching at Leiden and his clinical course regularly appeared as part of the curriculum. Boerhaave apparently presented a single patient at a time to a group of students. He explained why he had recommended particular drugs, diet, and regimens, and students recorded the master's words. This was, then, a revamping of the traditional lecturing procedure; students did not get "hands-on" training.

Clinical teaching was not unique to Leiden. In 1717, Johann Juncker (1679–1759) established a *Collegium clinicum* in Halle. In Halle (as elsewhere), the goal of such clinics was not primarily, or perhaps even principally, better medical education. Rather the Collegium clinicum was closely joined to poor relief. From Halle, the system spread to Berlin, and later to Göttingen, Jena, and Erfurt. Ernst Baldinger's (1738–1804) *Institutum clinicum* in Göttingen extended the clinic founded by Rudolf Augustin Vogel (1724–74). It, too, had a double purpose: medical education and charity. (For more on the charitable functions of such clinics, see chapter 6.)[13]

In Edinburgh, clinical teaching began at the Royal Infirmary in 1748 with John Rutherford (1695–1779), a pupil of Boerhaave's. Rutherford's preface to his first clinical lecture states his objectives and describes the aspirations early clinicians cherished:

I shall examine every Patient capabel of appearing before you, that no circumstance may escape you, and proceed in the following manner: 1st, Give you a history of the disease. 2ndly, Enquire into the Cause. 3rdly, Give you my Opinion how it will terminate. 4thly, Lay down the indications of cure yt [that] arise, and if any new Symptoms happen acquaint you them, that you may see how I vary my prescriptions. And 5thly, Point out the different Method of Cure. If at any time you find me deceived in giving my Judgement, you'll be soo good as to excuse me, for neither do I pretend to be, nor is the Art of Physic infallible, what you can in Justice expect from me is, some accurate observations and Remarks upon Diseases.[14]

In France, forms of clinical teaching had existed in Strasburg since 1729 and students at Aix-en-Provence and Avignon could find clinical teaching at hospitals there. Similarly Anton de Haën (1704–76) ran a

---

[13] Wolfram Kaiser, "Theorie und Praxis in der Boerhaave-Ära und in nachboerhaavianischen Ausbildungssystemen an deutschen Hochschulen des 18. Jahrhunderts," in *Clinical Teaching, Past and Present* (special issue of *Clio Medica*, 1989), 71–94.

[14] Quoted in H. P. Tait, "Medical Education at the Scottish Universities to the Close of the Eighteenth Century," in F. N. L. Poynter, ed., *The Evolution of Medical Education in Britain* (London, 1966), 64.

clinic in Vienna from 1754 which sought to unify theory and practice. The Viennese model was introduced at Pavia in 1770; Freiburg im Breisgau in 1780; Prague and Pest in 1786.

All of these examples (and one could draw more illustrations from elsewhere in Europe) make it clear that at least some form of clinical teaching was downright common if not universal in eighteenth-century medical schools. Two questions, however, remain as yet unanswered. First, was the "Boerhaavian tradition" the direct forerunner of the Paris clinic? And, second, what impact did such teaching have on students?

Many scholars (including Foucault, who coined the term protoclinic) quickly concede that clinical teaching existed, predated the Paris school, and reached a goodly number of students. Nonetheless, they perceive a major qualitative gap between protoclinics and "the" (real) clinic. Simply put, the numerical dimensions of the Boerhaavian clinics were too small. They drew on a very limited number of cases. University towns often had no hospitals or only very modest ones and these demographic realities restricted, sometimes severely, the numbers and types of cases available for clinical evaluation. Only great cities, like Paris, could deliver pedagogic raw materials in bulk. A close analysis of the Leiden clinic, for instance, shows that between 1699 and 1753 the number of patients fluctuated. The total was 832 – an average of 15.4 a year. However, the general trend was downwards. Between 1700 and 1710, 43.4 patients were admitted annually, then the numbers declined significantly (with, however, another peak from 1737 to 1742). The most was in 1704 with eighty-seven patients.[15]

Moreover, few students had an opportunity actually to treat patients even under the professorial eye. Most attended something similar to rounds, where the professor explicated the case and outlined therapy. Only very late in the century, probably in Pavia under the direction of first Samuel Tissot (1728–97) and then Johann Peter Frank (1745–1821), did a hands-on approach take hold. Similarly, the intention of the Boerhaavian clinic was to *transmit* rather than build up knowledge. Students were passive observers: "Preservation, not substitution of the existing paradigm was the intended goal of [these] educational programs."[16]

According to this line of argumentation, what happened in Paris was quantitatively different and this quantitative difference engendered a

---

[15] Harm Beukers, "Clinical Teaching in Leiden from Its Beginning Until the End of the Eighteenth Century," in *Clinical Teaching*, 146.

[16] Guenter B. Risse, "Clinical Instruction in Hospitals: The Boerhaavian Tradition in Leyden, Edinburgh, Vienna and Pavia," in *Clinical Teaching*, 15; Luigi Belloni, "Italian Medical Education After 1600," in O'Malley, *History of Medical Education*, 109–10.

qualitative one. Paris's public hospitals offered a vast number of patients, about 20,000, for teaching purposes. Students attended at the bedside and were confronted with an incomparable range of cases. The minute examination of patients was succeeded by investigative postmortems with an emphasis on pathological anatomy and the isolation of lesions. The purpose of the "Parisian clinic" was not only to disseminate existing knowledge to students, but to produce knowledge. In Paris, the "objectification, standardization, and quantification central to modern medicine" were first fully expressed.[17]

While these arguments seem quite cogent, the story presented above is not universally accepted. Some scholars, for instance, point out that, rather than one dominant clinical tone, there were variations on a theme. It has been argued, for instance, that enough pedagogic raw material existed before the 1790s and outside Paris to begin generating knowledge. Moreover, it is not clear that the rise of hospital or scientific medicine on the Paris model was ubiquitous in Europe. An examination of the rather different story of what happened in England alerts us to the problems of advancing European-wide generalizations.

English exceptionalism?

How different was England? Through the eighteenth century, the two English universities – Oxford and Cambridge – alone granted medical degrees. By the middle of the eighteenth century, however, only a very small portion of English practitioners had studied at either place. Englishmen now preferred other European venues such as Padua, Leiden, and, later, Edinburgh. In England or rather in London by the middle of the eighteenth century, private teaching and medical education outside universities had come to dominate medical training. Students frequented any one of a number of private schools or "walked the wards" of the city's hospitals with the attending physicians and surgeons. Thus, universities became increasingly incidental to medical education in England, whereas on the continent medical education, despite the changes traced above, remained firmly tied to universities.

London had no university, so it was not possible to link university teaching with the great metropolitan hospitals or with any of the charitable hospitals which had been established in the eighteenth century. Still, there was not a total divorce between universities and hospitals. Cambridge students, for example, attended at St. Thomas's Hospital in London to study there

---

[17] Susan C. Lawrence, *Charitable Knowledge: Hospital Pupils and Practitioners in Eighteenth-Century London* (Cambridge, 1996), 15.

with the best-known practitioner of his time, Richard Mead (1673–1754). Thereafter private teaching – both in hospitals and in schools – became widespread in the capital. A leading surgeon, William Cheselden (1688–1752), known for his skill in cutting for the stone, offered lectures on anatomy and physiology at St. Thomas's. Richard Kay attended the London lectures of Samuel Sharp and John Girle in 1743 and 1744. From August to December 1743, for instance, Girle presented on "Anatomy, Aliment through body, Slink calf [aborted fetus], Eye, Ear, Amputation of a leg, Cranium, [and] Teeth and bones of lower cranium."[18]

In the eighteenth century, a bevy of private teachers offered training in the form of fees-for-services. The most famous of these was the Great Windmill Street School, founded by the Scot William Hunter (1718–83). Hunter gave instruction in anatomy and midwifery (he was a famous man-midwife and wrote a important study of the pregnant uterus), and was more than ably assisted by a series of talented collaborators, including his own brother, the great surgeon John Hunter (1728–93), William Hewson, and William C. Cruikshank. Between 1710 and 1810 at least twenty-seven schools provided lectures in anatomy with opportunities for dissection. Some survived the competition for only a year or so. Others were hardier perennials. Joshua Brooks opened a school in 1785 that was still function-ing in 1820. Private *medical* teaching, on the other hand, seems to have been monopolized by George Fordyce from 1764 through 1802. All these medical entrepreneurs advertised in the capital's newspapers.

Finally, whereas in France and elsewhere the hospital and a hospital post became the *sine qua non* for medical prestige and a thriving career, the conjunction proved less relevant in England. In England, as W. F. Bynum points out, the hospital appointment at a voluntary (i.e., charita-ble) hospital could be of great importance for a physician because it gave him access to the upper crust and also endowed him with the cultural good of appearing in the humanitarian and beneficent role that character-ized an elite group. In addition, the opportunity to teach from the hospital was often a source of welcome income to a physician. Nonetheless, "British hospital physicians and surgeons almost always had at least one eye on their private consulting rooms, for it was here that the wealth that spelled professional success was to be had." Moreover, the kind of medical research that conferred professional respectability on French physicians, for instance, was less determinant in England. Modern medi-cine in England developed differently than on the continent and that

[18] F. N. L. Poynter, "Medical Education in England," in O'Malley, *History of Medical Education*, 238; Joan Lane, "The Role of Apprenticeship in Eighteenth-Century Medical Education in England," in Bynum and Porter, *Hunter*, 101.

difference did not merely derive from the relative weakness of English medical faculties, but from the very structure of a medical career. Perhaps it should also be mentioned that a more consumer-oriented, free-wheeling society fostered a "more piecemeal, informal and individualistic development of the medical profession" in England than elsewhere.[19]

On the other hand, we might argue that the differences between England and the rest of Europe are not, in fact, meaningful. It is possible that a whole string of institutions, including hospitals, infirmaries, dispensaries, and private schools, all served the identical purpose of clinical teaching. Thus, there may have been less to choose from between England and continental states than historians have insisted.

Private medical teaching was, after all, by no means exclusively English. Older historiography has frequently overplayed English singularity. In France, private medical tutelage had begun in the early eighteenth century and was, effectively, the only feasible way for students to receive clinical teaching. Everyone knew that the best *surgical* instruction was to be obtained in Paris's private schools. By the middle of the century, medical students in Paris typically attended private courses. Antoine Petit (1718–94), for example, lectured on anatomy, surgery, and obstetrics, and attracted most of the leading physicians to his private amphitheater. By the end of the century, many professors and members of the Academy of Surgery, like Petit, gave such courses. In order to gain clinical experience before the clinical revolution, most students had to pay a physician or surgeon to allow them to accompany him on his hospital rounds. By the 1780s a rather informal system of walking the wards was being transformed into a more elaborate system of medical tuition at the hospitals. This setup pertained not only in Paris but to other university cities as well. Private medical education, however, does not seem to have been as popular or widespread in central Europe as in either France or England.

Medical students

The purpose of university medical education was, of course, to produce physicians, and the definition of physician as it changed from 1500 to 1800 was reflected in altered educational objectives. For most of this period, learnedness was the key. Physicians used "their credentials as learned gentlemen" to separate themselves "from others lower down the social hierarchy." Still, the image of the physician did change and two things were especially apparent even before the clinical revolution. First, greater emphasis came to be placed on practice and on therapeutics. Second, the physician

---

[19] Bynum, "Physicians, Hospitals and Career Structures," 107–09, 119, 122.

was being given – at least theoretically – more multifaceted responsibilities which were now to "embrace the novel and crucial function of a medical administrator; he was to become the leader and supervisor of a team of trained subordinates," including surgeons, apothecaries, and midwives, although this vision was hardly achieved before the close of the old regime.[20]

So where did medical students come from and what were their ambitions? While it is hard to generalize about medical students over the course of some three hundred years, it seems that most students were recruited from the ranks of the bourgeoisie and from families of clerics, physicians, and lawyers. In France, for instance, students were sons of bourgeois families and families of magistrates, physicians, merchants, and lawyers. Only very rarely did the nobility send forth medical students and only then from its lower ranks. Poor students might study medicine, but this was unusual, because medicine was one of the more expensive degrees. In Germany, for example, the majority of needy students supported by private benefactions tended to study theology, not medicine. A number of countries and territories (some German and Italian states, as well as Spain) forbade their subjects to matriculate at foreign institutions. Others, like Russia in the eighteenth century, encouraged students to do so. In Catholic countries, Protestants might have trouble obtaining a university place while the same barrier constrained Catholics in Protestant areas. Jews were restricted until well into the eighteenth century almost everywhere. In some places bastards and the children of hangmen or those with fathers in other "dishonorable" occupations were barred from universities.

What sketchy evidence exists for the second half of the eighteenth century in Germany offers a comparable picture. Many students of medicine had fathers, uncles, or other close male relatives who were physicians; many more had such relatives who were surgeons, apothecaries, or even horse-doctors. In Protestant areas, a goodly number of clergymen's sons studied medicine. Children of merchants and tradesmen were fewer in number and only very few members of the nobility thought medicine an appropriate career for their sons. Students tended to attend local universities where they could forge or strengthen alliances.

Women generally did not study at universities (there were some exceptions), and so, at least until the nineteenth century, they were also excluded from obtaining a medical degree. There is, however, some evidence to suggest that, at least through the sixteenth century, some women served surgical apprenticeships. Of course, the tradition of women *in* medicine was ancient and many female healers were fully conversant with

---

[20] Broman, "Medical Sciences"; Laurence Brockliss and Colin Jones, *The Medical World of Early Modern France* (Oxford, 1997), 476.

Table 4.1 *Medical graduates in Great Britain*

Years	Oxford/ Cambridge	Continental	Scottish	Total
1500–1550	150			150
1551–1600	280			280
1601–1650	599	36		635
1651–1700	933	197	38	1,168
1701–1750	617	385	406	1,408
1751–1800	246	194	2,594	3,034
1801–1850	273	29	7,989	8,291

Source:
A. N. T. Robb-Smith, "Medical Education at Oxford and Cambridge Prior to 1850," in F. N. L. Poynter, ed., *The Evolution of Medical Education in Britain* (London, 1966), 49.

the learned medical theories of their day. The publishing midwives (see below, pp. 116–19), for instance, explicitly sought to introduce contemporary medical beliefs into the practice of midwifery.

The domestic popularity of universities ebbed and flooded, as did their ability to attract foreign matriculations. Padua, for instance, was fashionable in the fifteenth century, Paris in the sixteenth and seventeenth, and Leiden at the beginning of the eighteenth century. Thereafter, the torch passed successively to Göttingen, Vienna, Erfurt, Erlangen, and – most importantly – Edinburgh. Edinburgh was very well attended in the second half of the eighteenth century, boasting a truly international student body. From 1726 to 1799, 1,143 men took the M.D. degree there. Of these, 639 came from Scotland, England, or Wales; 280 from Ireland; 195 from the West Indies and North America; 2 from Brazil; 1 from the East Indies; and 26 from Europe.[21]

At the turn of the eighteenth century, London and Paris again drew students in large numbers. Table 4.1 indicates the number and origin of medical graduates in Great Britain from 1500 to 1800.

Student life at early modern universities exhibited the high spirits that one might expect of a relatively young (aged between seventeen and twenty-three years old) group of men, often living away from home for the first time. One celebrated example is that of Felix Platter (1536–1614) of Basel.[22] Felix Platter came from rather humble origins. His father,

---

[21] Tait, "Medical Education at the Scottish Universities," 65.
[22] All quotes from *Beloved Son Felix: The Journal of Felix Platter, a Medical Student in Montpellier in the Sixteenth Century* (London, 1961), esp. 46–47, 54–55, 75, 88–89, 115, 124–25.

4.1 Felix Platter (1536–1614), "Archiater Basileensis."

Thomas, was born in very low circumstances, although by the time Felix was growing up Thomas had established himself as the director of a boarding school and proprietor of a publishing house. He was never rich, but he was ambitious enough to think of sending his son to France to study medicine. At the age of sixteen Felix arrived in Montpellier to "began without delay to follow the curriculum of the school." Felix's diary, which covers the next five years of his life, records much of what living in a sixteenth-century town was like in an age of upheaval. The entries on his studies are relatively sparse, and the rest of the journal is filled with his friends, their outings and pleasures, political events, and the execution of heretics and criminals.

Lectures were an important part of his curriculum and Felix "attend[ed] two or three lectures in the morning, and as many more in the afternoon":

In the morning there were those of Sabranus, Saporta, and Schyronius, and at nine o'clock that of Rondelet. In the afternoon there were those of Fontanonus, Bocaudus, Guichardus, and Griffius.

A little irreverence and horse-play were not unknown: "We breakfasted during Schyronius's period, for he was very old," Platter records, "and one day he filled his breeches in his professorial chair" – much to the amusement of his listeners, one assumes. Nonetheless it seems that Platter worked hard. His father implored him "to be honest, pious, and studious, and . . . to apply myself especially to surgery, [for] the number of doctors in Basel was great, and I should never be able to make my mark there if I did not show more than the usual ability."

Felix was assiduous. Besides attending lectures, he frequented anatomical dissections of humans and animals. He was apparently dissatisfied with merely being an attentive observer, and went further, reporting how he not only "never miss[ed] the dissections . . . that took place in the College" but "also took part in the secret autopsy of corpses." Despite an initial repulsion, he even "put [his] own hand to the scalpel." Apparently, Felix and a group of friends took up the offer of a rich bachelor of medicine

to join him in nocturnal expeditions outside the town, to dig up bodies freshly buried in the cloister cemetery, and [carry] . . . them to his house for dissection. We had spies to tell us of burials and to lead us by night to the graves.

His efforts bore fruit, for on 16 May 1556 he sat for his bachelor's degree. The examination lasted from six until nine in the morning, during which time the "doctors of the university" argued against him. They must have liked what they heard because, after dressing in a red robe, thanking them in Latin verse, and paying eleven francs and three sols, he received his diploma "duly sealed." He had not yet taken the doctorate, which he would postpone until he returned to Basel. Although he admitted that "it would be no small matter to pass my doctorate . . . considering that I was yet scarcely twenty years old, and beardless," he was not particularly worried "as I had some practice in medical discussion . . . and had made distinct progress in every department of medicine, *in praxi, chirurgia, theoria.*" His confidence was justified, and Felix Platter enjoyed a fine, perhaps even a brilliant, career once settled back home. He became the city's principal physician, a professor at the university, and one of its rectors. He was in a position to marry, build a large, sumptuous house, maintain a fine collection of natural curiosities, and educate his half-brother, Thomas, as a physician.

A second Basel student, Daniel Bernoulli (1700–82), who lived some two hundred years later, exemplifies another, later course of medical study. After finishing the gymnasium in Basel, he matriculated at the university there and attained a "magister artium." Although he demonstrated the same great talent for mathematics that his father and brother possessed, his parents intended him to enter commerce. He hoped, however, to study mathematics and he and his father eventually compromised on medicine, which he studied first at Basel, then in Strasburg and Heidelberg, finally getting his doctorate at Basel in 1721 with a dissertation on respiration. He later became professor of anatomy and botany in Basel.[23]

Few early modern doctors found their professional feet as quickly as Platter and Bernoulli did. For most of them, especially those lacking influential friends or family connections, long, hard years of perseverance and penury awaited them before they became established. In the last quarter of the eighteenth century, Dr. Ernst Heim was more than thirty years old before he came to enjoy an income sufficient to support himself and his family. Even then only the help of a friend made it possible for him to get on. The timely intercession of mentors, old comrades, or family and acquaintances often was vital. For example, a young doctor in the small town of Schöppenstedt (Germany) was certainly helped along by his father, the pastor there. When his son returned from studying medicine, he circulated a personal note to all his clerical colleagues and to the schoolmasters recommending his son to them and asking them to endorse him to their congregations and pupils' families. For many of these men, in fact, attaining an official post – such as a town doctor or physicus (see chapter 5) – was essential to their occupational survival.

[23] Friedrich Huber, *Daniel Bernoulli (1700–1782) als Physiologe und Statistiker* (Basel and Stuttgart, 1959), 12–16.

The training of surgeons

One way to distinguish between surgeons and physicians is to argue that until almost the very end of the eighteenth century these were two separate occupations and surgeons were trained, while physicians were educated. That is, surgical instruction occurred within guilds, while physicians studied at universities. While this statement contains more than a grain of truth, it also privileges physicians over surgeons in ways that are not justified historically. For instance, many physicians trained as apprentices and never attended university courses. Many more received instruction at universities but never took a degree. Moreover, surgical training was neither inherently simpler nor less rigorous than medical education. While a dichotomy existed between surgical and medical schooling, we should not, as Susan Lawrence reminds us, convert this dichotomy into a hierarchy, i.e., assume that medical education was somehow better than surgical, merely because medical men – as members of a learned profession – enjoyed more cultural authority.

From the sixteenth century to the end of the seventeenth, most surgeons trained as artisans within the framework of the guild system. In the eighteenth century, however, the "rise of surgery" (or "rise of the surgeon") culminated in the reunification of physick and surgery. Surgical and medical education had progressively become more alike and in most European countries the difference between surgeons and physicians vanished entirely at the end of the century or early in the next one. Medical men were acting ever more like surgeons in their concentration on organs as the sites of disease.

The older historiographic tradition that values the admittedly remarkable John Hunter as the first of the "scientific surgeons" overstates the case. Many older histories have insisted that only with Hunter did "surgery [cease] to be a mere technical mode of treatment." Even before Hunter, however, surgery was not purely empirical in nature, for "*all* surgical practice was to a degree dependent on some theoretical notions of the working of the animal economy."[24] Greek and Arabic medical writings had included surgical topics and such works had become quite routine in the 1300s and 1400s. And the tradition of academic surgery continued in Italy and even spread to France in these years.

Most surgeons belonged to and received their education within *guilds*, however. Guilds, like universities, were a great medieval institution.

---

[24] Fielding Garrison, *An Introduction to the History of Medicine* (4th edn., Philadelphia and London, 1929), 344; Stephen Jacyna, "Physiology Principles in the Surgical Writings of John Hunter," in Christopher Lawrence, ed., *Medical Theory, Surgical Practice: Studies in the History of Surgery* (London and New York, 1992), 136.

Guilds were made up of masters, journeymen, and apprentices. Guilds were polyfunctional and not merely economic in character, but rather had a "comprehensive, binding lifestyle that encompassed everything."[25] They offered sociability and social security (many guilds had their own saints, their own chapels, and their own pensions, charitable provisions, and sick insurance schemes) and were at the same time educational institutions. Of course, the economic function of guilds was always pivotal. Guilds regulated prices, controlled access to occupations, and assured that each master would command an appropriate and suitable income. Guilds tried to divide the economic pie (or market share) equitably. One way to do so was to manipulate entry.

Guilds, however, were not a law unto themselves. They needed a charter (granted by the monarch or a city government) and royal or municipal officials supervised their activities. This management was most acutely felt in food provisioning – by setting the price of bread and specifying the weight of loaves – but it was almost as strong in the regulation of medical practice. Guilds worked best in relatively small, homogenous, and stable societies, such as in the medieval and early modern cities which governed themselves. Guilds were, in fact, almost exclusively urban institutions. With the expansion of markets, with the introduction of new means of production (proto-industrialization and factories), with accelerated demographic growth, and with the development of consumer mentalities, guilds could no longer maintain an economic edge. Their enervation worsened in the seventeenth century, when rulers interested in gearing up the productive capacities of their states showed less concern with maintaining guild privileges and protecting guildsmen. Guilds increasingly tended to be regarded as antiquated institutions that dampened a spirit of industriousness and braked economic growth.

Surgical guilds often combined surgeons, barber-surgeons, and bathmasters. In 1268 the Collège de Saint Côme was organized as a guild in Paris with two levels: the clerical barber-surgeons "of the long robe" and the lay barbers "of the short robe." The former were to examine and certify the latter. These combinations often led to conflicts, especially when surgeons wanted to distance themselves from their artisan-like brethren. Such internal wrangling often paralyzed the guilds and made them unable to resist pressures from outside.

Guilds also offered a form of quality control. Any one who practiced with the authorization of the guild was assumed to have realized a certain

---

[25] Hans-Ulrich Wehler, *Deutsche Gesellschaftsgeschichte*, vol. I, *Vom Feudalismus des alten Reiches bis zur defensiven Modernisierung der Reformära, 1700–1815* (Munich, 1987), 191–92.

degree of skill. Second, and closely related to the first, guilds had their own systems of education. Apprentices and journeymen had to fulfill the demands of the guilds to gain admittance to mastership. In the sixteenth and seventeenth centuries, it became more common for governments to insist on granting a license or examining candidates themselves before allowing them to practice.

While there were, of course, variations in surgical education in different European countries, the general setup was roughly similar. Early in adolescence, male children would be apprenticed to a master-surgeon for a period of time (in Württemberg, for example, for three years). The apprentice (or, more usually, his family) paid a fee to the master and, in return, he received board, lodging (usually in the master's household), and instruction. The apprenticeship contract signed by John Beale of Woolscot (Warwick) in 1705, for example, specified the length of his surgical apprenticeship at four years. During that time,

the apprentice shall faithfully serve his master, his secrets keep, his lawful commandments gladly obey; the apprentice neither to do damage to his master nor see it done . . . The apprentice not to commit fornication nor contract matrimony during the term; the apprentice not to play at cards or dice or any unlawful games that may cause his master loss. The apprentice not to haunt taverns nor alehouses nor be absent unlawfully day or night from his master's service but in all things behave as a good and faithful apprentice.

For a fee of £53 16s, William Edwards promised to teach Beale "all the art he uses by the best means he can." He also agreed to provide "meat, drink, washing and lodging."[26]

After successfully completing his apprenticeship, the young man became a journeyman for another, usually longer term (in Württemberg, for six years). During this time, he was expected to "wander" (hence, the term *Wanderzeit*) from place to place, laboring for other masters and sharpening his skills. Journeymen were not permitted to set up independently as surgeons and generally were forbidden to wed. After the Wanderzeit was over, the journeyman would usually return to his home or place of apprenticeship (the two were frequently the same) and stand for his mastership. Early in our period, the guild itself, or rather a group of masters, administered the test. As time passed, however, it became customary to involve others – physicians and members of the city magistracy – in the examination process. Thus local *collegia medica* (boards of health) would examine surgeons and then distribute a license. Increasingly, therefore, becoming a surgeon meant that one must become a member of a guild *and* satisfy a medical executive organ. After successfully passing

[26] Lane, "Role of Apprenticeship," 100.

his examination and paying a set fee, the newly minted master-surgeon was allowed to set up his own practice, take on his own apprentices and journeymen, and so the process reproduced itself.

The mastership examination itself blended the demonstration of practical knowledge with a viva: the latter was sometimes held in Latin. Although much emphasis was laid on the prospective surgeon's ability to prepare, for example, a poultice, or to show his facility in bandaging, applying a truss, or opening a vein, a modicum of theoretical knowledge was also demanded. Surgical training was never completely devoid of theory, even if that theory might be rudimentary in the case of barber-surgeons and bathmasters. In eighteenth-century Württemberg, for example, such theoretical knowledge included anatomy, osteology (bones), myology (muscles), splanchnology (internal organs of the abdomen), and the circulation. Especially in the eighteenth century, surgeon-candidates might also be asked questions about obstetrics.

Over the three hundred years which interest us here, heterogeneity characterized the training of surgeons and the skills they attained. While most barber-surgeons might have received only a practically oriented education, many surgeons possessed a greater trove of theoretical knowledge. Certainly, in many places, the time spent becoming a surgeon exceeded that for a physician. Numerous students, before they were apprenticed, had acquired a reasonably good education, and sometimes an outstanding one. Many had learned Latin and attended a secondary school.

Limited work at best has been done on the social origins of surgeons, and much of what there is pertains to the eighteenth century. In Württemberg, from 1742 to 1792, the percentage of surgeons' sons who also became surgeons exceeded half. Other fathers were artisans, a few were pastors, and, perhaps somewhat surprisingly, an equally small handful were apothecaries. In Braunschweig-Wolfenbüttel, apprentices with the necessary qualifications seemed hard to attract, at least in the middle of the eighteenth century. Two surgeons claimed that they had no luck finding suitable apprentices "although they demand from them nothing more than a Christian upbringing, that they understand the rudiments of German and Latin, and that they are able to pay fees of forty to fifty thaler." Few children of prosperous parents chose surgery, and those from inferior backgrounds lacked the preparatory education or the wherewithal to apprentice themselves. Another problem was that many "surgeons are satisfied with a smaller fee, and do not really care if an apprentice can read and write properly. If he can do the housework and within three months can give a good shave and help earn the bread he eats," then these masters were content. The education given surgeons (or surgeons and barber-surgeons) varied, but the need to pass a mastership test and, increasingly, the demand for licensing and examination by territorial health authorities meant that most surgeons were by no means ill prepared for their subsequent careers.[27]

The quality of surgical education and the overall status of surgery rose perceptibly from the late seventeenth century onwards. New and improved surgical methods expedited this elevation. The move toward more active surgical intervention, however, can be traced to the fifteenth century and, especially, to the introduction of gunpowder. Warfare itself required, or at least fostered, innovative surgical techniques. Ambroise Paré (1510–90) was the most illustrious of all early modern surgeons. Trained as a barber-surgeon in the French provinces, he became an army surgeon in the wars between the Habsburgs and Valoises. He penned works on monsters, discredited the use of mummy and unicorn's horn in medicine, and wrote voluminously on surgery as well: on the treatment of gunshot wounds, on the use of vascular ligature (tying off veins and arteries) rather than cauterization to halt bleeding from amputated limbs, and on how to turn a fetus in the womb to present its head. In 1564, he produced a massive tome on general surgery.

Military surgeons, like Paré, worked out better ways to treat the wounds of war and these procedures often had immediate civilian applications. Several people seconded Paré's stress on the simple treatment (i.e., noncauterization) of gunshot wounds, as Thomas Gale (1507–86?) described in *An Excellent Treatise of Wounds made by Gonneshot* (1563). Elaborate surgical procedures supplemented battlefield treatments, such as those which Hans von Gersdorff (d. 1529) advocated in his *Feldtbuch der Wundartzney* (Field guide to surgery, 1517). Gaspar Tagliacozzi (1549–99), in an early work on the use of skin and flesh grafts to rectify mutilations, delineated methods of *rhinoplasty* (surgery to alter the shape of the nose). Interestingly, these procedures were not Tagliacozzi's invention, but rather his publication of the "secret" held by a Sicilian family of itinerant operators, the Brancas. Such exposés spread knowledge of a series of carefully concealed practices, and the widespread implementation of these helped raise the status of surgeons and give surgery its increasingly good repute. One can mention here the most famous of "family secrets": the obstetrical forceps that Peter Chamberlen, senior, had developed in the 1620s or early 1630s. The Chamberlen family successfully hid their technique and their instrument away from curious eyes

---

[27] Sabine Sander, *Handwerkschirurgen: Sozialgeschichte einer verdrängten Berufsgruppe* (Göttingen, 1989), 141; Mary Lindemann, *Health and Healing in Eighteenth-Century Germany* (Baltimore, 1996), 191–92.

La figure d' vn homme situé comme il faut quand on luy veut extraire la pierre de la vessie.

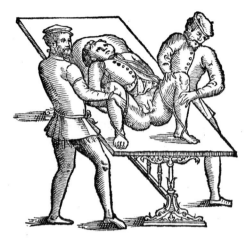

4.2 A male patient on a table being held in the lithotomy position by two assistants, 1628.

until early in the eighteenth century (although other forceps had come into use by then). Obstetrical forceps allowed man-midwives to deliver children otherwise undeliverable, thus saving some mothers and infants. Many, however, criticized the use of instruments altogether as dangerous for mother and child alike. Such forceps, often padded with leather and impossible to keep clean, must have spread infection.

A French family of lithotomists named Colot worked out a new way of cutting for the stone (*grand appareil*), and this procedure, too, remained undisclosed from the middle of the sixteenth century until early in the 1700s. The Colot method reduced tissue damage and complications as well as deaths from infection and shock. By the 1720s in the French capital, grand appareil lithotomy was widespread and relatively safe. These and other surgical successes contributed to the growing reputation of French surgery as the best in the world, or at least in Europe.

Equally effective were innovations in cataract surgery. Cataract operations had always counted among the most successful of the procedures specialists and itinerants performed. "Couching" a cataract, which consisted in depressing the lens of the eye, had achieved good results as early as the sixteenth century. Several operators and surgeons, including most famously the German Georg Bartisch (1535–1606), dedicated themselves to eye operations and a number of works, such as the *Traité des maladies de l'oiel* (Treatise on diseases of the eye, 1585) by Jacques Guillemeau (1550–1613), focused on the subject. In the middle of the eighteenth century, Jacques Daviel (1696–1762) developed a means of extracting rather than depressing the lens and this procedure remained the basis for cataract operations until lasers came into common use in the late twentieth century. Toward the end of the eighteenth century, surgeons occasionally even performed caesarian sections on living mothers with some (albeit very limited) success.

Surgery, therefore, offered sufferers a number of treatments that promised a reasonable degree of safety and chance of cure or at least alleviation of painful conditions. Such improvements embellished the prestige of surgery and, perforce, that of surgeons as well. Surgeons could reasonably claim that they proffered more effective aid than physicians and enlightened opinion tended to agree.

Several forces had combined to transform surgery. Although apprenticeship systems (and guilds) persisted, surgeons – often backed by royal or ducal governments – began to sever their ties with barbers and barber-surgeons. In eighteenth-century France, surgical education broke out of the guild system. Lectures and practical demonstrations, combined with walking the wards of hospitals, were how the "modern" surgeon was educated. Surgeons, too, entered the academy and, as early as 1672, the surgeon Pierre Dionis (1643–1718) lectured in anatomy and surgery in the capital. Governments hoping to augment the size of their populations quickly moved to establish a whole series of surgical colleges or academies, which combined theoretical and practical knowledge and which were in no way inferior to the medical faculties. Surgical schools, such as the Royal College of Surgery in Madrid (1788), appeared in many European capitals. Surgeons were, moreover, increasingly appointed to hospitals and offered instruction there. Hospitals also developed in-house lecture courses on surgery and students paid fees directly to teachers. Private schools sprang up in many places but especially in metropolitan hubs like London and Paris.

Changes in education helped eradicate the still-existing divisions between medicine and surgery. The late eighteenth-century revolution in Paris disestablished medical schools, and the laws reestablishing them in the early nineteenth century combined the education of surgeons and physicians. Even before then, dual medical/surgical degrees were coming into vogue. As early as 1728, Montpellier offered a degree in surgical medicine for physicians who wanted greater qualifications in surgery and in the second half of the century more and more students were choosing this option. By 1794, 627 surgeon-physicians had graduated from the university there.[28] (Apothecaries sometimes trained as surgeons or physicians, as well.) This trend was repeated elsewhere, although the timing was somewhat different. Nonetheless, by the early decades of the nineteenth century, medicine and surgery had come together again and medical education produced physicians and surgeons with the same basic skills.

Midwifery and man-midwifery

For our period, and in many parts of Europe until well into the twentieth century, midwives delivered the vast majority of infants. The training of midwives generally fell within an apprentice-like system where older, more experienced midwives passed their expertise on to younger women (not infrequently, their daughters, nieces, or other female relatives). (For more on the *practice* of midwifery, see chapter 7.) Experience was highly desired in a midwife and was often the only teacher, even in the late eighteenth century. In one rural area in northern Germany, many women explained their qualifications in just these terms. Elisabeth Heine had no formal training, her instruction having come from her own background of bearing eleven children and "having learned this and that from the other midwives." She, however (and not too unusually), had also obtained books from the local physician and read them and "the rest came with time and practice." By 1757, Catherina Gackens had been a midwife for seventeen years. Most of her knowledge came from what she had acquired in her own practice, and, she related, "if something happened that I felt unable to handle," she turned to "the famous midwife [in a nearby village], Mother Elisabeth, who died just last year." And, despite the widespread published criticism of midwives in just such rural settings, most communities appeared happy with their midwife and local physicians were by no means dissatisfied with them as individuals (although they were quick to criticize uncharacteristic arrogance and petulance).

Still, midwifery was not only learned at the bedside. As early as the sixteenth century, some cities ordered midwives to attend public dissections or obtain instruction from the city surgeon or city physician. Influenced by mercantilist and populationist thinking, the governors of many cities and territories began to institute more rigorous midwifery courses in the seventeenth century. Populationist writers, and especially the physicians among them, accused midwives of gross ignorance and held them responsible for much unnecessary infant death. Proper training was supposed to prevent such a "slaughter of the innocents." Dr. Lindemann in the small

---

[28] Brockliss and Jones, *Medical World*, 602–03.

German town of Königslutter, for instance, attributed the decline of population there "solely to the astonishing negligence" of local midwives. Another eighteenth-century observer believed midwives to be "the very death and destruction of the human race."[29] To improve midwifery, midwives might be, for instance, required to attend lectures on female anatomy and learn the methods of *version* (turning the child so that a safe delivery could be effected). Where special schools for surgeons existed, midwives were sometimes expected to train there. The German kingdom of Hanover established the first school exclusively for midwives in 1751. In France in the middle of the eighteenth century, the king licensed Madame du Coudray to travel through the provinces distributing instruction in the art of delivering children. She trained more than 5,000 women, and perhaps as many as 500 surgeons and physicians attended her courses as well. But she was not alone in making a great educational impact. Several midwives produced instructional manuals. Most famous were those written by Louise Bourgeois (1564–1640) in France, Sarah Stone (flourished in the late seventeenth and early eighteenth century) in England, and Justina Siegemund (1659–1705) in Prussia. Others of lesser fame enjoyed more limited, but by no means insignificant, reputations. The manual published by the midwife Anne Horenburg in Hanover in 1700 was used throughout northern Germany.

Cities and towns, as well as surgical colleges, had also set up courses to prepare men and women in midwifery. These efforts at improving midwifery by bettering the education of midwives did not have as their primary goal the suppression of women healers. While no doubt exists that midwifery was to some extent masculinized during the eighteenth century (and more rapidly, during the nineteenth), that was not the initial intent. Most physicians and surgeons wanted to control midwives, not displace them.

Midwives had, after all, never completely monopolized the birthing of children. Surgeons had always helped with difficult births. When fetuses proved undeliverable, for instance, the surgeon used an instrument to perforate the infant's skull (an operation called a *craniotomy*) and then removed the (now-dead) child piecemeal from its mother's womb. Beginning in the eighteenth century, however, men became regularly involved in the business of childbirth and more *accoucheurs* or *man-midwives* began to practice. These men assisted not only at dangerous births. Even before 1700, men gained some entry to the chambers of women in labor. In 1663 Louis XIV ordered a male midwife to the bed of one of his mistresses to deliver his child, and the same surgeon later attended the

[29] Quoted in Lindemann, *Health and Healing*, 205.

dauphine during her confinement. The forceps-wielding Chamberlens had enjoyed a fashionable and lucrative midwifery practice since the early decades of the seventeenth century. While it was highly unusual to have a man deliver a child before 1700, fifty years later it was by no means uncommon. If court circles and the aristocracy were the first to accept accoucheurs, the custom soon spread and by the late eighteenth century, at least in the northern, western, and urbanized parts of Europe, members of the bourgeoisie and even of the lower classes were having men deliver their children with greater frequency. This allowed some surgeons to specialize in obstetrics. In the French town of Reims, Pierre Robin was delivering about 200 infants a year in the 1780s. William Hunter built up an extensive obstetrical practice in London in the middle of the eighteenth century and trained man-midwives at his school. Man-midwives were generally surgeons with special training in midwifery often acquired at a school such as Hunter's or that of François Solayrès de Renhac in Paris.

Man-midwifery, then, became more familiar in the eighteenth century. This gradual infiltration of men into a field once overwhelmingly dominated by women has sometimes been interpreted as an attempt to force women out of the midwifery business, and is often seen as a process that went hand-in-glove with more general campaigns of professionalization. As the male physician or surgeon was raised to the status of expert, in this case, over the female body as well as over the rearing and education of children, women were pushed into subordinate roles. Thus, according to this argument, men gradually eliminated women from the world of legitimate practice and relegated female healers to the sphere of quacks and nonscientific practitioners. While one cannot dispute that more men were becoming involved in women's and children's health, it is not clear to what extent male crusading zeal caused the shift. It seems that many women themselves preferred the services of man-midwives partly because they had some better techniques, such as forceps, and partly because it was becoming fashionable to have a man-midwife attend at birth. Midwives were, to some extent, coming to be seen as practitioners for the poor or the ignorant, whereas the *bon ton* patronized the new accoucheur.

Of course, some people remained fixed in their prejudice against admitting men to the birth chamber on the grounds of morals and feminine modesty. These biases, too, were breaking down by the end of the eighteenth century. It is not clear that resistance to man-midwives was everywhere as strong as is generally supposed. One suspects that such moral arguments were advanced more forcefully in the nineteenth century. Populationists and members of the Enlightenment had launched a propaganda campaign against the ignorance of midwives and their "crimes" against humanity. Yet, as we have seen, many programs to improve midwifery were not directed at eliminating midwives, but rather at supervising them, although that management was, admittedly, to be male. Some policies designed to improve midwifery tried to lift the status of midwives by giving them salaries and official titles.

Finally, there were significant differences across Europe. Although man-midwifery became popular rather rapidly in England and France, it took hold somewhat less quickly in the Germanies, and even more slowly in the Italies, Spain, and eastern Europe. Especially in the vast expanses of Poland and Russia, it is very doubtful that any except the most westernized urban elites ever had a man attend at childbirth. A physician and a surgeon did receive payments for assisting at the birth of the Grand Duchess Elena Pavlovna in 1784, but the numbers of trained surgeons in Russia was so small that one cannot speak of any rise of man-midwifery there.

Medical theory and medical education, of course, developed in close step with one another at least for the academically trained physicians and surgeons of early modern Europe. Surgeons, apothecaries, and midwives, however, even when trained in an apprenticeship system, were rarely entirely untouched by theory. Moreover, we should not overvalue the acquisition of formal medical or surgical education. Many physicians, too, especially in the earlier part of our period, were trained as apprentices. And, as always, experience was a worthy mentor and only a few critics dismissed entirely the importance of the practical, hands-on experience of even women-healers as worthless, irrelevant, or possibly dangerous. If medical education was indeed becoming more formalized by the end of the eighteenth century, the teachings of experience were worked tightly into its fabric.

5   Hospitals and asylums

Hospitals are a measure of civilization.   (Jacques Tenon, 1788)[1]

The want of such hospitals [for sick and wounded seamen] is so sensibly felt, and Your Majesty's service suffers so greatly from the loss of seamen either by death or desertion, who are sent on shore for the cure of their distempers, that we think it our duty, humbly to renew our former application made to Your Majesty on that subject.
(Memorial from the Navy Board on subject of founding a naval hospital, 15 September 1744)[2]

Of rapacity and brutality, and all that is shocking to human feelings, a mad-house, that premature coffin of mind, body, and estate, is to an imputed lunatic, the concentration.
(William Belcher, "A Victim to the Trade of Lunacy," 1796)[3]

Properly speaking, the history of medical institutions is extremely broad and includes a consideration of "institutions *with* walls," i.e., hospitals, asylums, and poorhouses, as well as the many important "institutions *without* walls," i.e., medical guilds and societies, public health, nursing orders, poor relief, and charities. Not to be forgotten, certainly, is another institution: the state. There is, of course, much overlap here: early hospitals were charitable institutions and hospitals have always functioned as part of the whole apparatus of public health. This chapter will discuss hospitals, mental asylums, and their staffs and patients. Chapter 6 will then consider "institutions without walls."

Hospitals

Hospitals seem so fundamental to twentieth-century medicine that it is hard for us to realize that their powerful position today – as centers of

---

[1] Jacques Tenon, *Memoirs on Paris Hospitals*, ed. with an introduction, notes, and appendices by Dora B. Weiner (Canton, Mass., 1996), 43.

[2] Quoted in [P. D. Gordon Pugh,] *History and Haslar* (London, 1975), 1.

[3] William Belcher, *Address to Humanity: Containing, a Letter to Dr. Thomas Monro; A Receipt to make a Lunatic, and seize his Estate, and a Sketch of a True Smiling Hyena* (1796), quoted in Allan Ingram, ed., *Voices of the Mad: Four Pamphlets, 1683–1796* (Gloucester, 1997), 127–35 (quote, 132).

economic, scientific, and cultural authority – has been only recently achieved. In early modern Europe, the vast majority of people probably never entered a hospital for any medical reason; birthing and dying took place at home as did most medical care, including surgery. Nonetheless, even in early modern times, hospitals were neither irrelevant nor inconsequential to society. Many "hospitals," particularly those that dated from the middle ages and which originated as ecclesiastical foundations, owned large amounts of property, amassed fabulous wealth, and employed hundreds or even thousands. Others, especially those that functioned as poor- and almshouses, sheltered crowds of people, especially in winter. Thus, the hospital as an economic unit, or as a form of social housing, always assumed great significance in a community.

Generations of historians writing about hospitals tended to paint a very dark picture of medieval and early modern hospitals. Hospitals, according to this view, served as refuges for the outcast and impoverished, and medical treatment assumed a decidedly secondary role. Such histories stressed the noxiousness of early modern hospitals, branding them "gateways to death" or holding them partly responsible for the high mortality of early modern times. Accordingly, not until the late eighteenth century did improvements in construction, in nursing care, and in medical practice begin to transform hospitals into institutions of medical teaching, medical care, and cure. The major steps in this evolution were taken to be the introduction of bedside teaching in the eighteenth century and the rise of a clinical medicine based on morbid anatomy and pathology in the 1790s. The next strides were the bacteriological discoveries of the middle to late nineteenth century and the development of first *antiseptic* and then *aseptic* protocols near the end of that century. Equally important for the advancement of surgery, of course, was the discovery of ether anesthesia in 1846.

In such "triumphalist" hospital histories, physicians appear as the movers and the shakers, as those who successfully *medicalized* hospitals (i.e., turned them into institutions primarily devoted to medical care). Their admirers portray these men as stalwart champions who fought the combined opposition of nonmedical administrators, nurses, patients, and a wider unenlightened public that disputed such necessary procedures as postmortem examinations. Equally characteristic of older hospital histories was a pronounced emphasis on architecture and its evolution over time. While this is hardly a trivial pursuit (the construction of physical facilities and the provision of adequate ventilation and drainage significantly affected mortality), such historians often appeared to be more concerned with floor plans than people.

Radically different from the triumphalist school is the interpretation Michel Foucault voiced in *The Birth of the Clinic* (1963). Foucault, instead of tracing a progressive series of improvements in hospitals, postulated a profound break: a "birth" or "rupture" in the 1790s. From that point onward, the patient's place in hospital medicine was "objectified": he or she was opened up to the unobstructed gaze of physicians and became the target of an increasingly intrusive medical inspection and regulation. Second, whereas in the triumphalist version the ascendancy of medical science and the clinical method counted as an (almost) unreservedly positive phenomenon, Foucault reversed these polarities: it betokened not progress but a defeat for patients by solidifying the power of doctors over them. The development of hospital medicine was, therefore, altogether a bad thing for the freedom of the individual.

Since about 1990, a "new orthodoxy" on the history of hospitals has emerged which combines elements of both the approaches presented above. In particular, it has called for a broader chronological vision. Both the triumphalist and Foucauldian renditions focused almost exclusively on the closing decade of the eighteenth century. This newer approach takes a less blinkered view and surveys what happened in hospitals at least since the Renaissance. Research into early modern hospitals has strongly suggested that such institutions never functioned exclusively as refuse-heap relief. Although it is true that few hospitals before the eighteenth century employed many physicians (and some employed none), other practitioners – surgeons, apothecaries, and members of nursing orders – dispensed at least a modicum of medical care and sometimes much more than that.

Second, many studies have convincingly demonstrated that the exceptionally high mortality rates believed "typical" of early modern hospitals had already began to decline well *before* the clinical revolution. The "Black Legend" pertaining to hospitals, i.e., the argument that hospitals were mere "gateways to death" and cesspools of infection, seems to have been constructed in the late eighteenth century by Enlightenment critics. As we shall see, most eighteenth-century hospitals were far better providers of care and cure than the purveyors of "gloom-and-doom" depictions are willing to accept.

Today's hospital historians also tend to highlight the multiple functions hospitals fulfilled. Complex social, economic, and cultural forces converged in their administration, and, as Bernard Mandeville presciently observed, "Pride and Vanity . . . built more Hospitals than all the Virtues together." Hospital administrators were provincial or urban bigwigs and hospital financing overwhelmingly flowed from local benefactors. Whereas previous hospital history tended to concentrate on the heroic struggles of physicians, it is now usual to discuss how a *miscellany* of actors, including nurses, lay and ecclesiastic administrators, apothecaries, surgeons, and patients, together shaped hospital life.

The last of these, the patient, always sadly missing from triumphalist accounts because he or she was unimportant to the success of medical science except as a kind of "raw material," is becoming the centerpoint of many new-style hospital studies. Interest, always keen about mortality, has also turned to investigating how patients determined the care they received and manipulated staff and administrators to their own advantage. While the story of the "construction of the patient" is mostly yet to be written, the bricks-and-mortar approach has faded in favor of a more humane history rooted in flesh and blood.

Ancient and medieval precursors

The search for the recognizable roots of modern hospitals in the ancient world has produced only meager results. The founding of hospitals (as we tend to understand them) occurred in conjunction with the dissemination of Christianity, although not only Christians established them. For example, large hospitals called *bimāristāns* already existed in the tenth century in major Islamic cities such as Baghdad, Cairo, and Damascus. The first Jewish hospitals in Europe date from the thirteenth century: Regensburg (1210), Cologne (1248), and Mainz (1285).

Archeologists and historians have identified some pre-Christian institutions that might be viewed as either forerunners of hospitals or as institutions with analogous purposes: ancient Greek healing shrines (*asklepieia*) and Roman *valetudinaria* for soldiers and slaves, for example. The earliest Christian hospitals in both the eastern and western parts of the Roman empire date from the fourth century.

The term "hospital" in the middle ages actually embraced several related institutions: leper houses (*leprosaria*); almshouses; hospices for travelers and pilgrims; and institutions to care for the sick. By the end of the middle ages, there were quite a lot of them in Europe: in the fourteenth century, probably one for every 1,000 inhabitants. Leper houses sought to isolate the "unclean" from the rest of the population. They tended to be quite small and offered principally lodgings and food rather than medical treatment. Most were situated on the outskirts of town, often along main roads, and sometimes served as hospices for vagrants and the wandering poor. In their heyday, the number of leprosaria was huge. There were, for example, over 2,000 leper houses in France in 1225; there may have been as many as 19,000 in Europe. Because leprosy had almost vanished from Europe by the fifteenth century, in the

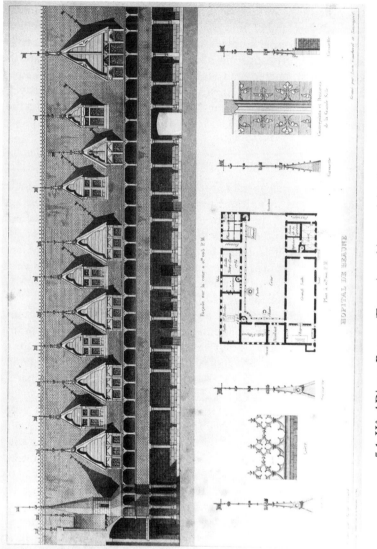

5.1 Hôtel Dieu at Beaune (France), architectural details of roof and floor plan.

sixteenth century almost all of the once flourishing leprosaria had fallen into disuse, were abandoned, or had been converted to other purposes.

Under the umbrella designation of hospital in the middle ages, we also find almshouses the principal function of which was to accommodate the poor, and hospices designed for travelers and pilgrims. Pilgrim sanctuaries dotted the road to the major shrine of St. James of Compostela at Santiago in Spain, for example. Neither almshouses nor hospices, however, offered medical assistance, as a rule.

The institutions that probably most closely resemble modern hospitals were those set up for the sick. These extended some medical care, although they also were retreats for the poor. Such institutions were scarce in medieval times and always fulfilled several functions. There was great variety in their size, administration, and conditions of endowment. Most were founded after 1200. England, for example, had several quite expansive institutions. The largest was probably St. Leonard in York with about 206 places. Besides these, a goodly number of more modest institutions, with room for between twenty and fifty inhabitants, as well as a number of very small ones, such as St. John the Baptist in Winchester, which catered to exactly six people, speckled the countryside. In fifteenth-century Florence, hospitals ranged from the huge San Maria Nuova with its 230 places to minuscule ones that accepted only a handful of sufferers at a time. Florence had at the time thirty hospitals for a population of about 30,000, about average for cities of its size and economic importance.

Many medieval hospitals evolved in lockstep with the western form of monasticism, i.e., groups of monks and nuns living communally (as distinct from the hermitical tradition of eastern Christianity). In the early ninth century, for instance, a plan for a model cloister at St. Gallen included the following: (1) an "infirmarium" for monks; (2) a "hospitale pauperum" for the poor and for pilgrims who "came on foot"; (3) a house for guests who "came mounted"; (4) a leprosarium; and, finally, (5) hospitals for novices, converts, and lay brothers. A Russian church statute of 996 erected sanctuaries for "unfortunates," a broad category of the ill, insane, possessed, and even criminal. Most were confined in monasteries and cared for by monks. Other western monastic orders, but especially the Cistercians, established cloister infirmaries on a similar design in the thirteenth and fourteenth centuries when medieval monasticism flowered.

Ecclesiastical influence was critical in the creation of medieval hospitals, but not all were founded by the church and its clergy. Lay donation was also common. Powerful nobles endowed a number of hospitals in the eleventh and twelfth centuries. William the Conqueror, in a pacific moment, had hospitals built in Cherbourg, Bayeux, Caen, and Rouen. One of the most famous and opulent of medieval institutions, the Hôtel-Dieu in Beaune, was built in 1443 by Nicolas Rolin, chancellor to the duke of Burgundy. Princes of the church were also active founders: the hospital of San Juan Baptista in Toledo (1542) was established by the most powerful, and perhaps also the wealthiest, prelate in Spain, Cardinal Juan Tavera.

Strong commercial, economic, and demographic growth characterized the late middle ages. Municipalities fed on the profits drawn from domestic exchange, international commerce, and craft production. Around 1300, cities, their wealthy inhabitants, and religious and guild fraternities expressed their religious piety and social standing by founding civic hospitals (what are called in German *Bürgerspitäler*). Dynamic commercial centers, such as Venice, Pisa, and Genoa in northern Italy, Augsburg in the prosperous German southwest, and the affluent Hansa cities of the north, all raised their own Bürgerspitäler. The buildings of a particularly fine example, the Heilig-Geist-Spital, still stand in Lüneberg.

These medieval predecessors are important because most did not simply disappear to be replaced by markedly different institutions after 1500. Rather, early modern hospitals were frequently the very same institutions, at least in name and often in physical structure as well. Hospitals erected during the middle ages resembled each other fairly closely. Generally we find an enclosed area set off from the rest of the city by walls and gates. The main building was usually rectangular or cruciform. Altars and chapels were identifying features of medieval hospitals. Beds, often large enough to accommodate more than one individual, were arrayed in rows down the length of the hall. Not until the middle of the eighteenth century did the typical structure of hospital buildings change. The new pavilion hospitals were clusters of one- or two-story edifices separated by open spaces. Large windows and properly placed doors allowed air and light to enter freely.

Just how much medical and surgical care medieval (and early modern) hospitals offered their inmates continues to perplex historians. This may be a poorly posed question, for medical care was never a hospital's sole raison d'être. Endowing a hospital was an act of piety that manifested the wealth, position, and power of sponsors. Charitable giving created and strengthened webs of obligations in a society which worked on the exchange of gifts, goods, and services. The right of benefactors to nominate people for beds, for instance, served several purposes at once: it was an expression of charity, a form of patronage, and a sort of insurance scheme for servants or clients. Hospitals continued to function in these ways well into the eighteenth and even nineteenth centuries. Roy Porter, for example, in writing about the *voluntary hospital* of the eighteenth century sees it as part of a long-term "gift relation" in western society and as a legitimate outlet for utilitarian charity.

Medieval hospitals and their earlier modern successors extended other services which may strike us as surprising. For instance, after 1464, the largest hospital in Florence, San Maria Nuova, acted almost like an investment bank, offering a return of 5 percent for any capital placed in its hands. The hospital of San Giovanni in Turin did something similar, and one in medieval Cambridge lent money to "men of substance" embarrassed by their debts. Hospitals assumed, therefore, an often central position in a community as property-owners, employers, and, occasionally, bankers.

Historians have generally concluded that the main function of medieval, and to a large extent, early modern hospitals as well was care not cure. Bedrest, clean linen, shelter from the elements, and a good meal were the "treatments" usually available. A recent study of hospital expenditures, for instance, lists outlays for fuel, food, linen, and candles, but only rarely for medicines. While it is true that custodial care was the most typical feature of medieval hospitals, such institutions were not totally lacking in medical treatments or even medical "research." Admittedly, the staff connected with hospitals were essentially caretakers, such as women servants and nursing sisters (and, in monasteries, monk-infirmarers). Yet one should not too quickly categorize medieval hospitals as *merely* custodial institutions. In the fourteenth century, for instance, San Maria Nuova paid a corps of visiting physicians and a surgeon as well as nursing sisters and servants. Most hospitals in Renaissance Florence kept a doctor and barber-surgeon on retainer, and these men visited patients regularly, sometimes even daily. Nurses (male and female), too, should not be dismissed as mindless drudges who only emptied chamber pots, made beds, prepared food, and lifted patients. Several hospitals had their own pharmacies and nursing sisters often ran them as well as administering medications to patients.

The older picture of medieval hospitals, therefore, needs substantial revision. Clearly these hospitals afforded more medical care than they were once credited with doing. Some treated a fairly wide social spectrum of patients as well. They catered to the acutely ill, as well as to the elderly, the destitute (especially widows and orphans), and the incurable. Patients did not invariably enter hospitals for life, or even for the rest of their lives. Some hospitals such as the Ospedale di San Paolo in Pistoia and San Maria Nuova in Florence boasted cure rates of 80 to 90 percent (although these figures should not be taken at face value). Short stays, of between eleven and fifteen days, were the norm. By the end of the medieval period, many hospitals employed a professional administrative staff, or at least a director, either lay or religious. He was not a medical person, however, but a man skilled in finance. Nurses and patients determined daily routines within the hospital more forcefully than did physicians. Regional differences played a clear role with more sophisticated and more medicalized institutions existing in the larger, more commercialized cities and, it seems, especially in Italy.

About the patients admitted to medieval hospitals we still know little. We cannot even say with much confidence to what extent they died in hospitals. Estimates of mortality range widely, if not to say wildly. All we can reasonably venture is that mortality rates probably improved in the Renaissance, and then throughout early modern times, if only gradually and with setbacks. Mortality experiences, moreover, varied enormously from place to place.

In terms of social class, however, most historians agree that inmates of medieval hospitals were poor, although not necessarily destitute. Especially in the commercial centers, artisans, domestic servants, and their families might go to a hospital when ill as, for instance, part of their rights as guild members. Especially toward the end of the middle ages, more sick people (rather than just poor people) were entering hospitals for acute care, although the category of the sick-poor contributed the greatest number of hospital-goers well into the eighteenth century.

Still, mounting evidence also suggests that the clientele of late medieval hospitals may have been socially quite diffuse. In a careful study of the Santa Cruz hospital in Barcelona, Uta Lindgren charted the backgrounds of 2,696 patients admitted between 1401 and 1499. Most of the patients admitted came from two groups: farmers and foresters (which demonstrates how the hospital drew from a large catchment area around the city), and other respectable workers. The total of beggars and vagabonds admitted was small – about the same as that of patricians. Likewise, while the number of hospitals in fifteenth-century Florence that catered to the "poor of Christ" was the largest (eight), seven hospitals existed for the care of the sick, six for specific occupational and professional groups, and five for women.

Medieval hospitals avoided admitting sufferers from contagious diseases. Nonetheless, the pesthouse or *lazaretto*, as a special institution for those afflicted with a catching or a "loathsome" disease, began to appear in the middle of the fourteenth century: in Geertruidenberg (Holland) in 1356, Dubrovnik in 1377, Marseilles in 1383, Venice in 1423, and Milan in 1488. All were cities that plague had ravaged in the fourteenth and fifteenth centuries, and all bustled with the movement of people, animals, and goods. Syphilis, too, once it became a problem in Europe, also prompted hospitals to exclude its victims. Special hospices appeared, however, to deal with this new type of patient. The Hôpital Saint-Louis, for instance, was established in Paris in 1607 for syphilitics and those suffering other contagious diseases. Similarly, in Germany, a number of hospitals were set up expressly for syphilitics in the sixteenth century.

By the end of the middle ages, then, most towns of any consequence boasted a range of hospitals which catered to the poor as well as to a growing number of others, generally drawn from the lower orders of society. There were, for example, about ninety hospitals in Spain before 1500. Burgos and Cordoba, typical regional hubs, each had eleven. While we should certainly not romanticize the quality of medical care in medieval hospitals, neither were they killing bottles. Increasingly hospitals were involved in serious medical care and increasingly people left hospitals "cured." Moreover, whereas hospitals such as San Maria Nuova had originally been "founded to serve the poor, with special emphasis on the sick, by the early sixteenth century it was serving the sick, with special emphasis on the poor."[4] The relative heyday of the medieval hospital was disturbed by the coming of the Reformation and even more by the structural economic and demographic crises of the late sixteenth and seventeenth centuries.

Hospitals from the sixteenth to the middle of the eighteenth centuries

The advent of the Reformation in Europe had radical consequences for poor relief and medical care. In the countries that sheered away from popery – in many German states and cities, in Denmark and Sweden, and in England – the disestablishment of the Catholic church was paired with a dissolution of monastic and ecclesiastical institutions, including hospitals. The impact proved most severe in England where Henry VIII indiscriminately broke up cloisters, religious foundations, and charitable establishments, and sold their lands. Hardly any medieval hospitals survived this assault. Of course, the decline of English hospitals had begun long before and so perhaps it is a bit unjust to rest all the blame for England's dearth of hospitals on the meaty shoulders of its Reformer King. In any case, the effects of the Reformation's pruning lasted only briefly. Hordes of the impoverished and homeless quickly overran cities. London's poor relief almost collapsed under the pressure, and in the

---

[4] Katharine Park, "Healing the Poor: Hospitals and Medical Assistance in Renaissance Florence," in Jonathan Barry and Colin Jones, eds., *Medicine and Charity Before the Welfare State* (Cambridge, 1991), 33–34.

1540s and 1550s monarchs reestablished the "Five Royal Hospitals": St. Bartholomew's and St. Thomas's for the sick-poor; St. Mary of Bethlem for the insane; Christ's for orphans; and, finally, Bridewell for miscreants. All received a medical staff consisting of a number of physicians and surgeons. Once one left London, however, the situation was much bleaker and the refounding of provincial hospitals had to wait until the voluntary hospital movement of the eighteenth century, although some survived as almshouses.

On the continent, the Italian wars of the late fifteenth and early sixteenth centuries and the religio-political unrest that disrupted the seventeenth century affected hospitals more adversely than did the disestablishment of religious orders. Hospitals in the suburbs of Montpellier, for instance, were razed during a siege in 1562 and the chronic battling among French, Imperial, Papal, and Italian troops severely disrupted the running of Italian hospitals. The sixteenth-century religious strife in Germany interfered less with hospitals than did the more sweeping dislocations of the Thirty Years War (1618–48).

Catholicism, after the middle of the sixteenth century, experienced a rebirth and a reanimation (institutionalized in the decisions of the Council of Trent, 1545–63) that was not solely a response to the challenge the Protestants posed. The Council helped rekindle a Christian charitable impulse that had never been as effectively dampened as it had in Protestant countries. Tridentine religious revivalism and the renewed drive of Catholic princes and prelates led to the foundation of numerous hospitals: the Juliusspital in Würzburg (1576); the Great Poorhouse (Großes Armenhaus) in Vienna (1693); the Hospital of San Maurizio and Lazzaro (1575); the Ospedale di Carità in Turin (1629); a hospicio in Zamora, Spain (1629); and the Albergo dei Poveri in Genoa (1635). Although hospital endowment in this period was not uniquely Catholic, the number of Catholic foundations greatly exceeded Protestant ones. Still, one can point to the Great Friedrich Hospital (Großes-Friedrich-Hospital) opened in Calvinist Berlin in 1697.

The largest number of new hospitals were established in seventeenth-century France, mostly by government fiat. In 1676, Louis XIV ordered that each city of a certain size must build and maintain a *hôpital général*. The nominal aim of the hôpitaux généraux was to immure the disorderly poor. Within their confines, administrators were to apply strictly regulated patterns of working and living to root out evil, profane, or merely unsocial behaviors and to habituate the poor to lives of thrift, diligence, and proper belief. Similar institutions existed in other European countries: in England, the *workhouses*; in German-speaking areas, the *Zuchthäuser*; in the United Provinces, the *tuchthuizen*; in Italy the *ospedali di carità*; in Spain, the *hospicios*; and in Russia, the *smiritel'nye doma*. The wonderfully baroque name of the Pforzheim institution (1714) – the "house for the orphaned, the mad, the sick, the criminal, and the poor" (Waisen-, Toll-, Kranken-, Zucht- und Arbeitshaus) – reflects its many missions. This was, according to Foucault, the prime instrument of "the great confinement" (see chapter 1); the coordinated attempt to incarcerate all those society defined as "deviant" and to apply the same remedies to all of them. Such institutions often swelled to gargantuan proportions. The Paris hôpital général, opened in 1656, had several buildings: among them, the Bicêtre for men, the Salpêtrière for women, and the Pitié for children. The Ospedale di Carità in Turin held almost 2,300 inmates in 1737 and the Hamburg Pesthof housed between 850 and 1,000 in its labyrinthine structure.

Despite their stated goals, the hôpitaux généraux never offered an effective form of repression and control. After scrutinizing the admission registers of the Ospedale di Carità, Sandra Cavallo concluded that "the violent repression of begging via arrest and punishment seem . . . to be of marginal significance in the hospital's overall activities, and was resorted to only in moments of acute crisis."[5] Nor was the control of undesirables usefully centralized. Most hôpitaux généraux in France, as elsewhere, were funded and run by locals. By the middle of the eighteenth century, hôpitaux généraux had largely shed their police functions. Most had also been medicalized at least to the extent of having physicians on retainer, surgeons on staff, and, often, a trained corps of nursing sisters in the wards (especially in Catholic regions). Furthermore, it is by no means certain that the efforts of the French government to close down thousands of smaller institutions in the name of greater efficiency was ever fully implemented. Vigorous opposition at the local level arose from those involved in traditional charitable undertakings or those excited by the message of the Catholic Reformation, as well as from the women of religious congregations and nursing orders, and from provincial elites who sought to preserve "their" charitable enterprises.[6]

Eighteenth-century reformers were unrelentingly harsh in their condemnations of early modern hospitals:

Most of the patients are incurables who either pass away soon [after being admitted] or draw out their lives with no attempt being made to treat their afflictions, or [they] are released on the slightest show of improvement . . . Not a small portion

---

[5] Sandra Cavallo, "Charity, Power, and Patronage in Eighteenth-Century Italian Hospitals: The Case of Turin," in Lindsay Granshaw and Roy Porter, eds., *The Hospital in History* (London, 1987), 97.

[6] Daniel Hickey, *Local Hospitals in Ancien Régime France: Rationalization, Resistance, Renewal, 1530–1789* (Montreal, 1997).

of the patients are insane . . . the quiet ones are kept in the wards . . . idiots wander about as they please . . . [and] the raving are chained to their beds.[7]

Still, the reformers' attack on such "spitals" as almost worse than useless ignores several points and distorts others. First, institutions such as the Hamburg Pesthof described above afforded safety from the elements for the homeless, food for the needy, and rest and warmth for the ill; one should not underestimate the worth of such aid. The Pesthof, like the hôtels-dieu and the hôpitaux généraux, served as a waystation for the poor, who migrated through it seasonally. Moreover, many inmates moved in and out rather more freely than one might imagine: leaving at dawn to go work, beg, or attend church, returning at night for a bowl of hot soup and a place to sleep. Even late in the eighteenth century the poor might well view refuge and sustenance as a hospital's real benefit. An Edinburgh medical student in writing up the case of "a poor indigent man without house or family" noted that "what he seemed most to want was shelter and protection during the severe winter months."[8]

We need to keep in mind, therefore, the mixed character of these institutions when we seek to judge the quality of medical care. What value we should place on mortality rates in this context is not clear. Much negative comment came from the reformers of the late eighteenth century. The statistics they marshaled tended to be dire in the extreme; mortalities of 25 percent or even more are cited as "typical." The most famous commentators, the English philanthropist, John Howard (c. 1726–90), and the French encyclopédist, Jacques Tenon (1724–1816), took firm aim at the Paris Hôtel-Dieu. Tenon, for example, found

no hospital so badly located, so cramped, so unreasonably overcrowded, so dangerous, so filled with causes of ill-health and death as the Hôtel-Dieu. Nowhere in the whole universe is there a hospital building that combines such an important purpose with results so deadly to society.[9]

These reformers thus painted a very dark picture of hospitals as the "very gateways to death." But, as Laurence Brockliss and Colin Jones insist, "the black legend of hospital care needs substantial modification and nuancing." A die-off of anywhere from one-quarter to one-third (and sometimes even more) might have pertained in some hospitals. By the middle of the eighteenth century and in the best-run hospitals, however,

---

[7] Johann Jakob Rambach, *Versuch einer physisch-medizinischen Beschreibung von Hamburg* (Hamburg, 1801), 411–12, 416–17.
[8] Quoted in Guenter Risse, *Hospital Life in Enlightenment Scotland: Care and Teaching at the Royal Infirmary of Edinburgh* (Cambridge, 1986), 8.
[9] Tenon, *Memoirs on Paris Hospitals*, 299.

those rates had often dropped to under 10 percent. In the teaching wards at the Royal Infirmary at Edinburgh, for example, mortality ranged from a low of 4.7 percent to a high of 10.5 percent. At the Bristol Infirmary, 86.5 percent of patients left as "cured," and a further 2.6 percent as "relieved." Death rates at the San Juan de Dios Hospital in Murcia, Spain, at midcentury were 19.5 percent and, by the 1790s, 18.6 percent.[10]

Caution is called for here, of course. Some hospitals remained desperately awful. Regional differences were probably enormous and death rates presumably rose as one moved away from the centers of culture and progress, although one can only venture this most tentatively as the research on these areas remains to be done.

The quality of staffing, its numbers, and the presence (or absence) of adequate funding could drastically affect mortality rates. Especially in Catholic countries, the nursing orders – in France, the Daughters of Charity, the Sisters of Saint-Thomas of Villeneuve, and the Brothers of Charity – came to dominate hospital routines. Sisters supervised the wards, ran hospital pharmacies, and even performed minor surgical operations. Not until the eighteenth century did physicians and surgeons challenge their authority with any success. The nursing orders brought a regimen of cleanliness and order to the hospitals and probably bore a good measure of the responsibility for improvements in hospital environment and perhaps, therefore, even for slight declines in mortality rates. At the same time, governments organized better training for lay nurses.

Even in the seventeenth century, hospitals began to hire permanent medical staff. The Hospital del Amor de Dios in Seville had employed two physicians since 1603 (as well as surgeons and apothecaries). The trend toward a "professionalization" of medical staff in hospitals greatly accelerated during the eighteenth century. By midcentury, hospitals commonly contracted with a physician to visit at stated intervals, engaged full-time surgeons, hired a pharmacist, and perhaps even provided in-house education for candidate surgeons and apothecaries. Local lay directors often used such appointments to exercise their rights of patronage. The locus of power in such institutions in no way rested with physicians. Lay administrators, house surgeons, and even nursing sisters decided policy and practices more actively than physicians did. The time when physicians would call the shots had not yet come and perhaps their dominance,

[10] For an intelligent and balanced treatment of the "Black Legend," see Laurence Brockliss and Colin Jones, *The Medical World of Early Modern France* (Oxford, 1997), 717–25; on mortality at the Royal Infirmary, Risse, *Hospital Life*, 264; at San Juan de Dios, José J. Garcia Hourcade, *Beneficencia y sanidad en el s. XVIII: el Hospital de S. Juan de Dios de Murcia* (Murcia, 1996), 160–61; at the Bristol Infirmary, Mary E. Fissell, *Patients, Power, and the Poor in Eighteenth-Century Bristol* (Cambridge, 1991), 107–08.

which seems so secure in the late nineteenth and twentieth centuries, was never as absolute as we tend to believe.

The patronage exercised by benefactors reminds us that hospitals were not untouched by greater political, economic, and social forces. Population growth, religious shifts, and material conditions powerfully affected the pace and timing of hospital foundings. A rise in general levels of prosperity, especially in rapidly developing commercial centers, such as England and Holland, generated great pools of wealth waiting to be tapped for charitable and medical purposes. Counter-Reformation piety also spurred benefactions. Equally obvious were broad governmental programs of state-run charity and social control. Wars, too, drove medical innovations forward. More specific political machinations could be just as decisive in determining how life in hospitals bumped along. For example, during the Restoration in England, Charles II vigorously intervened in the running of particular hospitals, purging his political opponents from the governing board of St. Thomas's Hospital which they had long dominated.

Patients remain the unknown element in this discussion. While we still do not know much about the patients who populated the early modern hospitals, some things seem clear. First, the old interpretation that early modern hospitals were crowded with the poor is generally correct, although it needs some qualification. By "the poor," we do not necessarily mean the absolutely indigent. Investigations of poor relief policies have shown that a large group of the so-called laboring poor (those who could normally make their way, but who fell into destitution during crises, whether personal or societal) often used hospitals to tide them over until better times returned. Children dropped at orphanages, for instance, were often "marked" with a token so that parents could identify and claim them later (as they often did). Orphanages also admitted children on the understanding that parents would eventually retrieve them. Likewise, hospitals of the late seventeenth and middle of the eighteenth centuries spent more time treating the ill and returned ever more patients "cured" or at least "improved" to the productive world of work and normal life.

European hospitals in an age of reform

The reform of hospitals in the eighteenth century proceeded in two ways: with the founding of new hospitals and the transformation of older ones. As we have seen, eighteenth-century reformers sharply asserted that existing institutions were totally unsuitable for the practice of medicine and, worse, actually frustrated the purposeful treatment of patients. Others argued that hospitals in fact engendered diseases, such as typhus and similar distempers. Some reformers advocated the abolition of hospitals altogether and advised that care outside hospitals would prove more beneficial and economical.

Around 1800, home care was eloquently championed, and partially implemented, by the French Hospital Council charged with reforming the nation's old hospital system. Keeping patients out of institutions was deemed the best way of preserving their health and of returning them to gainful employment speedily. The Council supported traditional venues of aid, such as soup kitchens and welfare centers, but also tried more novel approaches, such as the establishment of a series of dispensaries and infirmaries, as well as providing nursing care at home. More will be said about this and similar schemes in the following chapter.[11]

The early eighteenth century witnessed renewed interest in the founding of hospitals that can be attributed both to new ideologies (to the Enlightenment, for example) and to broader social, economic, and religious shifts. It seems evident that the mercantilism and populationism of the late seventeenth and early eighteenth centuries strongly affected plans to revise social welfare and flowed into the new hospital movement of the eighteenth century. The mercantilism of western Europe and the cameralism of the German-speaking countries were predicated on the idea that state action could bring about the general prosperity and well-being of the nation. In the realm of health, several cameralists sought to inject mercantilism into medicine in the form of *medical police*. (The term "medical police" is rather misleading. Under it one should understand a series of policies rather than a group of police agents or officers.) Johann Peter Frank, in his monumental *System einer vollständigen medizinischen Polizey* (A system of complete medical police, 1779–1825) detailed projects for state intervention into all areas of health. Frank viewed hospitals as integral components of a comprehensive medical police and wrote extensively on them. Another medical author, tellingly, compared hospitals to military defenses: "If a soldier may design fortresses which cost millions in order to protect countries; why should not a physician be permitted to propose a hospital in order to save people from devastating diseases?"[12]

Medical police had its greatest impact in Germany and Austria where the "well-ordered police state" (a sort of proto-welfare state rather than a dictatorial one) sought to enhance the health of the population as well as

---

[11] Dora Weiner, *The Citizen-Patient in Revolutionary and Imperial Paris* (Baltimore and London, 1993), 133–65.

[12] Quoted in Johann Peter Frank, *A System of Complete Medical Police: Selections from Johann Peter Frank*, ed. by Erna Lesky (Baltimore, 1975), 407; George Rosen, "Cameralism and the Concept of Medical Police" and "The Fate of the Concept of Medical Police, 1780–1890," both in Rosen, *From Medical Police to Social Medicine: Essays on the History of Health Care* (New York, 1974), 120–58.

to boost its size. Still, such thinking was not exclusively Teutonic. Similar notions fired the imagination of reformers and bureaucrats in almost every European country. Mercantilism and cameralism later blended smoothly into the Enlightenment.

The mercantilist principles of rational organization and purposeful charity fed into planning for new hospitals (as, more generally, they determined new forms of charity and medical care; see chapter 6). One of the best-documented hospital movements of the eighteenth century is the creation of *voluntary hospitals* in Britain. The term may baffle the uninitiated: it refers to nothing more than hospitals founded by individual and group, rather than by state, initiatives. These private enterprises may seem to fall well outside the realm of mercantilism in that the state assumed no active part. In fact, however, secular philanthropy and rational religion fostered an array of projects designed to advance the "glory of God by promoting the usefulness of man."[13] The founding of voluntary hospitals was a marvelously apt solution to the charitable quandary of the eighteenth century: how to deal with a greater poverty without providing handouts to the deceitful and comfort to the unworthy. Not only in England did such ideas find fertile ground in which to germinate: similar institutions cropped up almost everywhere in Europe.

The first voluntary hospital in Britain, the Westminster Infirmary (London), began admitting patients in 1720. By the end of the century, there were several others in England's grandest city (St. George's founded in 1733, London Hospital in 1740, and the Middlesex Hospital in 1745) and thirty in the provinces of which perhaps the best-known were in Edinburgh (1729), Winchester (1736), Bristol (1737), York (1740), and Liverpool (1749). Only two of the hospitals built in these years – Guy's Hospital in London (1726) and Addenbrooke's in Cambridge (1719) – were endowed by individuals: Thomas Guy, a wealthy bookdealer and Dr. John Addenbrooke, a physician. Philanthropic organizations established all the others on what Roy Porter has termed a "joint stock principle." Groups of philanthropically and practically minded men collaborated in drafting plans and raising funds. The milieu that fostered such engagement was that of the growing public sphere of the late eighteenth century. Informal exchanges of ideas in reading groups, coffeehouses, and gentlemen's clubs paved the way. The plan for the Westminster Infirmary, for instance, first saw the light of day in a Fleet Street coffeehouse. For England the landed gentry, the mercantile middle classes, and a savoring of parsons were the ones who contributed time, energy, and money to the cause. Elsewhere in Europe, respectable

[13] Quoted in Risse, *Hospital Life*, 17.

laypeople and clergy also took the lead. Patrons or benefactors either gave lump sums or paid regular subscription fees to fund the edifice and to offset its running costs; patients paid nothing. Those who donated large amounts tended to become members of the managing board of the hospital; but even those who enrolled only the minimum subscription enjoyed the right to distribute patronage in the form of "nominating" the sick-poor to a bed. Thus, subscribing to a hospital was a rational form of philanthropy that fitted well into the mercantile world and conformed neatly to middle-class social and religious mindsets.

Typical of the solicitation among friends and colleagues that could facilitate entry to voluntary hospitals was the mediation the novelist (and physician) Tobias Smollett (1721–71) undertook on the behalf of an acquaintance. In 1750 he wrote to William Hunter about the son of one Mr. Louttit, an apothecary:

> Mr. Professor,
>   Louttit was with me Saturday last, earnestly solliciting my Interest with Dr. Pitcairn in behalf of his Boy, who is (it seems) afflicted with scorbutic, lep'rous, or scrophulous ulcers, for which he desires the child should be admitted in Bartholomew's Hospital . . .
>   Louttit has been advised to have Recourse to the Doctor by a Gentleman belonging to the Hospital, who assures him that the Boy will be admitted, should our Friend [Dr. Pitcairn] make a Point of it, tho' otherwise, objections might be made to his Reception on account of the circumstances of the Disease. In the name of God, use your Influence with the Doctor; for Louttit is very clamorous and importunate, and will consider the favor as an indelible obligation.[14]

Hospital foundations on voluntarist principles were not, however, uniquely British. Even in countries where historians have judged state influence to be decisive, such as in the German and Italian states and in Russia, private efforts were never inconsequential. Privately devised and funded programs won acceptance in Hamburg, Lübeck, and Kiel, where commercial interests dominated.

German territorial states, often ruled by "rationalizing" princes or their bureaucrats, recast older institutions or established new ones under the rubric of general hospitals (*Allgemeine Krankenhäuser*) but which, despite the name, were not identical to the hôpitaux généraux. The purpose of these institutions corresponded to that the voluntary hospitals had undertaken, although here the state generated the power. New hospitals sprang up in eighteenth-century Germany beginning with the St. Hubertus Hospital in Düsseldorf (1709), followed by the St. Rochus Hospital in

---

[14] *The Letters of Tobias Smollett*, ed. by Lewis M. Knapp (Oxford, 1970), 16.

Mainz (1722–28), the Charité in Kassel (1772–84), and the hospital in Karlsruhe for civilian and military patients (1785). Venerable institutions, dating from the middle ages or the sixteenth century, such as the Juliusspital in Würzburg, underwent major renovations. We can also identify some privately founded hospitals such as the one the physician Johann Christian Senckenberg established in Frankfurt in 1763.

The greatest foundation of the eighteenth century in the German-speaking territories was the General Hospital (Allgemeines Krankenhaus) in Vienna (1784). Two students of Herman Boerhaave, Gerard van Swieten (1700–72) and Anton de Haën (1704?–76), had floated plans during the reign of Maria Theresa (1740–80). Founded by Joseph II, the Viennese general hospital fits snugly into the series of academic and teaching hospitals that midwived the "birth of the clinic."

In France, reform initiatives came first from private individuals and groups. In Paris, for example, several small pilot projects marked the 1770s and 1780s. One can point to, for instance, the *hospice de perfectionnement* set up by the Academy of Surgery for surgical or trauma cases of a difficult or peculiar nature; the Necker Hospital organized by Suzanne Necker for the parishes of St. Sulpice and du Gros Caillou; or the hospital built by the Paris priest, Jean Cochin, from his own funds for the needy parishioners of the faubourg St. Jacques. Such "neighborhood houses," small, intimate, "knowable," and staffed with good nurses, afforded a preferred solution to the dual problems of poverty and illness during the closing years of the French Old Régime.[15]

Where commoners led, however, royalty soon followed: the French crown transformed a house on the rue St. Jacques into a hospital for the venereally diseased and set aside room for a school for the deaf. Early in the reign of Louis XVI, reformers opened a debate on the dynamics of medical improvement. During the French Revolution, it culminated in the setting up of a special committee charged with evaluating all charitable institutions, including hospitals, and with drafting plans for correcting their flaws.

The Italian pattern also blended state and private initiatives. In a twenty-year period around the middle of the century, several new institutions were endowed in Turin, such as a ward for contagious diseases at the Ospedale di Carità in 1733 and a shelter for "fallen women" there in 1747. Whatever the objects of such charity, the donors remained the same: merchants, bankers, and well-off shopkeepers. Motives coincided with those that had moved the founders of the British voluntary hospitals: the exercise of rational charity and the desire to display one's wealth, acquire social prestige, and peddle influence.

---

[15] Weiner, *Citizen-Patient*, 36–40.

One of the first principles to which all (or almost all) these new hospitals adhered was medical exclusivity: they were not designed to be all-purpose institutions like the hôtels-dieu or the hôpitaux généraux. John Aikin, a proponent of voluntary hospitals in England, insisted on the name "infirmary" to distinguish them from either "almshouses" or old-fashioned "spitals." Besides the social and religious benefits the new hospital dished up to its benefactors, it was above all a place to heal the sick. Voluntary hospitals enacted restrictive admission procedures, and, broadly speaking, sought to admit only the curably ill: "I would wish to enforce as much as possible," Aikin said, "the idea of a hospital being a place designated for the *cure of the sick*."[16] Generally excluded from new-style hospitals were the incurably or chronically ill, fever cases, pregnant women, and the venereally diseased. Practice always made exceptions to even the most stringent rules. The Edinburgh Royal Infirmary, for example, contracted with the navy and army to take on sailors and soldiers for a fee; a goodly percentage of these suffered from venereal ills and fevers. Furthermore, as these hospitals worked to exclude certain groups, special hospitals followed to absorb those newly denied admission.

Important alterations in hospital building and administration slowly accumulated over the course of the century and the characteristics generally linked to the genesis of clinical medicine in the 1790s – bedside teaching, medical experimentation, clinical observation, and statistical evaluation – were already present earlier, at least in their rudiments. We have observed how many hospitals, even medieval ones, took pains to provide at least morsels of medical care, although success in those undertakings was less than stunning. Some hospitals quickly institutionalized teaching. The Quaker merchant, John Bellers, in a 1714 essay promoting the foundation of "new hospitals," based his appeal on the hope that "these hospitals will breed up some of the best physicians and chirurgeons because they may see as much there in one year as in seven anywhere else."[17] At the Hospital of San Giovanni in Turin, a physician or surgeon had been visiting patients twice a day since the sixteenth century and three apprentice, or student, surgeons, known as "dressers," resided and worked there; by 1730, there were thirteen. Finally, university reforms enacted in Italy between 1720 and 1739 mandated attendance on the wards for all students in medicine and surgery. The hospice de perfectionnement was, as Tenon recognized, "a unique and invaluable

---

[16] John Aikin, *Thoughts on Hospitals* (1771), quoted in Porter, "Gift Relation," in Granshaw and Porter, *The Hospital in History*, 150; Risse, *Hospital Life*, 23.
[17] Quoted in Risse, *Hospital Life*, 18.

institution . . . to make the art of medicine progress and to help humanity." And, from its very beginnings, the Royal Infirmary of Edinburgh was
devoted to clinical instruction and housed students. Ledgers and admission books recorded cases with some meticulousness and publications
drew on the experience garnered by students and professors walking the
wards. It was thus possible to "see" thousands of cases and draw lessons
for the advancement of medical knowledge from them. Similar trends are
observable in the Berlin Charité. Around 1730, the attending physician,
Johann Theodor Eller (1689–1760), published a series of clinical cases
selected from daily practice at the Charité.

The new eighteenth-century hospitals regarded patients as the legitimate objects of medical experimentation. Yet this statement cannot stand
without further clarification. Careful clinical trials were by no means the
rule in eighteenth-century medicine. Experimentation never proceeded
without restrictions. Local benefactors were chary about having "their
patients" delivered up to the whimsy of wild-eyed physicians and knife-
crazed surgeons. Governors also remained quite sensitive to patients'
complaints of brutal treatment. Thus, physicians overwhelmingly practiced what Susan Lawrence has labeled "safe science" on their hospital
patients and sought "to balance appropriate conservatism in practice –
one does *not* experiment on patients – with a properly innovative spirit –
one *does* experiment judiciously on patients – or else how would medicine
advance?"[18]

Scholars have been slow to acknowledge the longterm unfolding of
hospital medicine because the reformers of the late eighteenth century
very successfully projected an image of what even twentieth-century historians are inclined to refer to as "the grim reality of the public hospital."[19] To strengthen their position, reformers presented grisly tales of
hospital mortality, physical abuse, and mental suffering. Few simply lied.
Rather, each critic picked his material carefully with an eye to convincing
the public of the pressing need for change. And there certainly were
wrongs to be righted. Howard had indefatigably catalogued abuses. The
hospital for women at Malta, for example, was so malodorous that "the
governess [who] attended me through every ward . . . was constantly
using her smelling bottle; in which she judged very properly, for a more
offensive and dirty hospital for women I have never visited." He generally
praised hospitals in Italy, and especially those at Genoa and Pisa. The
French *Encyclopédie*, in its article on "Hôtel-Dieu," fixed on the Paris
Hôtel-Dieu with its truly shocking mortality and disgusting conditions.

---

[18] Susan Lawrence, *Charitable Knowledge: Hospital Pupils and Practitioners in Eighteenth-Century London* (Cambridge, 1996), 21.   [19] Weiner, *Citizen-Patient*, 45–76.

Another French writer, Louis-Sébastien Mercier (1740–1814), chronicled horrifying conditions in the Bicêtre: that "terrible ulcer on the body politic, broad, deep, and full of pus." Many health reformers, therefore, rejected large hospitals as irremediably bad and pursued other solutions, such as smaller institutions or health care without hospitals (see chapter 6).[20]

In fact, however, clinical medicine was coming to be practiced at numerous hospitals. The Paris legend is not false, although it should be ranged alongside what happened in other hospitals elsewhere in Europe. It is perhaps best understood as an example rather than a prototype. The history of Paris hospitals, moreover, cannot be disengaged from the history of the French Revolution. The revolutionary governments championed a range of social reforms that had far-reaching implications for hospitals and for medical education. Erwin Ackerknecht contended that only the Revolution made "the new teaching and the new school" possible. We have already reviewed how medical education (chapter 4) was revitalized and reformed in the wake of the French Revolution, and these same reforms could not but transform hospital life for patients and physicians.

In 1790, the French National Assembly empowered a Committee on Poverty (Comité de mendicité) to review the nation's sprawling array of charitable institutions. Its members assembled a massive factual base concerning hospitals in Paris and, less comprehensively, those in the provinces. After evaluating the information gained and visiting many hospitals in person, committee members proposed sweeping changes. Above all, they wished to limit admission to the curably ill and to secularize the hitherto religious direction of hospitals. The hostility of physicians on the one hand and, perhaps even more palpably, the exigencies of war on the other hampered or delayed many sound innovations. If the 1790s forced a hiatus in the period of civilian hospital reform, the French and Napoleonic wars quickened the expansion and improvement of military hospitals and military medicine already in progress.

Military hospitals

We tend to undervalue the caliber of military medicine and military hospitals grossly. Anyone teethed on tales of Florence Nightingale at the Scutari Hospital during the Crimean War might find it hard to believe

[20] John Howard, *An Account of the Principal Lazarettos in Europe; With Various Papers Relative to the Plague: Together with further Observations on some Foreign Prisons and Hospitals, and additional Remarks on the Present State of those in Great Britain and Ireland* (2nd edn., London, 1791), 60 and passim; Brockliss and Jones, *Medical World*, 717–25.

that, in the eighteenth century, military hospitals stood out as paragons of order and competency.[21]

The rise of army and navy hospitals was intimately tied to the fortunes of war in early modern Europe and to the presence of standing armies. Equally germane to the history of military hospitals was the consolidation of governmental activities in the seventeenth and eighteenth centuries. The states that first founded military hospitals and activated regular medical care for the troops were also those which first developed standing armies: France, Spain, and some German territories. Countries that centralized governmental tasks more belatedly, and introduced standing armies only rather late, for instance, England and the United Provinces, also lagged behind in organizing efficient systems of military medicine.

Throughout the middle ages, neither armies nor navies had any orderly form of medical care for combatants. When Henry V invaded France in 1415, for instance, only one "medicus," Thomas Morestede, and a group of surgeons who ranked with the commonest soldiers, accompanied him. Wounded soldiers and sailors were expected to help themselves, or solicit the aid of comrades-in-arms, relatives, or sympathetic (sic!) bystanders. Often they were required to pay for that assistance and, while convalescent, generally forfeited their wages. If lucky they might benefit from the largesse of officers, monarchs, or nobles. Toward the end of the middle ages, governments and commanders-in-chief occasionally arranged to have soldiers and sailors admitted to civilian hospitals.

The titanic struggle between the Habsburgs of Austria and Spain and the Valois of France in the sixteenth and seventeenth centuries saw the establishment of a permanent military hospital in Spain in 1570; of a guesthouse for soldiers (Soldaetgasthuis) in Amsterdam in 1587; and of the first military hospital in France in 1629. Care for veterans dates from slightly later and was measurably advanced when Louis XIV founded the Hôtel des Invalides in Paris in 1670. Like many other French hôpitaux généraux, the Invalides formed part of a royal campaign to control vagabondage and dissolute conduct. Strict house orders in the Invalides reflected the attitude of government administrators toward these "patients."

France had a extensive system of military hospitals (and a set of naval hospitals at the important French bases of Brest, Rochefort, and Toulon) in place by the middle of the eighteenth century. Other countries followed not far behind and sometimes actually forged ahead (although the French

---

[21] The story presented here relies heavily on the interpretation advanced by Brockliss and Jones, *Medical World*, 689–700.

5.2 Surgeon operating on the battlefield.

system in its entirety seems to have offered the best care for eighteenth-century soldiers and sailors). Berlin boasted the great Charité since 1725. During the Seven Years War (1756–63), Friedrich II founded permanent military hospitals in six garrison towns and set up field hospitals. Castile enjoyed pride of place with a field hospital dating from the reign of Isabella the Catholic in the late fifteenth century and with the first permanent army hospital from 1579 in Pamplona. Spain's preparations for the Armada (1588) included a medical staff of over eighty surgeons and two fully fitted hospital ships. Austria did not have a permanent military hospital until the reign of Joseph II (1780–90), whereas Peter the Great (1672–1725) had founded a military hospital in Russia almost three-quarters of a century earlier.

Several things typified the march of military medicine. The founding of specialized hospitals was important but so, too, were attempts to recruit well-trained and experienced medical personnel. During the eighteenth century, almost every country instituted separate educational facilities to train medical men for the requirements of war.

Equally critical to good military medicine were attempts to elevate the status of the medical corps. During the Mantuan wars of the middle of the seventeenth century, French army surgeons received the title of *chirurgiens-majors des camps et des armées*; in 1731 Prussian military surgeons came to enjoy the rank of *Unterofficier* (roughly, a lieutenant); and, after 1742, Spanish surgeons were allowed the genteel title of *don*. The erection of autonomous hierarchies of command within the medical services freed physicians and surgeons from the interference of nonmedical staff in medical and sanitary affairs. Control over the fine French system passed to medical *inspecteurs-généraux* in 1708 and supervision over all surgeons in the Prussian army to a surgeon-general in 1716. Another way in which governments bettered the lot of military medical men was to grant fixed salaries more consonant with what gentlemen-officers enjoyed.

Status and standing, of course, depended on the skill of medical men and their degree of education. By the eighteenth century, almost every European country required its military physicians and surgeons to be qualified and often expected them to pass an examination expressly focused on military medicine. Governments nurtured new generations of surgeons and physicians in special schools. In 1775 the French royal government laid down guidelines for the training of army medical personnel in the military schools at Metz, Lille, and Strasburg, and of naval personnel at Toulon, Brest, and Rochefort. In Prussia, the *theatrum anatomicum* created in 1713 grew into a *collegium medico-chirurgicum* designated for the instruction of military physicians and surgeons while teaching took place in the recently refurbished Charité. Seventy years later, the

Pépinère was founded in Berlin as a college for military and civilian surgeons. Spain opened a Royal College of Surgery for naval surgeons in 1747, one for military surgeons at Barcelona in 1760, and a school for military doctors by 1760. (Portugal, however, did not have schools for training military surgeons until 1825.) In 1786, the Austrian medical-surgical institute that had been training physicians and surgeons for the army since 1784 was advanced to the level of an academy and renamed the Josephium after the reigning Holy Roman Emperor, Joseph II. Even in Russia, the same trends existed. Peter the Great, in the wake of military disaster during the initial stages of the Great Northern War (1700–25), charged the Dutch physician, Nicolaas Bidloo (1673–1735), with the planning of a medical school and hospital for Moscow. The Moscow General Infantry Hospital opened in 1707. Also founded during Peter's reign were the Petersburg Admiralty and Infantry Hospital and the Kronstadt Naval Hospital which added formal medical and surgical schools in 1733.

The two countries that trailed behind in centralizing government and in instituting standing armies – England and the United Provinces – also delayed setting up orderly military medical services. In England, standing armies were of virtually no consequence at least until the second half of the seventeenth century and, even during the war-torn 1790s, remained at only a fraction of the size of the Prussian military machine. Despite some early attempts to care for the wounded and invalid, little was accomplished. Still, even in the sixteenth century, England was moving toward maritime greatness and it is therefore not surprising that the first English initiatives broached plans for sailors. As early as the fourteenth century, King Edward II had set up hospitals for the poor that were also to serve the wounded, such as St. Bartholomew's Hospital in Sandwich "fyrst ordened for maryners desesed [diseased] and hurt." Most care for soldiers and sailors, however, was organized through a contracting system: brokers arranged for sailors to be carried to private lodgings when the few available hospital beds were full. This system proved corrupt and inefficient. Though some thought was given to sending physicians and surgeons to sea during time of war (surgeons were even conscripted during the reign of Elizabeth I) and the wounded and invalid were sometimes admitted to civilian hospitals on the coast, the general level of care for Britannia's sailors was pretty poor. Drawing on his own experiences, Smollett vividly portrayed very bad conditions on board ship as seen through the eyes of his fictional creation Roderick Random:

[As I] observed the situation of the patients, I was much less surprised that people should die on board, than that any sick person should recover. – Here [in the sick bay] I saw about fifty miserable distempered wretches, suspended in rows, so huddled one upon another, that not more than fourteen inches space was allotted for each with his bed and bedding; and deprived of the light of day, as well as of fresh air; breathing nothing but a noisome atmosphere of the morbid steams exhaling from their own excrements and diseased bodies, devoured with vermin hatched in the filth that surrounded them, and destitute of every convenience necessary for people in that helpless condition.[22]

Only two institutions existed before midcentury for the injured and the invalid: the Chelsea hospital (1682) for soldiers and the Greenwich hospital for naval veterans (1696).

A report from the First Lord of the Admiralty tendered to the Crown in 1740 was a watershed event. As a result of that document, the government eventually constructed three more marine hospitals, one each in the naval ports of Portsmouth, Plymouth, and Chatham. The hospital in Portsmouth – the Royal Hospital Haslar – opened for patients in 1754 and, when completed seven years later, could house about 1800. The first director at Haslar was James Lind (1716–94), a man famous for his work on scurvy. British army hospitals did not really get going until the Napoleonic wars and their history properly belongs, therefore, to the nineteenth century.

What was true for England also held – in the main – for the United Provinces. Institutions of central government evolved even more fitfully in the United Provinces than in England. Interest in medical care for combatants noticeably waxed and waned with intervals of war and peace. As early as the 1570s, the States-General had arranged for ailing and injured soldiers and sailors to be admitted to civilian hospitals, but not until 1673 – in the wake of the French invasion of the previous year – did the States-General institute a regular system for recruiting, training, and compensating medical men. The first permanent military hospital also opened then. Not until the French invasion of 1795 was the system rationalized along French lines.

Even where the number of military or naval hospitals remained small, seldom did this mean that no care whatsoever was available for injured or ill warriors. Civilian hospitals sometimes contracted with the army and the navy to supply care for fees. Guenter Risse has traced this sort of relationship between the army and the navy on one hand and the Royal Infirmary of Edinburgh on the other. The Royal Infirmary began admitting soldiers regularly after the 1745 Scottish Rebellion. The number of soldier-patients remained high for the rest of the century: in the 1760s they made up about one-third of all patients; thereafter, the figure stood between 11 percent and 25 percent. Sailors, too, contributed a significant percentage of inpatients to the Infirmary in the 1760s. Soldiers and sailors suffered the injuries and wounds characteristic of their callings,

---

[22] Tobias Smollett, *The Adventures of Roderick Random* (2 vols., London, 1794), vol. I, 188.

but also had frequently contracted venereal infections. The recovery rate of soldiers was the highest in the hospital at 81 percent and that of the sailors, the lowest, although still about 60 percent. By the middle of the eighteenth century, the Spanish army had struck a similar bargain with the Hospital of San Juan de Dios in Murcia, although the numbers of soldiers admitted remained relatively small throughout the century: never more than fifteen or sixteen a year.

To end where this section began we need to assess the overall record of military hospitals. The best authority here is the work of Brockliss and Jones on military hospitals in early modern France which they esteem as "models" for civilian hospitals, where "the fundamentals of a creative and investigatory anatomo-clinical medicine were falling into place long before the 1790s."[23] It was in the military hospitals, with their strict organization and orderly regimen, that hospital medicine first arose. Most patients were available for experimentation; surgeons and physicians were able to make bedside observations undisturbed; and plenty of corpses could be postmortemed. Medicine, and especially surgery, flourished in the military hospitals and some of the greatest contributions to the surgical and medical literature of the day came from the circle of military surgeons and from the pages of the first periodical for military medicine: the *Journal de médecine*.

Insane asylums and hospitals for special patients

For much of the early modern period, care of the insane was a matter thought best left to the discretion of family and friends. Nonetheless, even in the middle ages, some institutions incarcerated the mad, such as, most famously, St. Mary of Bethlem in London. In early modern Russia, monasteries cared for the mad. Much later, Peter the Great ordered the setting up of *dollgausi* or "madhouses" on the German model. The German, Johann Peter Frank, saw the "guiding principle in the organization of the insane asylum" not merely in rendering lunatics harmless, but in fulfilling "another sacred duty": that of returning the insane cured to society.

Therapy for the mentally ill, therefore, was perhaps more closely linked to buildings per se than for other illnesses. Asylums themselves radically altered as ideas about the origins of madness and opinions about prognoses changed. Traditional care for the mad had tended to be ad hoc; the nonviolent were mostly left to wander about freely and only the raving and the dangerous were locked away. The nobility and the well-to-do maintained their deranged relatives at home or paid others to mind them.

---

[23] Brockliss and Jones, *Medical World*, 700.

Members of less prosperous groups, too, might tend their mad themselves, but, if this were not possible, often packed them off to an hôpital général. Cities sometimes designated towers or parts of thick walls – known as "Mad-Towers" or "Mad-Boxes" (*Tollkisten* in German) – for this purpose or relegated these unhappy individuals to basements and special cells in existing hospitals, pesthouses, or prisons. Seldom was treatment attempted and, if it was, it took the form of purges, emetics, and bleeding to counteract what were generally believed to be the physical causes of the disorder. The general dominance in the seventeenth century of the notion that madness was "associated with irrationality and the improper sense of the will" probably helped reduce interest in treatment and spurred on the crusade to lock the mad away with other rowdy social elements in the hôpitaux généraux.[24] By the middle of the eighteenth century, however, a groundswell of criticism attacked such arrangements for the insane as inhumane and counterproductive.

Thus, long before *psychiatry* (the medicalization of mental illness) was born, modifications in the treatment of the insane were already underway. Gaining the upper hand was a sense that the mad were not brutes. Numerous physicians and others writing on the handling of the insane all advocated a mix of decency and compassion. As early as 1758, William Battie (1703/04–76) insisted that "management did much more than medicines" and refused to administer harsh drugs to his mad patients or to allow them to be beaten. In Florence, Vincenzo Chiarugi (1759–1820) sketched out a series of "soft" restraints that he much preferred to chains. The Brothers of Charity at the Charenton in Paris tenderly nursed the insane men entrusted to them, neither stinting them on food nor denying them adequate shelter. In Germany, too, while asylum attendants were not specially trained, they were not "rough torturers" either.

Simultaneously, the belief arose that the mad should be secluded from other types of patients or recipients of poor relief not merely for society's protection but for their own benefit. What was needed were separate wards or even detached institutions. (This development not only touched the insane, of course: at the same time wards or homes for lying-in mothers, fever cases, sufferers from skin diseases such as scabies, the venereally diseased, and certain categories of incurables were also set up.) Many institutions in the course of the eighteenth century began to add rooms for the insane. A kind of halfway solution was attempted in Württemberg when Duke Karl Eugen set up a *Tollhaus* in 1746 for "the

---

[24] Ibid., 443; Christine Vanja, "Madhouses, Children's Wards, and Clinics: The Development of Insane Asylums in Germany," in Norbert Finzsch and Robert Jütte, *Institutions of Confinement: Hospitals, Asylums, and Prisons in Western Europe and North America, 1500–1950* (Cambridge, 1996), 117–32.

melancholic and idiotic, the *maniaci* and *furiosi*" and affiliated it with the combined prison-workhouse erected ten years previously.

Most important of these special facilities were the private charitable and private commercial institutions that shot up like so many mushrooms in the eighteenth century. Some were undoubtedly dreadful but others were demonstrably excellent.

Private madhouses (at least in England) began to open in the seventeenth century. Keeping a private madhouse required little investment and a couple of specially fitted rooms was quite enough. Mad-minding was a money-making proposition and madhouse keepers advertised their services, as did James Newton for his business in Clerkenwell Close. His bill read:

[there] liveth one who by the blessing of God cures all Lunatick, distracted, or mad people; he seldom exceeds three months in the cure of the Maddest person that comes in his house; several have been cured in a fortnight and some in less time; he has cured several from Bedlam, and other mad-houses in and about the city, and has conveniency for people of what quality soever. No cure – no money.[25]

The number of for-profit madhouses was probably greatest in England, although England was not unique in having them. The French capital contained at least eighteen toward the end of the century. All of these latter were quite small, but seemingly competently and humanely managed. In England where private madhouses were most abundant, the frequency of abuses was also most striking. Violations of individual liberty, as well as physical maltreatment and inhumane conditions, were by no means unknown. Not until Parliament passed the Act for Regulating Private Mad-houses in 1774 did the mad receive rights to prevent extreme cruelty or abusive incarceration. Before then, a person could be carried off and confined on the authority of two justices of the peace and often for petty reasons: to curb a wife's extravagance, to prevent an unfortunate love-match, or to forestall a lawsuit. People caged arbitrarily often suffered gross indignities and physical brutality. Samuel Brucksaw (who may or may not have been mad – it does not matter) was held for 284 days in a private madhouse in Yorkshire by a man named Wilson:

When Wilson shewed me to bed, he carried me up into a dark and dirty garet, there stripped me, and carried my cloathes out of the room, which I saw no more, for upwards of a month, but lay chained to this bad bed, all that time; ... they gave me bad victuals, short allowance, with sour beer, oftener water, and sometimes

---

[25] Quoted in Dale Peterson, ed., *A Mad People's History of Madness* (Pittsburgh, 1982), 40–41.

not that; no attendance, but what was as contradictory and provoking as they could possibly invent, and frequently the most barbarous stripes [marks left by beatings]; and to keep these inquisition-like transactions a secret from the world, Wilson's wife does the office of a barber.[26]

Some private madhouses existed at the opposite end of the spectrum and some of the greatest innovations in *moral treatment* occurred in privately run asylums. Moral treatment "as it was understood by its practitioners in the eighteenth and early nineteenth centuries meant that psychological methods were employed to help in what was seen as a mental disorder."[27]

The Retreat in York, proposed by William Tuke (1732–1822) in 1790 and opened by the Quaker community in 1792, institutionalized the moral treatment of the insane. The Retreat emphasized a range of non-medical remedies applied within a home-like environment. Gentleness and authority were to work together to obliterate whatever mistaken ideas had lodged in the patient's mind and which caused his or her derangement. Patients lived in a pleasant brick building set in a park, associated with other Friends (i.e., Quakers), and enjoyed plenty of opportunity to work in the asylum's gardens and wander about outside (under supervision, of course).

The emblematic moment of moral treatment, however, is generally taken to be the now almost legendary "freeing of the insane" from their chains. Supposedly the first man to accomplish this was the French physician Philippe Pinel (1745–1826), who struck the manacles off woman lunatics at the Salpêtrière in 1800. In fact, others had done virtually the same thing before him: the superintendent of the Bicêtre, the nonphysician Jean-Baptiste Pussin (himself a one-time inmate of that hospital), and the asylum director Abraham Joly in Geneva.

As the insane became objects of treatment rather than custodial care, so, too, did a number of others come to seen as amenable to medical intervention. Special institutions were proposed as ways to help them overcome their disabilities. Perhaps the most important were centers for the deaf, the blind, and the mentally retarded. The 1780s and 1790s, for example, saw the founding of Valentin Haüy's school for the blind in France, the Royal School for the Blind in Liverpool, and of the School for the Indigent Blind in Surrey. Some "institutions" were not in fact heaps of bricks and mortar, but services and methods of training. Enlightenment pedagogy pioneered methods to teach the blind to read with their fingers and the deaf to speak with their hands. The abbé Charles de l'Epée (1712–89) established one of the first schools for deaf children in

---

[26] Quoted ibid., 60.
[27] Anne Digby, *Madness, Morality and Medicine: A Study of the York Retreat, 1796–1914* (Cambridge, 1985), 33.

1755. Almost simultaneously, others devised touch-reading techniques that antedated the celebrated "cell" system Louis Braille (1809–52) later invented. Mentally retarded and autistic children, too, won their advocates and teachers, such as the physician, Jean-Marc Itard (1775–1838), who worked with Victor, the famous "wild boy of Aveyron." While many of these initiatives in education and, to some extent, institutionalization date from the eighteenth century, and while the strong populationist and philanthropic concerns of that century cultivated a preoccupation with children and their health, the story of hospitals for children does not properly begin until the nineteenth century with the opening of the Hôpital des enfants malades in Paris in 1802. Few children were hospitalized before then for medical care, although, of course, poor children might very well end up – with or without their parents – in the hôpitaux généraux or other multipurpose institutions.

Patients

As we have seen, the demographics of hospital populations changed over time as the character of the institution itself altered. As hospitals became, in Tenon's words, "machines for healing" (*machines à guérir*), they shed their identities as multipurpose institutions. They no longer admitted the merely destitute, the elderly, homeless, or incurable. As hospital administrators and physicians became ever more painfully aware of the prevalence of "hospital distempers" (i.e., diseases which crowded conditions and the "want of fresh air and cleanliness" seemed to breed), they also sought to exclude contagious cases – like smallpox and "fevers" – or, if they did admit them, took care to isolate these patients. Likewise, hospitals tended to exclude venereal sufferers and pregnant women. Those perceived as curably ill now formed the principal objects of hospital care.

While there is still not a great deal of material available on patients in early modern hospitals, tables 5.1 and 5.2 – for the Bristol Infirmary and the Royal Infirmary in Edinburgh – indicate that the majority of people admitted were those suffering acute illnesses thought to be curable or at least amenable to remedies. They also demonstrate, however, that the exclusion of "fever" patients was never fully accomplished.

In general, patients did not linger for months or even weeks in hospitals. At the Edinburgh Infirmary, for instance, the average stay did not exceed thirty-one days. Those who had undergone major surgery, such as amputations, or who were being treated for particularly obdurate complaints, like leg ulcers, tarried longer – anywhere from forty to more than fifty-five days. At the San Juan de Dios hospital, the length of stay in the middle to late eighteenth century was significantly longer for women than

Table 5.1 *Diagnostic categories – Bristol Infirmary*

Fever	16.6%
Respiratory	15.1
Trauma	13.9
Abscess, ulcer	13.2
Miscellaneous	10.1
Rheumatism, muscular	7.6
Skin problems	7.6
Digestive	5.7
Reproductive	3.8
Venereal	2.4
Operative conditions	2.4
Dropsy, etc.	1.5

Source:
Mary E. Fissell, *Patients, Power, and the Poor in Eighteenth-Century Bristol* (Cambridge, 1991), 107.

for men: 45.2 days in 1740 for women, 18.3 days for men; in 1790, it was 41.7 and 23.3 days respectively.[28]

Some have placed the shift toward hospital medicine and the "construction of the hospital patient" in an essentially dismal light: patients' own voices were silenced and they were subjected to strict regulations imposed by physicians and surgeons. Mary Fissell, in evaluating the medicalization of the Bristol Infirmary toward the end of the eighteenth century, shows how physicians and surgeons began to speak differently about diseases than their patients did. These medical men "disparaged or dismissed patients' own accounts of illness and replaced them with signs and symptoms unavailable to the patient, but meaningful within an emergent profession."[29]

Nonmedical or nonsurgical staff, such as nursing sisters, also purportedly experienced a sharp decline in their authority and in their ability to dictate daily institutional routines. Patients became objects and staff automatons. As charity became more "specialized" in late eighteenth- and early nineteenth-century Bristol, the governors and subscribers supposedly became more distanced from the everyday life of the hospital, abdicating control to medical men and surgeons.

[28] Hourcade, *Beneficencia y sanidad*, 220.
[29] Fissell, *Patients, Power, and the Poor*, 162.

Table 5.2 *Diagnostic categories
– Royal Infirmary, Edinburgh*

Venereal	14.67%
Fever	12.20
Pectoral	4.56
Rheumatism	4.56
Stomach	3.93
Ulcers	2.72
Sores on legs	2.39
Ague or intermittent fever	1.90

Source:
Guenter Risse, *Hospital Life in
Enlightenment Scotland: Care and
Teaching at the Royal Infirmary of
Edinburgh* (Cambridge, 1986), 120–21.

Patients and staff were, however, never mere pawns of medical men. Lay administrators maintained control of hospitals well into the nineteenth century, continued to appoint house physicians, and largely directed the rhythms of hospital life. Staff, too, were never easily elbowed aside. Nursing sisters, for example, quite masterfully held their own on the wards and in matters of patient care. Alliances of staff and lay administrators often thwarted the medical wishes of physicians and surgeons. Patients and their families were scarcely powerless. Patients could – and did – leave hospitals on their own, but they (or their friends and relatives) also vigorously resisted treatments and protested vehemently against improper, impolite, or cruel handling. These complaints were rarely dismissed out of hand. In the realm of patient experiences, however, we know more about people incarcerated for insanity than for other ailments, as these men and women often published their memoirs or legally protested their sequestration.

In conclusion, then, one sees how hospitals underwent a extended course of medicalization lasting three centuries or more. The word "hospital" increasingly came to refer to a place where medical care and cure were the paramount concerns. Hospitals were split off from larger, multipurpose institutions like the hôpitaux généraux (paralleling other campaigns to separate the care of orphans from criminals and to remove minor offenders from the deleterious influence of hardened malefactors). Specialized institutions – like the insane asylum or the lying-in hospital – cropped up in ever-growing numbers.

All these trends did not, however, surface with explosive suddenness at the end of the eighteenth century. Each was rooted in the hospitals of the early eighteenth century and even before. Some tendencies were already apparent in the late middle ages. Hospitals were never utterly lacking in medical care. Many hospitals employed permanent medical staff already in the sixteenth century and some even dispensed basic medical education. Care in hospitals was not unrelievedly awful in the "bad old days" before the *machine à guérir* motored onto the stage; it was often surprisingly good. Mortality rates in many hospitals had begun to drop long before one can reasonably date the "birth of the clinic." In short, the medicalization of hospitals was a gradual accomplishment the beginnings of which can be traced back into the middle ages, even if one must admit the hastening of that process during the eighteenth century. Just as important, it is necessary to see hospitals as institutions embedded in, and reflective of, the greater social, economic, political, and religious movements that had, over a period of almost three hundred years, markedly transformed European life.

6 Health and society

[P]ublic health is perhaps the most important of all subjects. If men are poor, the sovereign protects only the wretched; if they are sickly, he conserves only the ill. (Denis Diderot, 1775)[1]

Medical Police, like all police science, is an art of defense, a model of protection of people and their animal helpers against the deleterious consequences of dwelling together in large numbers, but especially of promoting their physical well-being so that people will succumb as late as possible to their eventual fate from the many physical illnesses to which they are subject. (Johann Peter Frank, 1779)[2]

All the infections that the sun sucks up,
From bogs, fens, flats on Prosper fall and make him
By inch-meal a disease. (*The Tempest*, ii, 2)

Today we accept as axiomatic that health is a community concern. This awareness, however, has not always characterized western civilization. To be sure, early societies were not ignorant of the consequences of bad sanitary facilities – the Romans were, after all, famous for their drains – but the present-day sense that health is a matter for public attention and *state* intervention is an understanding that has slowly matured since the middle ages. Part of the story, therefore, of health in society is the history of state intervention in matters of public health, for instance, in maintaining the cleanliness of towns, ordering quarantines during epidemics, draining and sewering, but also in setting building codes, laws to protect food and water supplies, rules about traffic, and fire-fighting.

The story of health in society is woefully incomplete if we think merely in terms of state action, however. Private initiatives and corporate endeavors (i.e., guilds and societies of physicians, surgeons, and apothecaries

---

[1] Diderot, "Plan d'une université par le gouvernement de Russie ou d'une éducation publique dans toutes les sciences," quoted in Laurence Brockliss and Colin Jones, *The Medical World of Early Modern France* (Oxford, 1997), 378.

[2] Johann Peter Frank, *A System of Complete Medical Police: Selections from Johann Peter Frank*, ed. by Erna Lesky (Baltimore, 1975), 12–13.

were known as *corporations*) were equally decisive. Thus, our investigation will embrace an array of "institutions without walls" by focusing on the multiple mechanisms of public health: demography, vital statistics, corporations, and humanitarian undertakings. The meaning of institutions might be broadened even more to include "a generally accepted mode of behaviour" in matters of health and we will pursue this topic as well.[3]

The history of health in society has generally fixed on state initiatives and urban conditions. An exceedingly rich literature on "the health of towns" exists. Largely neglected, however, are the private and philanthropic efforts that frequently pioneered innovations. The division into private, on the one hand, and public (or state) on the other is, however, an artificial one. Crucially important was the private/public combination – *private* institutions erected for *public* benefits, for instance, a foundling home, like that set up by the sea captain, Thomas Coram, in London in 1741, for a public purpose. Equally slighted has been the story of rural health, although it fascinated late seventeenth- and eighteenth-century policy makers because that was where the majority of the population lived.

The history of health in society has also been closely linked to the European epidemic experience. A recent study of medicine in early modern France divides the period from 1500 to 1800 into a time "beneath the shadow of plague" (i.e., before the last major incident in Marseilles in 1720) and "beyond the shadow of plague." To be sure, epidemics catalyzed many public health measures, and yet to write the history of public health as merely "epidemic-driven" is inadequate. Public health is, admittedly, always a defensive act – whether *reactive* or *proactive*. Over time, however, the proactive goal of public health, i.e., the attempt to prevent rather than merely respond, gained increasing relevance and has now come to be expected by the wider public as a legitimate field for state intervention as well as for constant societal attention.

The health of the population

Chapter 1 discussed sickness and health as they affected individuals during their life-cycle, and chapter 2 looked at the European epidemic experience as a whole. Here I will discuss themes relevant to the health of *populations*. Public health, after all, deals with aggregates rather than individuals, and we must therefore also concern ourselves with *demographic profiles* and *vital statistics*.

[3] Daniel M. Fox, "Medical Institutions and the State," in W. F. Bynum and Roy Porter, eds., *Companion Encyclopedia of the History of Medicine* (2 vols., London, 1993), 1206.

Demographers still find it difficult to say precisely what killed our ancestors, how rapidly, when, and with what efficiency. Even thornier has been the task of measuring *morbidity* (i.e., sickness). Once-accepted verities, such as that people in "the past" inevitably succumbed to ever-present disease and that life-spans were invariably short and disease-ridden, have now fallen to the more sophisticated demographic investigations of the past ten to fifteen years. Death and disease had differential impacts depending on age, sex, occupation, and location. We tend to believe that people in early modern Europe were always ailing, but James Riley warns us that we must distinguish between the risk of *falling* sick – which was high – and the risk of *being* sick – which was low. Most prevalent diseases were acute and rapid; people got them and either recovered or died within a relatively short span of time. Childhood was the most dangerous interval of life. Once people reached adulthood they had become hardened survivors. One cannot therefore conclude that "ill health prevailed among the people that survived"; rather, the opposite was probably the case, although one cannot discount the widespread existence of conditions like lameness that were limiting if not necessarily incapacitating.

Epidemic diseases waxed and waned in their intensity, and mortality in Europe did not decline in a smooth curve. Mortality dropped from the end of the sixteenth century through about 1800, then significantly rose and actually came to *exceed* the peaks of the sixteenth and seventeenth centuries in the first half of the nineteenth century. Thereafter, mortality rates fell again and have continued to decline since then.

The modern rise of population, therefore, occurred either because epidemics themselves had diminished in virulence or rate of occurrence, or because fewer people came in contact with disease. Quarantine or travel restrictions contained some epidemics to limited regions, and public health initiatives, like draining and street-cleaning, reduced the dangers from insect-borne diseases (like malaria) and water-borne diseases (like typhoid fever and bacillary dysentery).

The legacy of plague

Generations of scholars who have addressed the history of public health generally agreed with Carlo Cipolla that "it all started with the great pandemic of 1347–51." Accordingly, the fear and reality of plague prompted the development of *boards of health*, i.e., of the first administrative mechanisms for addressing the health of society. There is some justice in this view for many characteristic traits of public health – quarantines, *cordons sanitaires*, isolation techniques, and boards of health – took on recognizable forms then.

But Cipolla's clear statement is too simple. He is, of course, right that most boards of health first saw the light of day in the fourteenth and fifteenth centuries, but the process was not quite as linear and transparent as his easy formulation makes it appear.

All societies have rules about how to live together that touch on matters of sanitation and hygiene. The first settled peoples had to set aside places for dumping waste and performing excretory functions. These precepts may not have produced results to the taste of twentieth-century fastidiousness, but our ancestors were less fussy about hygiene and cleanliness – both personal and public – than we are today (although we should not overestimate the dissimilarity). City environments swarmed with hazards and reeked with smells. Rural areas were equally malodorous and filthy: manure piled high outside every door, unpaved streets filled with animal excrement, cottages roofed with thatch, and the close proximity of domestic animals and vermin were typical conditions.

It was, however, in the cities where the buildup of debris had become most offensive and noticeable. A report from Pisa in 1612 noted that:

None of the houses has a privy with its own underground cesspit but they shit between the houses where there are gaps between the walls . . . and there are hundreds of turds to be removed which, as well as stinking horribly, present an extremely disgusting sight to those who pass by in the street.[4]

The growing congestion within the confined space of medieval and early modern cities exacerbated the problem and made closer regulation of basic environmental conditions imperative.

Four things combined to initiate public health measures in medieval cities: economic growth, guild expansion, population aggregation, and governmental aggrandizement. Economic growth generated the wealth necessary for public works projects. Medieval guilds were always involved in the regulation of trade and competition as well as in a sort of licensing. Most important, however, was the rise of a rudimentary administrative science and the development of a corps of city managers trained in law and finance.

These men took actions that eventually improved the urban environment aesthetically and biologically. Medieval cities paved streets (Paris began in 1185, Prague in 1331, Nuremberg in 1368, Basel in 1387, and Augsburg in 1416); introduced canalization for drainage; supplied water; prohibited the dumping of garbage and offal onto streets or into rivers; erected municipal slaughterhouses; and designated special places for

---

[4] Carlo Cipolla, *Miasmas and Disease: Public Health and the Environment in the Pre-Industrial Age* (New Haven, Conn., 1992), 16.

particularly noxious or dangerous trades. Butchers' shops and tanneries were major offenders of the civic nose, as well as significant health hazards.

Medieval cities laid the groundwork for the further expansion of municipal public health. Milan, for example, had already by the fourteenth century appointed officials to supervise street cleaning and markets. In Amiens, various councilors (or *échevins*) watched over the baking of bread, the sale of fish, and the vending of meat. *Aldermen* in English towns and *Ratsherrn* in German cities assumed identical tasks. Admittedly, much of this regulation had to do with economics, such as setting fair prices and assuring precise weights and measures, but the quality of foods – whether they were fresh or spoiled – was also a major consideration, as was the general cleanliness of market stalls.

Undoubtedly, the arrival of the Black Death and its subsequent incursions quickened the expansion of public health. In these centuries, public health remained mostly reactive and defensive: a wall to keep the enemy out. The main goal of public health was the prevention and control of epidemics. Yet if plague was the ogre that frightened people out of their lethargy, it was not the only factor, and public health did not merely pop into existence in the fourteenth century. Health measures matured gradually. It took the *repeated* experience of *several* epidemics to generate real public health programs. Factors other than disease – such as changing attitudes toward the poor, social deviants, and strangers – appear to have played an equally decisive role.

When plague struck in the middle of the fourteenth century, cities were by no means totally unprepared to deal with it: some public health measures were in place and, more important, many cities had robust and well-developed city governments that responded with energy and imagination. Cities had dealt with menaces before – wars, famines, and fires – and were not simply thrown for a loss. If it took time to institutionalize the machinery of public health, it was not because civic leaders rulers were so paralyzed with fear that they could not think.

How did cities and territories react? The areas around the Mediterranean – Sicily, Sardinia, Corsica, Spain, and the north Italian city-states – were gripped first. Experiences there offer some idea of how cities answered the challenge. In general, the story runs thus. First, cities appointed officials to deal with the emergency. These men enjoyed broad emergency powers, which often included a form of criminal jurisdiction to punish those who refused to observe regulations. These posts, however, disappeared as the incursion subsided, and only after repeated attacks of plague did cities gradually empanel standing boards of health. Once boards of health became semi-permanent or permanent features of government, they acquired more extensive powers and slowly began to draft long-range plans to forestall new attacks of plague (or other diseases) rather than merely react to a present threat. Characteristically, early boards of health were primarily staffed by laypeople, either patricians who were already members of government or urban bureaucrats whom the city employed.

In Venice, as early as March 1348, the Large Council (Maggior Consiglio) chose three of its members (all, by definition, noblemen or patricians) "to consider diligently all possible ways to preserve public health and avoid the corruption of the environment." When plague passed, however, this commission dissolved, only be to revived when plague recurred in 1440. By the 1480s, it was plain that plague was not simply going to go away and obvious that averting epidemic outbreaks was a longterm, full-time occupation that demanded the attention of the Consiglio in the same ways foreign policy and justice did. As a result, in 1486, the Consiglio began selecting three members from its ranks annually to serve as commissioners of public health (*provveditori di sanità*). Once the board became a fixed part of Venetian government, its patrician members hired paid subordinates who gave a consistent life to the board of health. Although medical personnel might be consulted as to their opinion about matters touching on isolation or treatment, the surveillance of public health was viewed then, and for a long time thereafter, as a bureaucratic responsibility rather than a medical one. Venice also provided local boards for its mainland territories.[5]

The story for Florence is much the same, although the city on the Po moved more slowly. Fourteenth-century boards of health had finite lifespans and narrowly circumscribed powers. Not until 1448 did the governing council delegate authority to combat the plague to an already existing organ, the Otto di Custodia, for a period of three months. Only eighty years later did the city install a group of five men to deal with public health. Like the Venetians, the Florentines then organized local boards for their subject cities: in Pisa, Pistoia, and Leghorn. Yet neither Venice nor Florence could claim pride of place. Milan, under its capable and powerful Sforza dukes, seems to have set up a permanent board of health in the early fifteenth century.

While it is generally conceded that Italian cities moved at the forefront of public health, other places soon followed. Ordinances concerning plague appeared in France in the sixteenth century: in Troyes in 1517, Reims in 1522, and Paris in 1531. The "Plague Orders" of 1543 began

[5] Carlo Cipolla, *Public Health and the Medical Profession in the Renaissance* (Cambridge, 1976), 11–12.

public health in England. Sprawling territorial states faced a more arduous task. Late in the sixteenth century, various territories attempted to cordon off areas beset by plague (i.e., to erect cordons sanitaires), but not until the next century was the battle truly joined. In the late seventeenth century, additional legislation appeared. In moments of epidemic crises, fighting the plague could form the principal business of government, assuming a salience and urgency equaling that of impeding invasion by hostile forces.

Battling the plague depended to a large degree, of course, on how people understood its causes (i.e., its *etiology*) and how it spread. As we saw in chapter 2, interpretations varied and contemporaries mixed religious or providential explanations with other factors. Chief among the latter were *miasmas*, heralded by stench. If, however, cleaning up the environment was regarded as the major defense against plague, most people – and most governments – also believed that plague passed insidiously and directly from person to person. Thus isolation, cordons sanitaires, and quarantine were the stock weapons in any plague-fighting armory.

The plague ordinance (Pestordonnantie) of 1599 for the Dutch city of Hoorn nicely illustrates this range of options. The opening paragraph referred to the plague as the "fiery rod" of God and argued the necessity of establishing "a good order" in the city. Eighteen rules of conduct explicated usual rules of plague prophylaxis and set up fines and punishments for noncompliance. Persons with plague patients at home were to mark their houses with "a straw bundle about one-half ell long and as thick as a [man's] arm or with a straw wreath of the same dimensions." Those who died from plague were not to be buried before twenty-four hours had elapsed (to avoid burying someone alive) but bodies were not to remain more than twenty-*eight* hours above ground either. The ordinance prohibited inhabitants of "plague houses" from freely circulating among "the good people [of the town, or] in the markets, churches, or any other places" until six weeks after the last plague patient in their house had recovered or succumbed. Moreover, they should avoid the markets at busy times and must never handle foods displayed there. Householders were ordered to burn infected bedding, taking great care, however, not to let fire spread out of control. Dogs "large and small" were not to be permitted to run about loose, but were to be kept indoors and leashed. Carcasses, offal from slaughtered animals, or guts from cleaned fish were not to be thrown onto "streets, dikes, or in any canals or streams within the city." Likewise, barbers were forbidden to spill human blood out onto the streets or to pour it into the canals. In addition, the Pestordonnantie tightened up other measures of municipal housekeeping: fire-fighting precautions were doubled; all drains and gutters were to be repaired forthwith; and pigs were banished from the city.[6]

The measures proclaimed in Hoorn differ little from those found in almost any sixteenth- or seventeenth-century town or city. In England, for instance, in the 1630s, *Certain necessary Directions, as well for the Cure of the Plague, as for preuenting the Infection* (1636) outlined similar methods of plague prophylaxis. As in Hoorn, householders were to give notice of the illness, "assoone as any one in his house complaineth, either of Botch, or Purple, or Swelling in any part of his body." Moreover, "as soon as any man shal be found . . . to be sick of the Plague, he shall the same night be sequestered in the same house [and] . . . be shut up for a moneth." Detailed directions attended to the airing of the house and its contents, especially the mattresses of the sick, to burying the dead, and to marking the infected houses. Precepts of urban hygiene were enumerated. In particular, "it is . . . ordered, that euery house-holder do cause the Street to bee daily pared before his doore." In addition, "speciall care [must] be taken that no stinking filth, or unwholesome Flesh, or mustie Corne, or other corrupt fruits . . . be suffered to be sold about the City." Finally, "that no Hogs, Dogs, or cats, or tame Pigeons, or Conies . . . [are] to be kept within any part of the City, or any Swine to be, or stray in the Streets or Lanes." The loose swine were to be confiscated by the city's beadles, while "the Dogs [were to be] killed by the Dog-killers, appointed for that purpose."[7]

Municipal measures against plague could also include the naming of extraordinary medical personnel: plague physicians, plague surgeons, and plague midwives were all appointed in addition to lay "searchers" (known as *visitators* in the Low Countries), grave-diggers, and carters. Medical practitioners were usually involved in the execution of policy but not in its formation. Only rarely did physicians and surgeons sit on boards of health, and when they did so it was as advisors. Before the sixteenth century, special *physici epidemie* (the Italian name for them; the Dutch and Flemish called them *pestmeesters*; the Germans *pest-chirurgien* or *-medici*) cared for plague sufferers. They were forbidden to treat others.

The steps taken against plague, therefore, combined measures that sought to purify the atmosphere (by lighting fires, by shooting off cannon

---

[6] "Pestordonnantie" (1599) for Hoorn, printed in J. Steendijk-Kuypers, *Volksgezond-heidszorg in de 16e en 17e eeuw te Hoorn: een bijdrage tot de beeldvorming van sociaal-geneeskundige structuren in een stedelijke samenleving* (Rotterdam, 1994), 374–76.

[7] *Certain necessary Directions, as well for the Cure of the Plague, as for preuenting the Infection; With many easie Medicines of small charge, very profitable to his Maiesties Subiects; Set downe by the College of Physicians by the Kings* MAIESTIES *speciall command,* ... (London, 1636).

to agitate the air, or by burning aromatic herbs and spices) with those that aspired to reduce contacts with plague sufferers or contaminated goods. By the sixteenth century, cities and states were routinely issuing *health passes*. Although these measures were more or less ubiquitous, larger cities enforced them more vigorously than smaller towns and villages. Territories experienced greater problems of enforcement and control.

For individuals, the time-tested advice, passed down from antiquity, was "flee early, go far, return late," and many took that counsel to heart. In the middle of the fourteenth century, more elaborate recommendations on how to preserve oneself from plague or how to cure it began to appear. Printing proliferated such advice greatly. *Plague tracts* combined medical disquisitions on cause and propagation with guidance to prevention and cure. Learned works in Latin, such as Michele Savonarola's *De preservatione a peste* (On the preservation from plague, written between 1444 and 1449) or Fracostoro's classic *De contagione* (On contagion, 1546), reached a smaller audience than did the cheaply printed vernacular guides that flooded off the presses in the sixteenth and seventeenth centuries. Authors often proffered advice in the form of a dialogue or in question-and-answer format like a catechism, paralleling the manner in which Reformation churchmen sought to inculcate the true faith. Popular treatises, such as the "friendly conversation" between "Polylogum Curiosulum" and "Orthophilum Medicum" produced in 1681 or the earlier astrologically informed "Promptvarium" of 1576 written to inform "each and every health and sick person, old or young, man or woman," followed these conventions.

The city physician in Ulm, Heinrich Steinhöwel (1420–82), in his *Büchlein der Ordnung der Pestilenz* (Little book of rules for plague, 1473) laid out typical regimens. One should pay close attention to cleansing the air in houses: one should throw open windows and prop doors to allow light and air to penetrate. Bonfires expelled feculence from the atmosphere. Rooms should be thoroughly scrubbed with water and vinegar and strewn with "sour" and "cooling" plants. One should avoid living near slaughterhouses and cemeteries and shun contacts with beggars and foreigners. In general, one was to eat lightly, and consume nothing when not hungry nor until the previous meal had been well digested and "evacuated." In winter, one should choose warm foods; in summer, cool (but not cold) ones. Moderate exercise after meals was good; strenuous exertion, however, quite injurious.

Intricate dietary rules touched on almost all foods. For instance, Steinhöwel found black and blue plums to be good, but one must peel them and dust them with sugar before consuming them. Meat from pastured animals was far better than from those kept in stalls. One should avoid all organ meats with the exception of chicken livers, cock testicles, and sheep and goat brains, and all these should prepared with liberal quells of pepper and ginger. He advised, moreover, that one should quell strong emotions of all kinds and seek out "harmless pleasures." Moderate enjoyment of sexual intercourse was useful, but excess could bring one into great peril.

If a person fell ill, others must take care to purge the air of the sick room and do things to "strengthen the heart." Steinhöwel recommended smelling salts and witch hazel or "good old wine" with which one should rinse hands, mouth, nasal passages, and the face, sprinkle some behind the ears, rub with it under the arms and on the genitals, as well as drink some. He advised "pest tablets" and boluses as well.

Those who took ill must be treated rapidly if they were to survive: the first twenty-four hours were critical. The sick room must be carefully cleaned and aired, and a good, light diet (for example, composed of gruel, chicken broth, vinegar, delicate meats, and lemon juice in water) administered. The victim should be kept in good spirits with singing and pleasant conversation. On the first day of illness, the patient should not be permitted to sleep, because during sleep the "poisonous material" could move to the heart, thus killing him or her. Bowels should be kept open with mild laxatives (plums and tamarind) and bleeding in moderation was also endorsed. Once the buboes formed, they should be encouraged to open by applying "drawing" poultices; if necessary, they might be lanced, then dressed with egg white and a healing salve. These directions were by no means unique to Steinhöwel; all could be found elsewhere.[8]

Like Steinhöwel, magistrates fretted about the presence of vagabonds and beggars. Plague in fact played a major role in molding new forms of poor relief in early modern Europe. The *Certain necessary Directions* dealt with issues of poor relief and reflected how European attitudes toward beggars and vagabonds, once regarded as "the poor of God," had appreciably hardened:

Nothing is more complained on, then the multitude of Rogues and wandering Beggers, that swarme in euery place about the City, being a great cause of the spreading of the infection . . . It is therefore now ordered, that . . . no wandering Begger be suffered in the Streets of this City, in any fasion or manner whatsoeuer vpon paine of the penalty prouided by the Law to be duely and seuerly executed vpon them.

Appended to this was a "Proclamation for quickning the Lawes made for the reliefe of the poor, and suppressing, punishing and setling of the sturdy Rogues and Vagabonds."

---

[8] Karl Sudhoff, *Der Ulmer Stadtarzt Dr. Heinrich Steinhöwel (1429–1482) als Pestauthor* (Munich, 1926), 197–204.

The connections between mendicancy and disease, forged in the aftermath of the great waves of plague in the middle of the fourteenth century, held on tenaciously. Hamburg, like many ports, suffered several severe bouts of plague. Physicians and city fathers accepted the presence of a link between poverty and epidemic disease, having, they argued, "learned from experience . . . that such contagions spring from the poor and are spread by wandering rabble." In 1596, the city physician, Johannes Böckel, warned against beggars who carried the "plague seed" with them in their bodies or on their rags and transmitted it to those who generously gave them alms or sheltered them in their homes. The progress of the 1712–14 epidemic in Hamburg produced, it seemed, much additional evidence to support these theories because the most impoverished sections of the city succumbed first. A cruel combination of economic disruption, harsh weather, and endemic warfare drove thousands of starvelings into Hamburg, and poor relief soon became the most pressing affair of the city's newly reconstituted board of health.

It would be too easy from the perspective of the twentieth century to condemn the efforts of our ancestors. Obviously the rats–fleas–human chain of infection was unknown to contemporaries, who were more likely to attribute the contagion to divine wrath, stench, meteorological and astronomical events, or prodigies such as comets. We can, however, venture some ideas about the possible effect these measures might have had.

Today physicians can successfully treat plague with antibiotics, but no early modern medicine would have affected the responsible pathogen. Still, a light diet, sufficient water, rest, and cleanliness could not have hurt, and good nursing care might well have saved lives. Shutting up houses kept sick people off the streets, although it also locked the healthy in with the infected and with the fleas and rats who spread the disease. Killing off cats and dogs probably allowed the rat population to expand, but the fleas of domestic animals have not yet been totally exonerated from some role in the spread of the disease. Public health authorities in their attempts to interdict the movement of people and goods, scour streets, track new cases, and prevent gatherings of people were in some ways on the right track, although obviously many of the measures they condoned did little or nothing (or were even counterproductive) in stopping or checking the plague. Quarantines and cordons sanitaires, however, may have been another matter.

Evidence is mounting that the efforts of governments to block off cities and territories, to interdict the movement of people, and to disallow communication with contaminated places might have considerably reduced the speed at which plague spread. These regulations probably had little significance before the seventeenth century, but, with the growing centralization of government and general improvements in communication and transportation after 1600, such endeavors may have become more effective. Certainly, plague epidemics began to decline in frequency and virulence after about the middle of the seventeenth century before they finally vanished from western Europe after 1721. Countries, however, did not immediately dismantle their antiplague mechanisms. Europeans could not let down their guard and they knew it. When plague ravaged Moscow in 1771, the French observer Charles de Mertens commented that "to a country situated like our own, histories of this terrible disorder occurring in the northern parts of Europe are more particularly interesting, by holding up to our view a picture of what it probably would be, whenever it should visit us again." Fortunately, de Mertens was a better witness than prophet.[9]

While the prevention of plague remained an important function of public health, health in society always meant more than merely fending off biological foes. Let us now consider other aspects of communal health and trace their development from the late middle ages through the end of the eighteenth century: the appearance of a network of town and state physicians; the regulation of medical practice; medical care and charity; and, finally, the new environmentalism of the late seventeenth and eighteenth centuries that occasioned vigorous interventionism.

Town and state physicians

Medical historiography has traditionally connected the rise of the *medical officer of health* to the evolution of public health. Such administrative innovations, however, need to be firmly situated within the framework of broader historical change. The growth of cities and the increasing capabilities of states and territories shaped public health mechanisms as forcefully as did the theories of medicine and the exigencies of epidemic disease.

The term "medical officer of health" is perhaps not the most appropriate to apply here. It is an imperfect English translation for a variety of names – most common was either *physicus* or *medicus civilis* – that referred to men accorded particular administrative and medical functions. In fact, the earliest form of these, the town and state physician, did not always possess public health or administrative duties.

---

[9] Charles de Mertens, *An Account of the Plague which Raged at Moscow in 1771* (trans. from French, London, 1799; reprinted and annotated with a introduction and bibliography by John Alexander, Newtonville, Mass., 1977), iii.

The town physician (*medicus civilis*) can be traced back to the late middle ages. Such physicians appeared first in northern Italy. By the fifteenth and early sixteenth centuries, numerous cities throughout Europe had appointed them. Municipalities contracted with men who became known as civic doctors (*medici condotti* in Italian or *Stadtärzte* in German-speaking areas) to ensure the presence of a physician in the city. The scarcity of medical practitioners gave rise, therefore, to the medico condotto. The custom of hiring civic doctors faded whenever a city began to attract more academically trained practitioners. Exactly *when* this level was attained varied – earlier in Italy, later in northern and western Europe, and even more belatedly in central and eastern Europe, in Hungary, for instance – but the process was everywhere comparable. Two examples illustrate well the rise and fall of the institution of civic doctor: one comes from Italy and the other from the Low Countries.

Ugo Borgognoni of Lucca is traditionally deemed the first medico condotto. In 1214, he agreed with the city of Bologna "to provide free treatment for the army, and for all injured residents of the city and for those of the countryside who have been brought to the city, save for those with abdominal hernia."[10] This custom spread widely throughout Italy and by the fourteenth century many cities listed one or more medici condotti on their payrolls. As the number of trained physicians rose in a locality, the office of medico condotto withered away. Large Italian towns by the sixteenth century no longer felt it necessary to hire medici condotti. Venice, which during the fourteenth century had employed between seven and ten of them, had none in the sixteenth century. The practice continued and even expanded for the next two hundred years, however, in small towns that always experienced difficulties in attracting physicians. Surgeons were also hired on similar terms.

The same sequence of events can be traced in other places, although the timing differs. In the Dutch city of Hoorn, for example, the burgomasters lured a physician named Albert Dircxz. to the city by offering him a salary, citizenship, and tax relief. Around 1600 Hoorn had three such *stadsdoctors*. At the middle of the seventeenth century, however, there were only two and salaries had also been much reduced. Partly the decline of the stadsdoctor must be attributed to the mid-1600s economic malaise that enervated Hoorn, but it was also true that by then many more physicians lived there.

Here I have distinguished scrupulously between civic doctors and what were later called medical officers of health or *physici*. One should be

---

[10] Vivian Nutton, "Continuity or Rediscovery?: The City Physician in Classical Antiquity and Mediaeval Italy," in Andrew Russell, ed., *The Town and State Physician in Europe from the Middle Ages to the Enlightenment* (Wolfenbüttel, 1981), 26.

warned, however, that not everyone observes these niceties of language and one often finds the term physicus used unsystematically. One might usefully discriminate among several types of state-employed physicians as Norbert Zólyomi does in his study of Hungary: (1) those without a contract and without a fixed salary who were commissioned on an ad hoc basis to execute a particular task, such as frame a report on the water supply; (2) those without a contract who were employed and paid for a short period of time, such as during a plague attack; and, finally, (3) those possessing a contract with a city or state, a regular salary, and (to augment Zólyomi's specifications) a binding set of instructions delineating a series of duties – the *real* medical officer of health.[11] Medical officers of health were occasionally appointed in cities in the sixteenth century, but the establishment of a *network* of officers that covered a territory like Prussia, Hungary, or France did not occur until the eighteenth century.

Several examples illustrate the evolution from civic doctor to medical officer of health. Local conditions, the presence of powerful personalities, and social, economic, or even geographical peculiarities always occasioned differences. These instances do not, therefore, represent models, but rather illustrate the heterogeneous ways in which public health systems developed.

One set of examples comes from Germany. Two of the earliest Stadtärzte were Hermann "Medicus" selected by Wismar in 1281 and Master Berchtoldus by Munich in 1312. In the fourteenth century several cities established such posts: Cologne in 1371; Strasburg in 1383; and Frankfurt am Main in 1384. The orders of the Emperor Sigismund (1431) specified that "each imperial city should have a physician." Town physicians are recorded in Zurich from the fifteenth century and one can trace similar developments in other Swiss towns (Geneva, Bern, Basel). If one looks at Hungary, a like process occurred, although the introduction of physici took place two hundred years later than in western Europe: not until after 1735.

The duties of the early modern physici were many and they expanded over time. Cities began to promulgate comprehensive *medical ordinances* in the fifteenth century (in Nuremberg in 1478, for example) and territories in the sixteenth century (Würzburg in 1502, for instance). In general these documents charged the physici with caring for the sick-poor; with conducting forensic examinations (doing postmortems, viewing wounds, judging victims of sodomy – the delicate tasks of, for example, determining virginity or establishing rape were left, however, to midwives); with

---

[11] Norbert Duka Zólyomi, "The Development of the District Medical Officer in Hungary," in Russell, *Town and State Physician*, 133.

advising the political authorities; with supervising sanitary conditions (for example, testing well-water, patrolling markets to search out rotten fruit and spoiled meat, investigating animal diseases, and so on); and with instructing, examining, and superintending all subordinate medical personnel. For these tasks, physici received regular salaries. Sometimes the form of payment was exclusively cash, but most places provided physici with compensation in kind as well: loads of wood for fuel or an allotment of city wine or beer. More intangible, but equally meaningful in a world concerned with display and status, were grants of citizenship, marks of distinction such as invitations to city festivities or places of honor in city processions and at town meetings.

Town physici did not, however, bear the burden of responsibility for medical and sanitary affairs alone. They worked alongside, or rather, under civic officials. The tendency for medical men to dominate boards of health was not achieved until the latter part of the eighteenth century. Before then lay magistrates usually kept control. In a large town like Valencia, Spain, for instance, medical organization was already quite complex by the sixteenth century. In addition to physicians hired by the town, there were *examinadores* who granted permission to practice; *veedores* who supervised apothecaries; and *desospitadors* who dispensed medico-legal advice; as well as others with other special assignments. None of these were physicians. The coordinator of all these tasks was the *mustasaf*, a magistrate.

Medical conditions outside towns tended to be more haphazardly ordered and supervised. Before the middle of the eighteenth century, provincial physici were few and generally appointed only to cope with emergencies like plague in humans or rinderpest in cattle. Cities and city-states, like Hamburg or Venice, might make arrangements for rural areas attached to them. Florence, for example, dispatched help to the village of Monte Lupo during the plague epidemic of 1631. Creating the post of permanent resident medical officer of health for rural areas took much longer.

In France the organization of rural health in these centuries resembled a patchwork quilt. The first nationwide effort to centralize or coordinate medical care came quite late, with the founding of the Société royale de médecine in 1776. The Société, however, did not act as a national board of health, but rather as a sort of corresponding society among physicians for the purpose of gathering information. Earlier in the century, other pieces of a public health puzzle had fallen into place. The network of *intendants* set up by Cardinal Richelieu, and then expanded under his successors, facilitated the state's ability to cope with medical emergencies swiftly and with some degree of expertise. In response to the Marseilles plague of 1720, the royal government sent physicians and surgeons to assist and the overall effect was excellent.

These individual efforts continued to expand as the old régime drew to a close. In various généralités after about 1750, intendants commissioned epidemic physicians and surgeons. As in Italy and Germany, towns often contracted with local medical practitioners, offering them a supplementary wage in return for providing medical care in areas that might not otherwise attract physicians. Not only towns were busily involved in such initiatives. Provincial estates, the church, or "even socially aware local notables" might also employ physicians. Toby Gelfand, in surveying these arrangements, also points to the interesting example of Biarritz where 253 families paid 2 French francs each for the services of a surgeon. (Similar strategies developed elsewhere. The Fürstenberg porcelain manufactory, for example, organized medical care for its workers on a subscription basis.)

The French government's most sustained effort was, however, the distribution of boxes of remedies (*boîtes des remèdes*) from the late seventeenth century onwards. None of this, however, equaled a system and thus, as Gelfand concludes, "public medicine at the end of the Old Régime remained essentially an emergency measure designed to supplement other kinds of charity during a crisis such as an epidemic."[12]

Some places in Europe, however, had moved more rapidly down the road to coordinated medical provision and supervision. German territories probably went furthest in building up networks of state-appointed and state-salaried physicians. These men were, however, neither civil servants nor even employees.

The history of the *physicate* (i.e., the administrative district for a physicus) and the construction of a web of physici can be reconstructed for several German territories. While no territory is ever fully representative of the "German" experience, the history of what happened in the small duchy of Braunschweig-Wolfenbüttel nicely illustrates how such structures evolved. As in most places, physici first appeared in cities and in the penumbra of plague or other infectious diseases. The plague years of the late sixteenth and early seventeenth centuries, especially the epidemic years of 1577, 1597, and 1609–11 in Braunschweig (city), occasioned a number of new ordinances. After the Thirty Years War, renewed threats of plague and epidemic dysentery advanced the regulation of health to a more constant issue of governance. Particularly in large cities and towns,

---

[12] Toby Gelfand, "Public Medicine and Medical Careers in France During the Reign of Louis XV," in Russell, *Town and State Physician*, 101–03, 116.

it became less common for the office of physicus to remain vacant for years on end. Throughout the seventeenth century and, for that matter, well into the eighteenth, the appointment of physici remained a local prerogative, however, exercised by urban magistrates. After the passing of a comprehensive medical ordinance in 1747, the newly activated Board of Health regularly appointed physici to each of thirteen districts. Physici received salaries directly from the privy purse. The physicus was neither solely nor principally a *physician-to-the-poor* (although he did treat the poor and received reimbursements from poor relief funds), nor was he granted a monopoly of practice in his area.

Physici were, in many ways, outsiders in their districts. How well (or even if) they survived professionally depended on a constellation of forces and events. Their own personalities were critical as were their relations with a range of local notables. Some physici got along famously with the inhabitants of their districts, and often married into local families. Some did noticeably less well, and many seemed to have warred with everyone. Thus, the physicus must be placed within the fields of influence of local political, social, economic, and cultural forces and all these together accounted for his success or failure in a locality. The physicus filled multiple niches in a community, and his several roles often had little to do with medicine directly. The extraofficial and extramedical aspects of his life – his position as property-owner, as debtor and creditor, his propriety, his bearing, his piety, and even his dress and manners – largely determined whether his neighbors accepted him.

Before leaving the issue of state-organized medical provision behind us, two additional topics deserve consideration: (1) *auxiliary doctors* and (2) *veterinary medicine.*

Seventeenth- and eighteenth-century reformers vigorously debated how to disburse medical care in the countryside. One solution was to extend existing networks of physici. Another was more ingenious and advocated creating a corps of *routiniers* or auxiliary medical practitioners with less training than physicians, but who were also distinct from surgeons and apothecaries. In 1751, the Swedish botanist Carolus Linnaeus (1707–78) worked out a plan for involving rural clergymen in medical care (and even then the idea was not entirely new: seventeenth-century theology students in Lutheran Denmark had also studied some basic medicine). The priest-doctor solution gained favor in the closing years of the eighteenth and the opening decades of the nineteenth century, but it was actually tried in just one place. Nineteenth-century Sweden implemented a program for educating prospective pastors in medicine. The government abandoned the scheme, however, before the first students were sent into the field.

In France, however, things took a different turn. The revolutionary government had abolished older educational and regulatory structures. Early in the nineteenth century, the Napoleonic government stepped in to reestablish both of these. As a stop-gap solution, Fourcroy's Law of 1803 arranged for the instruction and placement of "practitioners of a lower degree." These *officiers de santé* learned by apprenticeship and were to be deployed in rural areas and during times of war. Officiers de santé continued to practice in France until the end of the nineteenth century, despite the growing opposition (and availability) of academically trained physicians.

"The practical problems of bringing health care to the countryside," as Caroline Hannaway observes, did not, however, stop with human beings. Yet, few people have made veterinary medicine the object of scholarly study. This is a rather curious omission. Horses were indispensable to the trades of war and peace, and treating equine diseases, as well as breeding better animals, was serious business. In the eighteenth century the accent switched from horses to other domestic animals and, in particular, to cattle and sheep. Not surprisingly, we can link this shift to prevailing concerns with improving agriculture (in France, known as *physiocracy*). An equally great role, however, was played by the several waves of *rinderpest* (i.e., cattle plague) that began in Italy in 1711 and then swept like wildfire over Europe in the 1740s and 1750s, and again in the 1770s and 1780s. In some areas, like the Netherlands, it became endemic. Cattle populations were decimated and huge economic losses recorded. Quarantines, the isolation of herds, large-scale slaughtering, and even experiments in inoculating animals were introduced to cope with the epizootic. This plague of cattle greatly encouraged the founding of schools for veterinary medicine. These appeared in several European countries during the eighteenth century, although France took the lead, establishing colleges in Lyons in 1762 and in Alfort in 1766.

The regulation of medical practice in early modern Europe

As boards of health became integral parts of governments, they took on more assignments. Under the impact of mercantilist and cameralist teachings, the health of the population became a central interest of the state. Detailed plans for the minute regulation of health and human welfare culminated in Johann Peter Frank's massive *System einer vollständigen medizinischen Polizey* (A system of complete medical police, 1779–1825).

Two issues were always important. One was the need to assure that enough medical personnel were available to serve the population and the other was to examine and license practitioners. Although several ancient peoples thought to compensate victims of malpractice (most famously in Hammurabi's code), none evolved a systematic form of education or licensing. Roger of Sicily (reigned 1130–54) and his grandson, the Emperor Frederick II (reigned 1212–50), framed rules for medical practice and specified that all those who wished to practice must obtain a license. It was, however, ecclesiastical authorities who issued the credentials.

An articulated and comprehensive concept of licensing, the idea of a sort of quality control, and attempts to regulate the marketshare developed in the middle ages with the rise of guilds. Guilds were sometimes called corporations, and thus much of the medical structure of early modern Europe was essentially *corporate* in nature. For example, by 1293, Florence had a guild incorporating *medici*, apothecaries, and grocers, while a College of Physicians for university-trained physicians existed in Venice by 1316. In France, the surgeons' and barber-surgeons' corporations in Montpellier (1252) and in Paris (the St. Côme corporation, 1268) were the earliest and most eminent. A similar college of physicians did not exist in England until 1518. Other northern and western European countries were even slower to call such bodies into being.

Corporations in one way or another attempted to monopolize medical practice. Some were quite successful; others appreciably less so. Corporations that brought together surgeons and physicians often became embroiled in bitter internecine feuds over rights and authority. Guilds generally excluded women, although the widows of surgeons, barber-surgeons, apothecaries, and bathmasters might be allowed to continue their spouse's practice with the aid of a journeyman. Midwifery, while not in fact guilded, was often organized in what might be called a semi-guilded manner: aspirant midwives trained by working alongside older midwives in an apprentice-like relationship.

Corporatism remained the most important form of medical organization until the very end of our period, when the corporate structure in medicine, like that in other realms of life, began to decay. There were, however, notable regional differences. Medical corporatism was never as strong in England as, for example, in France and the breakdown of corporate life there occurred earlier.

Corporatism produced in France what Brockliss and Jones have termed a "differentiated medical community," i.e., a community divided into several specific occupations, each with its characteristic rights and privileges, distinct fields of action, and proper means of defending its "territory" against the encroachment or trespass of others. There were separate corporations for physicians, surgeons (often surgeons and barber-surgeons were combined in the same corporation), and apothecaries. Still, this generalized corporate structure did not pertain everywhere. In Italy and Spain, for instance, the tendency that was so marked in the rest of western Europe (to separate physicians and surgeons) was never pronounced, at least not until well after the sixteenth century. Physicians and other practitioners, for instance, belonged to the same guild in Renaissance Venice.

By 1500, in France, corporations existed for both physicians and surgeons/barber-surgeons. Still, corporate life was not firmly planted by the beginning of the sixteenth century and considerable variations characterized different corporations. For instance, although theoretical training and university education generally distinguished physicians from surgeons, many physicians (just like surgeons) had learned their craft as apprentices. Moreover, there were far more corporations for surgeons than for physicians. During the sixteenth and seventeenth centuries, however, the pace of incorporation in France began to quicken due to the increased desire of the monarchy to foster it. English corporations likewise languished or prospered with the ebb and flood of monarchical power and support. Brockliss and Jones estimate that by the end of the seventeenth century in France there were between thirty-six and forty-three colleges of physicians or medical faculties, three hundred corporations of surgeons and about the same number for apothecaries. And yet, as we shall see in the following chapter, members of medical corporations by no means monopolized (or even dominated) the medical marketplace. Literally thousands of noncorporate practitioners thrived.

During the eighteenth century, three developments sapped the vigor of this corporate world. First, the medical faculties began to decline in relevance as educational organs. Private medical teaching and newer institutions (especially in the field of surgery) began to supplant them. Second, and at the same time, the corporations became more elitist in their orientation. Third, although there were always many noncorporate practitioners, their numbers rose strikingly. Thus, by the closing decades of the eighteenth century, the corporate medical world – and not only in France – was in crisis. The French revolutionary government razed the corporate structure in its entirety, and that demolition, of course, also affected medicine.

The history of medical corporatism in England and Germany demonstrates similarities to France, but also obvious differences. By 1550, three corporations controlled medical practice in London: the Society of Apothecaries, the Barber-Surgeons Company, and the College of Physicians (later the Royal College of Physicians). The first two had existed since the late middle ages. The College of Physicians, however, was newer and more unusual: it was chartered by Henry VIII in 1518 in answer to the requests of court and academic physicians under the leadership of the humanist physician Thomas Linacre (c. 1460–1524). In theory, the two older corporations bowed to the superior authority of the College of Physicians.

The College of Physicians functioned in several ways: it was a learned society, it was an organ representing the views of academically trained physicians, and it was a sanctioning agency. Full membership as *fellows* was possible only for men who had achieved the degree of M.D. at one of the country's two universities (Oxford or Cambridge). To become a fellow, the applicant must not only possess his degree but also submit to an examination in Latin based on his knowledge of Galenic and Hippocratic texts. Fees were charged for the examinations – in 1684, the by no means inconsiderable sum of £20. Practical experience was neither relevant nor tested.

By the middle of the seventeenth century, the College had significantly expanded its membership and began granting licenses to men with baser academic qualifications: these men received *licentiate* status. Licentiates were, however, not necessarily men of lesser skill or fame: Thomas Sydenham (1624–89) was perhaps the most celebrated licentiate of the College. On the whole, however, members of the College represented an academically trained elite. Throughout most of its early modern history, the College exercised the right to try cases of malpractice and, in particular, to proceed against illicit practice. Of course, the College exerted no control over practitioners outside the capital. There were, moreover, other ways to receive authorization to practice medicine. In 1512, for example, Parliament endowed bishops with the right to grant medical licenses within their dioceses. Thus, the sway of the College was imperfect even in London.[13]

Medical corporatism was never as resilient in England as in France, and what Harold Cook has called the "medical old regime" declined faster and earlier in England. The College of Physicians suffered a massive setback to its authority in 1704 in a famous case involving the apothecary William Rose, in which the House of Lords resolved that apothecaries, too, had right to practice medicine. By then several things had combined to weaken the power of the College and its ability to maintain control. As in France, the medical marketplace had greatly expanded and the party of physicians was more fragmented than ever before. Fresh currents in medical thought and theory were rapidly

---

[13] The most important sources for the history of the (Royal) College of Physicians in these centuries are: Harold J. Cook, *The Decline of the Old Medical Regime in Stuart London* (Ithaca, N.Y., and London, 1986), and George N. Clark, *A History of the Royal College of Physicians of London* (2 vols., Oxford, 1964–66).

eroding the pillars of academicism that had once undergirded the community of physicians. Those who planned for a Society of Chemical Physicians (1665), for example, emphasized experience and experimentation more than the academically trained, text-oriented members of the College did. In addition, by the final third of the seventeenth century, the College could no longer count on the unequivocal backing of the court. The College had been founded with the support of royal body-physicians, and monarchical protection had always been its mainstay. Royal support was no longer unquestionably enjoyed after the Glorious Revolution (1688). Moreover, many aristocrats and courtiers were great fans of the new science and were little attracted to the stale textualism of collegial orthodoxy. Thus, both the intellectual and medico-social world of eighteenth-century England was no longer congenial to the closed corporatism of the College, and the Rose decision was only indicative of that process.

The German situation defies easy categorization. "Germany" is, of course, unwieldy to deal with precisely because there were so many "Germanies" before 1871. Moreover, state power, even within territories that had undergone a process of centralization since the sixteenth century, was always diffuse. The peculiarity of this situation makes it hard to understand how important corporate life was for physicians. For one thing, in Germany physicians were never organized in guilds.

Other legitimate practitioners are easier to characterize. As in both England and France, the surgeons and barber-surgeons, apothecaries, and bathmasters had been organized in guilds since the fourteenth and fifteenth centuries. In places where these groups were joined in one guild, the relationships among them were often rocky. Jurisdictional conflicts over specific practices were *intra-* and *inter*-guild. Still, not until the seventeenth century did real clefts open up. Especially bitter were the protracted battles between bathmasters and barber-surgeons and between barber-surgeons and surgeons. In the duchy of Braunschweig-Wolfenbüttel, for example, a legal snarl over division of rights ignited in the middle of the sixteenth century, smoldered for decades, and finally burned itself out in the imperial courts between 1635 to 1738. The most important point at issue was the attempt of surgeons to peel away from barber-surgeons and to reduce the practice of the latter to nothing more than clipping hair, setting cups, and applying leeches. That goal was achieved by the end of the eighteenth century.

It is much more demanding to explain the corporate life of physicians in Germany. As we have seen, corporations in both France and England had two functions. On the one hand, they were the gatekeepers to the profession and their members decided who should be admitted (their licensing function). On the other, admittance to practice also meant that one became a *member* of that corporation, such as a fellow of the College of Physicians. The second function never existed in Germany (not even in Vienna or Berlin) perhaps because there was no such accretion of people, prestige, and power in one place in Germany as in either France or England. In Germany, of course, physicians just as readily defined their distinctiveness in terms of their learnedness and their training.

By the late seventeenth and early eighteenth centuries, the task of licensing came to devolve on new-style *collegia medica*. Most of these were set up by state authorities to function as boards of health. All physicians in an area were supposed to submit their credentials for approval to a collegium before settling down to practice, but the collegium itself did not at first proof candidates' competence or learnedness; instead they "checked their papers." Later, most collegia medica held viva voce (in Latin) as prerequisites for entering practice. Once a candidate passed the examination, however, he did not become a member of the collegium medicum (as one could become, for example, a fellow of the College of Physicians in London). Thus the German situation reveals many of the same traits that characterized German political structures as a whole: it was a hodgepodge. No clear division of responsibilities existed. A mix of privileges persisted and confused the relationships between governors and the governed.

Peoples and places

The history of health in society is to a great extent the history of peoples and places. Since antiquity, men and women have been aware that health somehow hinged on the state of nature. Even when ideas of contagion seemed to dominate, contemporaries still deemed environmental influences significant. The bacteriological age (beginning in the middle of the nineteenth century) helped push environmental concerns into the background, but this change may represent only a temporary hiatus in an age-old tradition. Certainly today we have lost our complacency about the environment and have become acutely sensitive to diseases caused by environmental pollutants such as asbestos and dioxins.

Few people used (and use) the terms "contagion," "infection," and "miasma" carefully. Roughly speaking, contagion means that diseases are passed from person to person, either directly or through water, air, or inanimate objects. Cause of disease interpretations that rely on the environment argue that something in the physical surroundings – and very often in the air – is responsible for illness. Unfortunately, many people apply these terms indiscriminately. Moreover, as Margaret Pelling has observed, such words were never exclusive to a medical vocabulary. Ideas of contagion, for instance, "are inseparable from notions of individual morality, social responsibility, and collective action." The tendency to reduce explanations to single causes is a product of the bacteriological revolution which implied that one thing – a germ – caused disease and that one thing – a drug (for example, an antibiotic or some other form of *magic bullet*) – would cure it. It does, of course, make a difference in public health policies whether one believes that diseases pass principally from person to person or diffuse through the subtle mechanism of the air.[14]

Ever since the Greeks, people have connected disease with their physical surroundings. The Hippocratic works, and particularly *Airs, Waters, Places* and *Epidemics I* and *III*, contrast the relative healthiness and insalubrity of places. Numerous factors were thought to affect environmental conditions: prevailing winds, native waters, character of the soil, seasons and their alteration, and sudden meteorological shifts or terrestrial upheavals, especially earthquakes. This mode of explanation held on doggedly through the centuries. When, for example, Professor Gottfried Beireis was asked in 1766 to explain an "alarming mortality" in the small town of Schöppenstedt, he identified a persistently damp environment which

weakens the mechanism of breathing, hinders the preparation of the blood in the lungs, and abruptly stops up the perspiration. [These] are the causes of the almost always fatal chest diseases, which continue unchecked throughout the year there, [and] of the irregular intermittent fevers, especially quartan fevers, of the preponderance of tumors and of dropsy, the last [of which] is almost endemic in Schöppenstedt and the cause of most adult deaths.[15]

Several decades earlier, the English physician John Arbuthnot (1667–1735), in observing an epidemic of catarrhal fever, emphasized the drought of the preceding year because such dry spells

exert their Effects after the Surface of the Earth is again opened by Moisture; and the Perspirations of the Ground, which was long suppress'd, is suddenly restor'd. It is probably that the Earth then emits several new Effluvia hurtful to Human Bodies.

[14] Margaret Pelling, "Contagion/Germ Theory/Specificity," in Bynum and Porter, *Companion Encyclopedia*, 310.

[15] All quotes from Mary Lindemann, *Health and Healing in Eighteenth-Century Germany* (Baltimore, 1996), 283–84.

These "Effluvia" harmed all nature, for a "previous ill Constitution of the Air" had attacked animals earlier and provoked "a Madness among Dogs." Moreover, "the Horses were seiz'd with the Catarrh before Mankind; and a Gentelman averr'd to me, that some Birds, particularly the Sparrows, left the Place where he was during the Sickness."[16] Neither of these analyses would have seemed odd to any western medical man writing since antiquity. Beireis and Arbuthnot, like the Hippocratic authors, affirmed a close affinity between the environment and the action of the humors within living bodies.

Equally important in this context was the idea of corrupt air, or *miasma*. Generally associated with the defilement of air were rotting vege-tation, decaying corpses, discarded entrails, and fetid excrement. People who were sick also breathed out transpirations that fouled the atmosphere and Mother Earth herself was not innocent: exhalations from craters and gaps in the earth occasioned, for example, by tremors were also widely believed to breed dangers. *How* corrupted air worked on the individual or on his or her humors was not exactly clear. It was widely accepted that even a small quantity of tainted air could sully the atmosphere, much as a particle of dye in water colored its entire volume. Such ideas underpinned the many measures taken during epidemic outbreaks to purify air, to keep it moving (still air was bad air), and to clean up things which emitted bad smells.

Not only the atmosphere made one ill. Other diseased people did so as well and, despite the lack of an explicitly articulated idea of contagion, most people accepted that many epidemic diseases were contagious. This deep-seated belief shaped public responses that sought to isolate the sick from the healthy or to prevent the ill from coming into contact with the well. Not all diseases, and not even all epidemic diseases, were viewed as equally catching, however. Smallpox existed at one end of the contagious-ness continuum, while diseases like malaria at the other. One malady, syphilis, had a strong impact on European society and helped bolster the logical force of contagionism.

The Veronese physician, Girolamo Fracastoro, who named syphilis, also introduced a term – *fomes* or *fomites* – to designate "inert carriers" of contagion. For this reason, Fracastoro has frequently been placed in a pantheon of scientific precursors that includes such figures as the Flemish anatomist Andreas Vesalius and the Polish astronomer Nicolaus Copernicus (1473–1543). George Rosen, writing in 1958, referred to Fracastoro's book as "one of the great landmarks in the evolution of a

---

[16] Quoted in James C. Riley, *The Eighteenth-Century Campaign to Avoid Disease* (New York, 1987), 25.

scientific theory of communicable disease." Such hero-making is, however, a rather questionable enterprise. Fracastoro, for example, did not perceive "the categorical distinctions between contagion, infection, and noncontagious disease which are so important from the modern point of view."[17] Thus, it is ahistorical to lift Fracastoro to the pedestal of scientific innovation or to transform him into an early bacteriological guru.

Throughout the early modern period, the dual strands of miasma and contagion combined and recombined in myriad ways to (1) explain the cause of various diseases and (2) suggest plans of action to cope with biological emergencies. Few, if any, public health programs rested exclusively on one or the other, as any quick perusal of plague ordinances demonstrates. The twin strands were always present, but by the late seventeenth and early eighteenth century the thread of environmentalism, or what has been called a *new Hippocratism*, was thickening.

By the beginning of the eighteenth century, many people were persuaded that disease could be avoided, even if it could not be cured.[18] This faith in an ability to manipulate the environment was new. The Greek view of the environment had been an essentially fatalistic one: physicians could treat the individual patient but nothing could be done to prevent epidemics. Eighteenth-century environmentalists thought otherwise, and set out on a crusade to change the world about them. They began by trying to assemble accurate information on physical phenomena. Then, they endeavored to uncover hidden patterns in that data. Once these patterns were exposed, they argued, it should be possible to learn what to avoid and what to alter in the environment, as well as how.

Improved methods of studying the atmosphere and the weather made the projects of the environmentalists seem feasible. New instruments (e.g., barometers and thermometers) made it easier to obtain a quantitative perspective on air pressure, temperature, rainfall, and wind velocity. From about the 1660s onward, those interested in the weather began to keep daily records of meteorological occurrences, often continuing them for years. This pursuit then expanded into a studied attempt to correlate weather and other environmental conditions with epidemic occurrences. The star of the new Hippocratism guided the writing of the *medical topographies* that then began to appear. These works typically reviewed climatic and environmental factors, patterns of illness, and the unique effects of certain localities.

[17] Pelling, "Contagion/Germ Theory/Specificity," 319.
[18] My discussion of the "new environmentalism" or "new Hippocratism" of the eighteenth century relies heavily on the work of Riley, *Campaign*. See also Caroline Hannaway, "Environment and Miasmata," in Bynum and Porter, *Companion Encyclopedia*, 292–308.

One of the pioneers of medical topography was the Italian physician, Bernardino Ramazzini (1633–1714). His account of Modena (1685) was followed by a series of others: Friedrich Hoffmann studied epidemics in Halle and Johann Philipp Burggrave and Johann Adolph Behrends wrote on Frankfurt am Main. As the Europeans stretched their influence over the globe and settled in climates they found strange and biologically perilous, medical topographies appeared for these places as well. Lionel Chalmers, for example, penned an account of South Carolina in 1776. Perhaps the most expansive of these efforts was that written by the father of *medical geography*, Leonhard Ludwig Finke (1747–1837), whose three-volume *Versuch einer allgemeinen medicinisch-praktischen Geographie* (Medical-practical geography) appeared from 1792 to 1795.

The medical topographers of the eighteenth century were far more successful in collecting information than deriving lessons from it, however. Part of the problem lay in the overwhelming size of samples, but another part in the lack of consensus on how to observe. Did one record temperature indoors or out? At 6 a.m. or 6 p.m.? Using which one of several competing scales? To say nothing about the inaccuracy of early scientific instruments and the absolute babel of terms for describing or specifying diseases. Attempts to quantify data and to develop what has been called an "applied environmental mathematics" remained crude and had no predictive value. Yet they deviated significantly from an older, qualitative emphasis on "airs, waters, places" and pointed toward a medicine based on the science of large numbers. These conclusions suggested to eighteenth-century observers that improvements in the environment would affect mortality and morbidity positively.

Riley distinguishes four initiatives for improving the environment: (1) draining; (2) lavation or the cleaning of streets, gutters, and other public facilities, such as privies; (3) ventilation; and, finally, (4) new burial practices. While none of these undertakings was novel, they were pursued with uncommon fervor in the eighteenth century and on a larger scale than previously dreamed possible.

The noisome exhalations from swamps and bogs were deemed especially harmful and large-scale projects to drain them had been going on at least since the seventeenth century. Equally rank were the closer environments of cities and towns. City streets often gave off overpowering stenches, and rivers like the Thames and the Tiber were little more than open sewers. In the sixteenth and seventeenth centuries, street flushing remained the responsibility of residents. In England, for instance, most towns required houseowners to sweep the streets outside their homes once a week and delinquents were fined. Minor criminal offenders might be sentenced to remove the accumulated mess from streets or to haul nightsoil away. Rather then hiring street-cleaners themselves, cities contracted with private individuals to perform these tasks, although such arrangements with individuals had significant drawbacks. Municipalities soon devised ways to flush the streets regularly and laid simple, open storm sewers to carry off the filth thus dislodged from the surface. In the nineteenth century, environmental engineers would accomplish massive works projects like that of watering and raising the streets of cities the size of Chicago.

Equally important was the attempt to provide adequate quantities of potable water. This proved a burdensome task especially for large cities as the nearest and most convenient supplies were often the same ones that conveyed away the city's filth: rivers. Paris had two major sources: the River Seine and an aqueduct which carried water in from miles outside the city. For London in the middle ages, wells were the first sources of water (besides the three rivers, the Thames, the Fleet, and Walbrook). In 1613, Sir Hugh Myddleton, a goldsmith, formed the New River Company to bring water to London. Although Myddleton's intent was clearly entrepreneurial, others undertook similar projects for beneficent and philanthropic reasons. This latter trend became especially apparent in the eighteenth century.

Throughout the early modern period, most city dwellers continued to obtain water from public pumps or conduits, while countryfolk relied on wells and convenient streams. Especially in cities, water rarely reached the consumer unpolluted. Systems of water filtration, although proposed in the seventeenth century, were not introduced on an urban scale until the nineteenth.[19] Yet the picture was not altogether dismal. Even the "great wen," London, had been much improved in the early eighteenth century through the initiatives of private persons and local governors. Indeed, in 1767, Dr. Thomas Short noted that

many of its Streets have been widened, made straight, raised, paved with easy Descents to carry off the Water; besides Wells in most public Yards; and Pipes for conveying Plenty of fresh Water to keep them clean and sweet.[20]

Because "air corrupted by putrefaction is the most fatal of all causes of illness,"[21] air too must be cleansed of its impurities. The best way was to keep it in motion. As the new science began to demonstrate that air was

---

[19] Jean-Pierre Goubert, *The Conquest of Water: The Advent of Health in the Industrial Age* (Cambridge, 1989); F. W. Robbins, *The Story of Water Supply* (Oxford, 1946).

[20] Quoted in Roy Porter, "Cleaning up the Great Wen: Public Health in Eighteenth-Century London," in W. F. Bynum and Roy Porter, eds., *Living and Dying in London* (London, 1991), 68.   [21] Quoted in Riley, *Campaign*, 97.

composed of many gases and capable of carrying particles in its "materia," its role in disease causation attracted more notice. Novel schemes for ventilating buildings where many people resided, such as jails, orphanages, workhouses, and especially hospitals, were based on just these principles of movement and openness. We have seen how reformers at the end of the eighteenth century stressed the value of good aeration in hospitals, but that need was equally vital for maintaining the health of any crowded population, whether on land or at sea. Inventors devised all sorts of mechanical fans which they then introduced to supplement simpler actions like flinging open doors and windows, shaking out bedding, and letting the sun shine into the dark and musty corners of old buildings. When, for example, the London aldermen became alarmed by the high mortality in Newgate prison, they consulted Dr. John Pringle (1707–82) who had written on the prevention of disease in the armed forces and Stephen Hales, a clergyman and avid experimenter with ventilating fans. Pringle and Hales recommended that ventilators be reinstalled in the prison. The Pringle/Hales team also demonstrates the mix of medical expertise and philanthropic concern characteristic of many eighteenth-century public health ventures.

Perhaps the most intriguing aspect of the four-pronged attack on filth was that connected with burials. For centuries the Christian dead had been immured in churches and sunk in churchyards, places where space was limited. Sepulchers and graves often had to be opened and the bones of ancestors moved to make room for their descendants. The stench arising from church floors and walls, and the juices oozing into the earth, greatly troubled eighteenth-century sanitarians. Around the middle of the eighteenth century, horrifying reports of multiple deaths resulting from the opening of church crypts sensationalized the matter. Very quickly a call arose to halt the practice of burials within church walls and to relocate cemeteries to the suburbs. The removal and reinterment campaign gained momentum throughout western Europe. Significantly, the first to be buried outside city walls were the poor.

The eighteenth century was fascinated with the moment of death. A series of humanitarian projects to prevent burial alive and to restore the seemingly drowned linked up with crusades to clean up burial grounds. Life-saving institutes – devoted to rescuing the drowning or restoring the "lifeless" by means of a "tobacco clyster-pipe" and other stimulating measures – cropped up first in towns with many canals and waterways, such as Hamburg, Amsterdam, and Haarlem, but then spread. Campaigns to prevent burial alive often violated the religious sensibilities and funerary rituals of Christians and non-Christians alike. It was thought necessary to wait at least twenty-four hours to see if a person was truly dead or had only slipped into a trance or coma: apparent death. Attempts to mandate more than a day's delay before interring the dead, however, jostled Jewish burial customs that required the deceased to be under earth within twenty-four hours.

The question remains: did these initiatives have any constructive impact on morbidity or mortality in early modern Europe? It is next to impossible to answer, mostly because we are not – or not yet – able to correlate improvements in environmental conditions with declines in either sickness or death. Perhaps more detailed local studies might in the future demonstrate these connections more effectively. Clearly, there is a correlation in time between the rise of the medicine of the environment with the decline of mortality. Coincidence does not equal cause and effect. It does seem probable, however, that cleanup drives removed many pathogens from the environment. Of course, contemporaries were mostly combating something that was, in and of itself, harmless: miasma. Yet, it seems indisputable that, as James Riley concludes, "useful measures were taken for the wrong reasons."

"The bookkeeping of the state"[22]

Modern demographers, of course, have different perspectives on disease than did early modern men and women. Yet, these people were not unaware of what killed them and their contemporaries. Their observations conditioned responses both as individuals and as a collectivity. Although governments started amassing "numbers" rather early to assess the impact of disease on their subjects (in terms, for example, of how many were buried in a given period of time, say, a week or a day), it was not until the seventeenth century that this attempt was ventured systematically.

Raw data for the quantitative analysis of the size and the health of populations first began to be generated in the sixteenth century. Some Protestant parishes began keeping information on births and deaths, or rather on christenings and burials, as well as weddings, before the middle of the sixteenth century. The Council of Trent (1545–63) required Catholic parishes to record christenings and marriages and, by the beginning of the seventeenth century, they were to record burials as well. One purpose of this effort at registration was religious, i.e., to document legitimate marriages and births within different Christian communities, and governments quickly recognized the political advantages in terms of, for example, taxation.

---

[22] "The bookkeeping of the state" is the phrase George Rosen applied to "political arithmetic": Rosen, *A History of Public Health* (New York, 1956), 87.

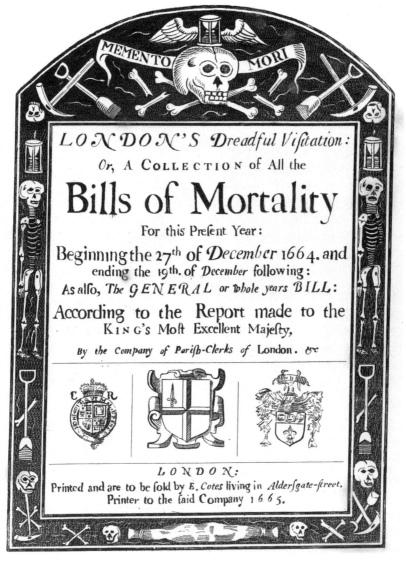

6.1 Bills of Mortality (London) from 1665.

In fifteenth-century Italy, another document arose that scholars have used to study the health, wealth, and demographic stability of a population: *bills of mortality*. Milan first began to record deaths from plague in 1452. Bills of mortality date from 1496 in Mantua, from 1504 in Venice, and from 1554 in Modena. The earliest bills in England, which appeared in 1538, noted only plague deaths. Causes of death other than plague were added in 1625. Such data was also collected in France after 1667 and in Sweden after 1686. Elsewhere in Europe efforts progressed more slowly and the process of collation, or even collection, on a grand scale lagged. Some German and Italian states were well on their way by the middle of the eighteenth century, although the fragmentation of both areas until the 1860s and 1870s frustrated larger compilations.

Private individuals, rather than governments, took the next step toward purposeful analyses of this data. William Petty (1623–87) was the first of these so-called political arithmeticians and, in fact, coined the term *political arithmetic*. Petty assembled an immense range of facts about England's commerce, population, and economic resources. His friend, John Graunt (1620–74), produced a *Natural and Political Observations on the Bills of Mortality* (1662), which correlated deaths to age. He figured that after age six one-third of all human mortality had taken place and thereafter the chances of dying in any decade between the age of six and seventy-six was roughly equal. Graunt – like the other political arithmeticians of his day, like Edmund Halley (c. 1656–1743; of comet fame) who studied in Breslau and like Johann Süssmilch (1707–67) in his *Die göttliche Ordnung in den Veränderungen des menschlichen Geschlechts* (The godly order in human affairs, 1756) – sought to illustrate the "grim regularity" of mortality statistics. Of course, no such uniformity exists. In Lorraine Daston's words, Graunt and others "as much invented as discovered" what Süssmilch would later refer to as "a constant, general, great, complete, and beautiful order."[23]

Why were these men so ardent about discovering *patterns* of mortality? While continued faith in the regularity of divine providence must have played a role for some, most were also intrigued by questions of political economy. Mercantilist views taught that the wealth of nations depended not only on their stores of precious metals, but also on the size, industriousness, and health of their populations. Vital statistics promised to allow for rational planning by determining, for instance, whether there would be enough recruits of a proper age for the army.

There were, of course, other uses for statistics and many of the political arithmeticians were concerned – like Halley who constructed a famous "life table" in 1693 – with assembling accurate tables so that insurance schemes and annuities could be properly calculated and paid out. A rash of financial failures involving pension plans calculated on faulty conjectures about length of life and chance of dying at any given age drove this pursuit along with some urgency. The term for all this cataloging and surveying came from the German: it was known as *Statistik* from *Staat*.

---

[23] Lorraine Daston, *Classical Probability in the Enlightenment* (Princeton, 1988), 127–30.

The most notorious early demographic analysis flowed from the pen of the Reverend Thomas Malthus (1766–1834). His *Essay on the Principle of Population* (1798) first conjured up the frightening specter of *over*population. Malthus argued that population, if unchecked, would outrun food supply resulting in widespread distress, famine, and death. Malthus, who lived at the very end of our period, represents a significant shift away from the perspectives of the early political arithmeticians. Those men had worried about the unpropitious *decline* of population and had hoped to *increase* its size. Malthus reversed the equation. To be sure, the political arithmeticians were not unaware that overpopulation could engender misery and they never foolishly accepted a maxim of "the more the merrier." Frank articulated what mercantilists and cameralists all understood, that, "if the increase in the number of people were left to the free play of the instincts of the sexes, we would soon attain a number that would cause mankind to suffocate itself."[24] While the vision of the cameralists led in general to expansion of public relief and medical care, Malthus provided *opponents* of charity with powerful ammunition for their case.

Medicine and charity

The connection between medicine and charity has always been intimate. In chapter 5, we observed how frequently private charity was responsible for the foundation of hospitals. The realm of charity, however, neither began nor ended with hospitals. Especially in the eighteenth century, medical charities of many kinds became a favored form for expressing a utilitarian type of benevolence. In exploring the affinities between charity and medicine, we are once again confronted with a complex relationship between the public and the private, for even private medical charities expressed civic desiderata and offered social benefits.

Almost no early modern writer on poor relief failed to count the ill among the fit beneficiaries of charity. The sixteenth-century Englishman, William Harrison, listed among the worthy poor: "the aged, blind, and lame," the "diseased person that is iudged to be incurable," "the wounded soldier," and "the sicke persone visited with grieuous . . . diseases," all of which he separated from the "thriftless" and improvident who merited no support.[25] The advent of Protestantism did not shift this orientation. The Swiss reformer, Huldrych Zwingli, for example, referred to the deserving poor as the "living images of God."

---

[24] Frank, *System*, 24.
[25] Quoted in Robert Jütte, *Poverty and Deviance in Early Modern Europe* (Cambridge, 1994), 11.

Recent investigations have shown that many of the changes once facilely labeled "reformed" can be traced back to the policies of medieval cities and found in the writings of fifteenth-century humanists. Perhaps the greatest contribution of the Reformation (in its Protestant and Catholic variants) was to ally poor relief more closely with governments. Many German and Swiss cities, for instance, as well as England as a whole, made poor relief districts coterminous with parishes.

Humanist and reformed writers on poor relief also sharpened the distinction between the deserving and the undeserving poor: the medically indigent, however, remained safely among the former. With the Reformation (although not solely *because* of the Reformation), medical care became a central ingredient of poor relief at least in cities. Most church reformers since Luther, like Johannes Bugenhagen and Martin Bucer, for example, argued for the creation of *common chests* to centralize funds for many communal activities, including poor relief. During the process of confessionalization, as religious lines slowly rigidified, poor relief and medical care entwined ever more closely with parish life. Some forms of medical relief were old. Yet, while numerous Protestant states continued to tend the poor in newly laicized hospitals, they also developed other types of medical care that the parish administered and that acted outside the institutional framework of hospitals and almshouses.

Church officers – usually *deacons* and *elders* – managed these programs. Generally, applicants had to petition for aid. Care might consist of arranging for a person to be admitted to a hospital, but it might also involve free medical care from physicians, surgeons, apothecaries, and midwives, who either contributed their services or whom the congregation compensated for their trouble. In Amsterdam during the 1630s, the well-known anatomist, Dr. Nicolaes Tulp, a physician *and* an elder of the Reformed church, helped draft a plan to employ physicians, a surgeon, and an apothecary to care for the poor. Similarly decentralized schemes were found in Groningen and in the three Lutheran cities of Hamburg, Lübeck, and Bremen. This alternative to institutional care reached a much larger number of the poor in the community than could be admitted to hospitals.

Territorial states, like Denmark, Sweden, and England, likewise began extending medical relief to people who were not hospital inmates. Much of this similarity of thought and simultaneity of action can be explained by the spread of a Protestant ideology, but also by the movement of people back and forth across borders. The influence of Dutch refugees who had fled the Low Countries to England, or Catholic areas for

Protestant ones, in the sixteenth century was critical here (as in so many other ways). While in exile, they (perhaps of necessity) created forms of medical care – small hospitals and the decentralized systems discussed above – for their own members, carried these ideas back with them when they returned, and left lasting impressions on their English hosts as well.[26]

The availability of care for the medically indigent was becoming ever more extensive. The definition of the medically indigent also widened. Charitable medical assistance was no longer just for the chronically ill, the invalid, and the elderly. A significant movement arose that sought to include more of those Jean-Pierre Gutton calls the *potential poor* (*paupéris-able*) or what others have come to refer to as the *laboring poor*. And, especially in the eighteenth century, we see a growing interest – among medical men and the medical laity alike – in experimenting with new forms of medical charity, such as *dispensaries* for this category of the needy.

Medical care for the poor was, of course, never value-free. Suspicion lingered that some medical conditions directly resulted from improvident lifestyles and willful vice. The existence of a direct tie between poverty and disease, or rather between disease and *impoverishment*, was, however, explicitly made and widely accepted. Moreover, while medical and charitable reformers spoke, by no means hypocritically, of the "reduction of human suffering" as their principal goal, they never lost sight of the need to "preserve the lives of the [laboring] poor [who] . . . are the hardest workers and thus the most valuable to the state." Christian Wilhelm Hufeland (1762–1836) insisted that "only the sick-man lacks all resources." Considerations of "capital" and "returns on investments" (frequently employed metaphors) informed thinking about medical relief.[27]

When the questioning of the old hospitals became more vociferous and harsher after midcentury, a whole range of plans for supplying medical assistance under the general rubric of *domiciliary care* (medical care provided at home by physicians-to-the-poor who either donated their time or were paid by the government) surfaced as a popular and economical solution to medical indigence. The debate over the best form of medical care for the poor took place almost everywhere in Europe, but nowhere was it

---

[26] Ole Peter Grell and Andrew Cunningham, "The Reformation," in Grell and Cunningham, eds., *Health Care and Poor Relief in Protestant Europe 1500–1700* (London and New York, 1997), 34–35; Jonathan Israel, "Dutch Influence on Urban Planning, Health Care and Poor Relief: The North Sea and Baltic Regions of Europe, 1567–1720," in Grell and Cunningham, *Health Care and Poor Relief*, 66–83.

[27] C. G. Hoffmann, "Ankündigung einer Anstalt für arme Kranke zu Altdorf im Nürnbergischen," *Journal von und für Deutschland* (January 1786): 100; Christian Wilhelm Hufeland, *Armen-Pharamakopäe entworfen für Berlin nebst der Nachricht von der daselbst errichteten Armenkrankenverpflegungsanstalt* (2nd edn., Berlin, 1812), 3.

more vigorously pursued than in the German states. Academic societies, such as the Göttingen Academy of Sciences, set essay contests on the topic. The most expansive and successful scheme was launched in Hamburg and it stood as a gleaming example of what domiciliary care could accomplish. The Hamburg experiment is equally instructive for the blend of public and private action that characterized it.

Until the end of the 1760s, Hamburg (then a city of more than 80,000) offered little medical care to the domiciled poor and still less to workers. Urban magistrates and parish officers could afford temporary assistance in emergencies, to be sure, but no system aided the sick-poor on a regular basis other than to dispatch them to the old Pesthof. (Of course, individual medical practitioners might well provide free care *pro bono*.) Then, in 1768, several physicians volunteered to offer medical care and medicines to the poor for a trial period of two years. Ten years later, some of the same men recast the plan, producing a more formal and better-funded Medical Institute for the Sick-Poor (Institut für kranke Hausarmen).

The explicit aims of this medical charity were "to save the lives and preserve the health of thousands," "to return many upright and honest workers to the state," and "to reduce the distress of suffering humanity." Its dimensions swelled to quite extraordinary limits. From 1779 to 1781, the Institute cared for about 3,500 patients, while the Medical Deputation of the General Poor Relief handled about 50,000 cases from 1788 to 1801 and then another 40,000 to 50,000 cases by 1815. Significantly, a goodly proportion of all these were *not* registered paupers, but members of the working poor who received free medical care *only* and not alms.[28]

Proponents of this kind of medical charity largely accepted *structural* definitions of poverty, i.e., that poverty was mostly caused by economic dislocations. Yet these reformers (like the founders of voluntary hospitals) never totally resolved the conflict between regarding poverty and illness as the product of impersonal forces that individuals could not control and seeing these conditions as emanating from moral flaws. The Medical Relief, for example, assured its supporters that it did not treat diseases arising from "criminal dissipations," from imprudence, or from lack of restraint, such as venereal diseases, alcoholism, and the pregnancies of unwed mothers. While they never quite dispelled the tension between their disciplinary and their humanitarian impulses, they often helped the "guilty" as well as the "innocent" victims of disease.

[28] Mary Lindemann, "Urban Growth and Medical Charity: Hamburg, 1788–1815," in Jonathan Barry and Colin Jones, eds., *Medicine and Charity Before the Welfare State* (London, 1991), 113–32.

Domiciliary care was, of course, not the only new form of medical charity in the eighteenth century. Other initiatives stemmed from concurrent transformations in medical education. Ernst Gottfried Baldinger, a disciple of Boerhaave, founded a clinic in Göttingen in 1773 as a school for medical students and a facility for outpatients. Students visited patients too ill to be moved at home and thus this clinic, like others, extended free medical care to some of the laboring classes, although patients tended to be regarded in the first instance as pedagogic raw materials. In somewhat similar ways (although within institutional walls), therapeutic experiments were tried out at Bethlem (London) on pauper lunatics.

During the eighteenth century, specialized medical benefactions became quite fashionable among medical men and the philanthropic public; they were a fad in the following century. Big cities were best endowed: between 1740 and 1770 Londoners founded at least two dozen such charities. Elsewhere a number of similar charities bound physicians and laypeople together in ventures typically titled "philanthropic" or "benevolent." The Philanthropic Society of Paris (1780) offered aid to artisans and shopkeepers struck by illness in order to avert their destitution. Provincial towns had their charities as well, even if the number and variety were more limited. Philanthropically motivated citizens and physicians frequently founded lying-in charities (i.e., for delivering pregnant women) in addition to smaller facilities for specific diseases such as the often unpleasant *lock hospitals* for the venereally diseased. Equally popular were the *dispensaries* that treated people on an outpatient basis.

Lying-in charities neatly fused ideas of populationism with the wish to restrict aid to the worthy poor. The London Lying-in Charity for Delivering Poor Married Women in Their Own Habitations (1758) exemplifies many similar charities. These lying-in hospitals and maternal charities usually assisted only married women and thus bore "open testimony" in support of marriage "on which not only the comfort, but the very support of human life so greatly depends; [and] which is the foundation of families and government." The Society for Maternal Charity (Société de charité maternelle) set up in 1788 served "a class of poor for whom there are neither hospitals nor foundations at Paris – namely, the legitimate infants of the poor." If these two charities concentrated on the legitimate offspring of the respectable poor, others accepted unwed mothers and their infants. The Hamburg poor relief paid midwives, surgeons, and accoucheurs to attend *both* married and unmarried women in childbirth. Several writers on medical police and medical reform – such as, most famously, Johann Peter Frank – explicitly advocated care for *all* mothers: "The condition of pregnancy in unwed mothers is as estimable as in married women; both carry a citizen and a creature of God's making under their hearts."[29]

A number of dispensaries proffered more general assistance. These catered to a broad range of the working poor by disbursing medical care and medicines (the latter often prescribed from "Pharmacopeia for the Poor") outside hospitals. While the rise of the *dispensary movement* has been studied most extensively for Britain, other countries also participated. Moneys for dispensaries were raised by subscription, but the influence of medical men was especially telling as they furnished the indispensable expertise and time. In 1769, Dr. George Armstrong (1720–89) established the earliest dispensary in England in Red Lion Square (London) for "the infant poor." Although Dr. Armstrong's project did not outlive its founder, other dispensaries took up the torch in the capital and in provincial cities, including Bristol, Doncaster, Liverpool, Newcastle, and Birmingham. All acknowledged the same purpose of "administer[ing] medicine and advice to the poor, not only at the Dispensary, but also at their own habitations."[30] These goals typified the dispensary movement whether dispensaries were founded solely by private initiative, as in England, or whether they also received the support of the state, as in some continental countries.

This longish history of health in society has been based on the premise that initiatives in public health came from several different directions. While the "state" in whatever form – urban, royal, parliamentarian, or republican – was never a trivial player, it is too simple to regard public health as solely the result of state impetus. In all European countries, albeit to a greater or lesser extent, private endeavors powerfully affected public health because they provided the wherewithal for charitable successes. If the relative abundance or scarcity of such undertakings varied from place to place, it is to their broader histories that we must look for explanations. Whatever we may conclude, there can be no denying that early modern society was never apathetic to the health of the people.

---

[29] All quoted in Donna T. Andrew, "Two Medical Charities in Eighteenth-Century London: The Lock Hospital and the Lying-In Charity for Married Women," in Barry and Jones, *Medicine and Charity*, 85; Stuart Woolf, "The Société de charité maternelle, 1788–1815," in Barry and Jones, *Medicine and Charity*, 100; Frank quoted in Mary Lindemann, "Maternal Politics: The Principles and Practices of Maternity Care in Eighteenth-Century Hamburg," *Journal of Family History* 9 (Spring 1984): 45.

[30] J. C. Lettsom, *Medical Memoirs of the General Dispensary in London* (London, 1774), 19. On the history of the dispensary movement, see Irvine S. Loudon, "The Origins and Growth of the Dispensary Movement in England," *Bulletin of the History of Medicine* 55 (1981): 322–42.

7   Practice

O *Thou Afflicted*, and under Distemper, Go to *Physicians* in *Obedience* to God, who has commanded the *Use of Means*. But place thy *Dependence* on God alone to Direct and Prosper them.

(Cotton Mather, "The Angel of Bethesda")[1]

Miss Nicholson, an Irishwoman, suffering from epidemic fever. A single woman of about 20, beautiful, lively, with a good temperament; suffering from some hardness of the breast; very fond of watery food and living a life of idleness. For some time she had been feeling depressed, then during the evening of July 7th she suddenly became very feverish, with vomiting and pain in her head and back. She took nothing but Sal Prunella. On the 9th of July she became confused: 10 oz of blood were removed. Immediately afterwards I was called to see her and found a weak, rapid pulse, deep laboured breathing, whitened tongue, thirst, constipation, urine stringy with slight whitish sediment. Delirium. The blood very slightly inflamed. At 10 in the evening her bowels moved and she became less confused.

(From the medical casebook of Dr. William Brownrigg)[2]

Today [11 November 1772] the master-carpenter Hermanus Mulder died. He was a great artist in his ability to set teeth in the human mouth and even created entire sets of upper and lower [teeth] and affixed them firmly with leather bands . . . He also invented a sort of machine that was very flexible and hollow in the middle like a pipe, which one could use to tap a man's urine when he was obstructed. Physicians and surgeons throughout the whole country bought it and he earned much money therefrom.

(Jacob Bicker-Raye, *Diary*)[3]

---

[1] Quoted in James H. Smylie, "The Reformed Tradition," in Ronald L. Numbers and Darrel W. Amundsen, eds., *Caring and Curing: Health and Medicine in the Western Religious Tradition* (New York, 1986), 213.

[2] *The Medical Casebook of William Brownrigg, M.D., F.R.S. (1712–1800) of the Town of Whitehaven in Cumberland*, ed. and trans. by Jean F. Ward and Joan Yell (London, 1993), 8–9.

[3] Jacob Bicker-Raye, "Notitie van het merkwaardigste, mij bekennd, dat er is voorgevallen binnen de stadt Amsterdam, zijn begin nemende met het jaar 1732 en eindigende met het jaar 1772," from 11 November 1772, in Dagboek Bicker-Raye, Gemeente archief, Amsterdam.

Millions of people practiced medicine in early modern Europe. This chapter considers the entire range of medical assistance from self-help to the university-trained physician.

It once seemed very simple to construct two medical worlds that faced each other as antagonists: that of the quacks and that of the few bona fide healers whose legitimation depended on their education, licensing, or admittance to a guild: physicians, surgeons, apothecaries, bathmasters, and midwives. Beginning in the 1960s, however, as social historians began to enter the field of medical history in greater numbers, the above dichotomy began to break down, and medical historians increasingly accentuated conflict between "elite" and "popular" medicines. At first, scholars tended to view these two "types" as isolated from, and inimical to, each other. During the 1970s and 1980s, however, scholars began to explore the multiplicity of healers and the heterogeneity of healing practices, emphasizing, for example, the role of apothecaries as "general practitioners"; the importance of surgeons and barber-surgeons; the functions of magic and astrology; and indeed the entire, vast, if often ill-defined area of "popular medicine." In addition, attention turned more and more to the multiple roles of the patient: sufferer, healer, patron, and client.

Gradually, historians began to perceive that "the frontiers between orthodox and unorthodox medicine have [always] been flexible . . . So mobile have been their boundaries, that one age's quackery has often become another's orthodoxy."[4] Thus the therapeutic practices and even, to a large extent, the medical "theories" of the village "quack," the sufferer seeking his or her own cure, the surgeon, the apothecary, and the university-trained physician did not differ all that much from one another.

Closely linked to these discussions, of course, are the issues of professionalization and medicalization that we have already assessed. By 1500, a university education had become to the physician a way to separate himself from artisanal healers and to situate himself among the intellectual elite. In this chapter, we will be interested in whether people used professional status or intellectual refinement as criteria in selecting a healer: whether people preferred physicians.

Once the academic study of medicine had been institutionalized in the medieval universities, the status of the physician derived from his reputation as a *litterateur*. The Dutch physician and philologist, Gisbert Longolius (1507–43), is a good example. A body-physician to the

---

[4] W. F. Bynum and Roy Porter, "Introduction," to Bynum and Porter, eds., *Medical Fringe and Medical Orthodoxy, 1750–1850* (London, 1987), 1.

archbishop of Keulen, he was also a well-respected teacher and translator of Greek. Not until the nineteenth century, and certainly not until the middle or even end of that century, were Europeans successfully medicalized to the extent that physicians became their clear first choice as healers. Before then people generally did not perceive physicians as especially or uniquely qualified to treat illness. Physicians, in short, by no means monopolized and controlled, or even dominated, the medical marketplace. Rather, physicians competed on equal or even disadvantageous terms with a wide range of other healers for the medical trade of the day.

Patients and practitioners

The doctor–patient relationship is an important one for the history of medicine, but it has proved difficult to open up to historical scrutiny. In the 1940s, the American sociologist, Talcott Parsons, addressed the reciprocity inherent in the doctor–patient arena. When ill, the patient assumes what Parsons called "the sick-role." Accordingly, the sick person is, on the one hand, excused his or her social responsibilities, but, on the other hand, is expected to desire a return to health and to comply unquestioningly with the directives of medical experts in order to achieve this goal.

More historically oriented is the work of Nicholas Jewson on the evolution of the role of the patient in European history. In two frequently cited articles, Jewson documents a shift from what he calls "bedside medicine" – in which the patient controlled the medical consultation – to "hospital medicine" – in which the patient was increasingly subordinated to the voice of a medical authority, generally that of the physician. (A third step in this process, toward "laboratory medicine," occurred in the late nineteenth and early twentieth centuries and further accelerated the alienation of the patient from his or her own perceptions of illness.)

In early modern times, however, the patient largely determined the dynamics of the medical encounter as well as the course of treatment. He or she functioned as a patron, who called the physician to the bedside. Because most people who consulted physicians (according to Jewson) were wealthy or at least prosperous, the patient's status often exceeded that of the attending doctor. Patients were quick to dismiss practitioners whose medicines did not work, whose cures they disliked, or if they found the man personally unpleasant. The early modern medical consultation, Jewson argues, also depended heavily on the patient's reporting his or her own case-history, known as the *patient narrative*. The patient's description of symptoms formed the basis for practitioners' decisions on diagnosis, prognosis, and therapy. Reliance on the patient narrative to a large extent reversed the roles we have come to expect: the patient, not the practitioner, was the active partner in the consultation. Not until about 1800, with the rise of hospital medicine and the clinico-anatomical method (see chapter 3), did the power relations move decisively in favor of the physician. Then physicians took center stage in the drama of medical practice. The patient's story became ancillary to, and thus less meaningful than, the physician's special knowledge gained from increasingly meticulous and intrusive physical examinations and clinical studies informed by morbid anatomy and pathology. The patient, once dominant in the medical encounter as the physician's patron, now became subordinate as the physician's client.

Jewson's paradigm – as sketched out above – has greatly influenced the writing of medical history. While the Jewson version indeed offers a useful way to link transformations in social and cultural authority with developments in medical knowledge and institutional change, it is perhaps too simply constructed to catch the complexities of early modern medical encounters, and it does not really address contacts between patients and *nonphysician* healers (which were more frequent than between physicians and patients), in which power and status relationships might have differed considerably from those Jewson describes.

Many factors, therefore, need to be taken into account in investigating early modern medical practices and in analyzing how such relationships worked. Availability of practitioners is one cardinal concern. Throughout our period, rural/urban differences remained significant. Writing in 1974, Jean-Pierre Goubert spoke of late eighteenth-century France as a *désert médical*. Goubert's striking phrase, however, has suffered much misinterpretation. Goubert was speaking of the dearth of *university-trained* physicians, and not of other practitioners who, he recognized, were plentiful in both country and city. Most historians writing on early modern medical practice now accept the position Margaret Pelling and Charles Webster laid out about two decades ago. They defined a medical practitioner as "any individual whose occupation is basically concerned with the care of the sick."[5] That occupation need not be (and, in fact, seldom was) a full-time "job" and often did not supply a majority, or even a goodly part, of the practitioner's income. Dr. Daniël van Buren, who lived in Amsterdam in the first half of the eighteenth century, served as physician to the city's *gasthuis* (a form of almshouse and hospital) and was an officer of the municipality's *Collegie medici*. He also owned a fleet of boats and barges and was a merchant contractor heavily engaged in the inland water trade,

[5] Margaret Pelling and Charles Webster, "Medical Practitioners," in Charles Webster, ed., *Health, Medicine, and Mortality in the Sixteenth Century* (Cambridge, 1979), 166.

from which he drew most of his considerable income. Likewise, in the 1620s and 1630s, the counter-remonstrant pastor, Henricus Alutarius, in Woerden and Rotterdam, combined his clerical role with that of *medicus*, at least on occasion.

The answer to the question of "how many practitioners" varied greatly throughout Europe. The provincial center and market town of Groningen in the United Provinces (with about 20,000 inhabitants), for instance, had fourteen physicians in the sixteenth century, fifty-three in the seventeenth century, and thirty in the eighteenth century. The town was also well stocked with nonphysician practitioners. There were, for example, between 1553 and 1594 thirty-seven barber-surgeons who served in the city and the guild of master-surgeons registered 171 members from 1597 to 1730. In about the same period (1578–1730) some sixty-five "traveling practitioners" (*reizende meesters*) – including dentists, corn-parers, cutters for bladder and kidney stones (*lithotomists*), and oculists who specialized in treating cataracts – applied to the city government for permission to practice; several peripatetics were female. Basically rural provinces, like Veluwe and Overissjel, had about one practitioner for every 1,400–1,700 inhabitants, while the more urbanized provinces of North Holland had one for every 500. Late sixteenth-century Norwich (England) had about one practitioner for every 200 inhabitants. In sixteenth- and seventeenth-century London, there were some fifty physicians, 100 surgeons, the same number of apothecaries, and 250 "other" practitioners. In sixteenth- and seventeenth-century France, for instance, only large towns like Paris, Montpellier, Lyons, and Marseilles supported many graduate practitioners. And the numbers fluctuated. Best-guess estimates suggest that there were about 400 such physicians in France in 1520, and 1,750 in the middle of the seventeenth century, but perhaps only 1,300 by the end of that century. Other countries seem to have also experienced rises and contractions at about the same times. Surgeons were more plentiful: there were around 2,000 in the 1530s and 1540s in France; more than 3,000 by the end of the sixteenth century; 8,400 in the 1650s; and 6,350 in the 1690s. This state of affairs changed dramatically in the eighteenth century. In France, as elsewhere (and especially in western and central Europe), the total number of practitioners expanded as did the number of physicians. Paris, for instance, with a population of 660,000, had 153 physicians (2.3/10,000 inhabitants), 192 surgeons (2.9/10,000), and 135 apothecaries (2.0/10,000), while Orléans, a city of 48,500, had similar proportions: 10 physicians (2.1/10,000), 16 surgeons (3.3/10,000), and 14 apothecaries (2.9/10,000).

Despite this evidence, the myth of medical insufficiency persists. In fact, however, the range and actual number of healers in early modern times were great. As Mary Fissell has observed for seventeenth- and eighteenth-century England, "someone who fell ill . . . found a profusion of health care providers eager for his or her custom." This plenitude of health care providers was not unique to that time and place. Matthew Ramsey points out that, while no one knows for sure how many practitioners were to be found in eighteenth-century France, "it now appears that by the end of the Old Regime the majority of Frenchmen may have been in a position to consult an authorized healer."[6] In addition, the number of university-trained physicians in rural areas by the 1700s was growing, especially in the German lands, parts of Scandinavia, and in some Italian states, where governments were beginning to erect networks of physici.

Even if the availability of physicians remained low in the sixteenth and seventeenth centuries, it had increased measurably by the middle of the eighteenth century. Moreover, the number of other licensed or legitimate practitioners – surgeons, barber-surgeons, apothecaries, midwives, bath-masters, and traveling *operators* (people who cut for kidney and bladder stones, "couched" cataracts, cut corns, or pulled teeth) – always far exceeded the number of physicians. Many others practiced medicine: among them we find cunning-men and -women, astrological healers, Catholic priests, Protestant clergymen, gentlefolk, executioners, and nobles, to name just some of those frequently involved. By 1800, almost all governments had regulations in place to define legitimate practice and practitioners. Still, these various ordinances seldom reflected the *reality* of medical practice. It did no good, for example, to restrict the treatment of internal ailments to physicians if no physicians were in the neighborhood. Moreover, the constraints governments set on practice did not necessarily coincide with popular understandings of "proper" or "appropriate" healers.

The selection of a healer turned on many variables: the perception of their abilities counted, of course, but so, too, did the healer's position in a community, personal habits, and fees. This last factor – expense – has often been evoked to explain the antipathy many people felt toward physicians. Whether such crude kinds of cost-accounting drove people's choice of healers is doubtful. Medical decision making was complex. People often paid what might (objectively) seem like exorbitant sums for

---

[6] Mary E. Fissell, *Patients, Power, and the Poor in Eighteenth-Century Bristol* (Cambridge, 1991), 37; Matthew Ramsey, *Professional and Popular Medicine in France, 1770–1830: The Social World of Medical Practice* (Cambridge, 1988), 62.

medicines and advice, and a simple correlation comparing, for example, the amount of a day's wage to the cost of a drug or a treatment misses the point.

Most important, early modern people were medically promiscuous. They often, perhaps usually, consulted several practitioners, serially or consecutively. Medical promiscuity was by no means limited to the lower elements of society; a monarch, a lord, or a wealthy patrician was just as liable to seek advice from a range of practitioners as was an artisan or a cowherd. It is simply not true that the well-to-do patronized "legitimate" practitioners, and especially surgeons and physicians, while the less well-off (or less knowledgeable) frequented the lower ranks of medical practitioners or visited "quacks."

Medical practice for everyone, however, almost always began at home. Self-help, of course, quickly shaded over into guidance sought from friends, neighbors, and family. Every household treasured its own assortment of time-tested remedies for everyday ills. Moreover, most people had a sense of what they needed to do to remain well, even if these ideas today might seem rather odd or even counterproductive. Daily habits depended heavily on individual differences. In other words, what was considered good for one person might prove harmful or even deadly for another. Joan Lane, in a review of the diaries and letters of the eighteenth-century English, refers to a man who blamed his bodily discomfort to eating "unwisely." He seldom found himself ill if he consumed only "plain foods," while "made dishes and sauces" always caused an upset. A sixteenth-century German refrained from cheese and any dishes containing it because he felt they gave him indigestion.

Clearly, as these examples show, the boundary between *preventive* and *therapeutic* care was smudgy. Regimens often rested explicitly or implicitly on the ancient medical doctrine of the six non-naturals and stressed moderation in eating, drinking, and sexual intercourse, and regularity in evacuations and exercise. Regimen books and self-help manuals prescribed the way to health and recommended methods to assure a long life (the science of *prolongevity*). Particularly popular, and often reprinted, were Thomas Elyot's *Castel of Helth* (1539); Luigi Cornaro's *Discorsi della vita sobria* (Sure and certain methods of attaining a long and healthful life, in twelve editions in several languages from 1558 to 1724; Cornaro seemed an especially good authority – he lived to be ninety-nine); George Cheyne's *An Essay on Health and Long Life* (1724); and finally, Christoph Hufeland's best-selling *Die Kunst des menschlichen Lebens zu verlängern* (The art of prolonging life, in eight editions from 1776 to 1860).

Choices

Several cases selected from differing geographical regions and varying socioeconomic milieux illustrate what people might do to remain well or regain their health. One must bear in mind, however, that medical choice always has an idiosyncratic character to it and that these cases offer examples, not models.

The sixteenth-century Cologne city councilor, Hermann Weinsberg (1518–97), filled more than 4,000 manuscript pages with his autobiographical "notes."[7] Weinsberg recorded 153 illnesses or afflictions affecting his family. In thirty-four cases he consulted a "Medicus," in twenty-five cases a surgeon, and in six cases an "Empiriker" or a wise-woman. Otherwise Weinsberg did nothing or relied on self-treatment and home remedies. When his nephew suffered "fever and chills," Weinsberg advised "good beer and bread and some wine and herbs mixed with sugar." Weinsberg possessed an herbal for reference and used vegetable remedies, either self-concocted or purchased from an apothecary or "root-wife." Such remedies made up a large part of the medical armamentarium of early modern peoples. Mary Fissell reminds us how familiar people in these centuries were with plants, and their prophylactic and curative powers. Common herbs – fennel, broom, rhubarb, mustard, and valerian, to name just a handful– were used to treat myriad ailments.

Because regularity of evacuations counted as one of the golden rules of regimen, many people believed that a periodic internal "cleansing" was essential to health. Purges and bloodletting made up part of the treatment Weinsberg's wife received when she fell seriously ill in 1557. First, she had blood let, then her urine examined (by a physician?), called in two or three "medici," and solicited the advice of a wise-woman. Another physician recommended a purge. All for naught; less than two weeks after falling ill, she died.

Samuel Pepys (1633–1703), surely the most famous of English diarists, commented frequently on health and illness, especially his own.[8] When Pepys began his diary in 1660, he was twenty-six years old. He had already survived a serious illness and undergone a major surgical intervention: four years earlier he had been successfully "cut for the stone." Urological complaints (perhaps exacerbated by bouts of gonorrhea?), however, recurred throughout the years of his diary (1660–69) and eventually led to his death in 1703. Like many contemporaries, he worried

---

[7] Material on Hermann Weinsberg is taken from Robert Jütte, *Ärzte, Heiler und Patienten: medizinischer Alltag in der frühen Neuzeit* (Munich, 1991), 12, 77, 82, 97.

[8] The standard edition is *The Diary of Samuel Pepys: A New and Complete Transcription*, ed. by Robert Latham and William Matthews (11 vols., London, 1970–83).

about chills and especially their effect on his "yard and stones" (penis and testicles). In 1666, he recorded being "in some pain of the collique [colic or belly-ache] – hav[ing] of late taken too much cold by washing my feet and going in a thin silk waistcoat, without any other coat over it, and open-breasted." Part of Pepys's normal precautions for preserving his health thus involved not "ketching cold."

Pepys's regimen was hardly unique; it was not even unusual. Besides avoiding drafts and damp, he also had blood let at irregular intervals. On Sunday, 4 May 1662, he called upon the surgeon, Mr. Holliard, to "let me blood, about 16 ounces" as he perceived that he was "exceedingly full of blood." Later, he turned to phlebotomy for therapeutic reasons and in summer of 1668 recorded that he "was let blood, and did bleed about 14 ounces, towards curing my eyes." Regimens could be preventive or therapeutic and the advice friends gave him in 1664 to "cure" his childlessness had embedded in it many widely accepted rules of regimen:

1. Do not hug my wife too hard nor too much. 2. Eat no late suppers. 3. Drink juyce of sage. 4. Tent [a Spanish wine] and toast. 5. Wear cool holland-drawers [loose undergarments]. 6. Keep stomach warm and back cool. 7. Upon my query whether it was best to do at night or morn, they answered me neither one nor other, but when we have most mind to it. 8. Wife not to go too straitlaced. 9. Myself to drink mum and sugar. 10. Mrs. Ward did give me to change my plat [diet].

In 1667 his eyes began to trouble him greatly, and diary entries from 1668 and 1669 record repeated bouts of eyestrain and his attempts to forestall what seemed approaching blindness. In June 1668, he consulted the celebrated eye specialist, Dr. Turberville, who recommended a physic – a laxative – and "also a glass of something to drop into my eyes." In spring 1669, on going to his haberdasher to pick up a belt "the colour of my new suit," he learned that "the mistress of the house, an oldish woman in a hat, hath some water good for the eyes, she did dress me, making my eyes smart most horribly," and yet he hoped that "it will do me good." Despite these efforts his vision deteriorated, leading him to abandon his journal a month later. Pepys did not, however, go blind and his eyes did improve, but fear of losing his sight made him dictate his journal to clerks thereafter and was content "to set down no more then is fit for them and all the world to know."

Liselotte von der Pfalz,[9] the second wife of Louis XIV's brother, always regarded doctors skeptically. When Liselotte first arrived at court in 1671, Madame de Sévigné noted that

---

[9] Elborg Forster, trans., *A Woman's Life in the Court of the Sun King: Letters of Liselotte von der Pfalz, 1652–1722* (Baltimore, 1984), and Forster, "From the Patient's Point of View: Illness and Health in the Letters of Liselotte von der Pfalz (1652–1722)," *Bulletin of the History of Medicine* 60 (Fall 1986): 297–320.

she has no use for doctors and even less for medicines . . . When her doctor was presented to her, she said that she did not need him, that she had never been purged or bled, and that when she is not feeling well she goes for a walk and cures herself by exercise.

Although she did submit – reluctantly – to the ministrations of physicians and surgeons on occasion (allowing herself to be bled prophylactically), she continued to believe that the best ways of preserving and recovering her health were to exercise regularly, drink lots of water, and to use only a few simple remedies such as an egg beaten with boiling water, sugar, and cinnamon for a cough or warm baked bread applied to an aching ear. In 1683, on the death of the queen, she castigated the royal physicians whose "ignorance . . . killed her as surely as if they had thrust a dagger into her heart." Moreover, "no child is safe [at court], for the doctors here have already helped five of the Queen's to the other world." Other court healers fared little better. In 1697 she tumbled with her horse while out hunting and broke her arm. She had the bone set by a country-barber in a nearby village and "it would have healed in two weeks if the court barbers had not practiced their art on me afterward, which, I believe, will cripple me for good." While Liselotte's dislike of doctors may have been more pronounced than was typical in the seventeenth century, many would have agreed with her. Liselotte's generally robust health and her attitude toward preserving it was echoed by the experience of another princess: Catherine the Great of Russia. Like Liselotte, Catharine often eschewed the treatments her physicians prescribed in favor of relaxation, bedrest, moderate diet, and mild exercise.

The journal of the Reverend Ralph Josselin (1616–83)[10] offers a picture of what a family of the "middling sort" might do when faced with illness or accidents. Lucinda Beier, who has analyzed Josselin's diary at length, counts 762 mentions of illness, but only seventy-nine times did Josselin record treatments and in only twenty-one cases does he indicate consulting a healer outside the family circle. He and his wife, Jane, diagnosed and handled most familial ills, dosing themselves, their children, and their servants. While they relied heavily on herbal remedies (Jane brewed common medicines such as hyssop syrup herself), they occasionally obtained preparations from an apothecary or used proprietary medicines such as Daffy's Elixir and Tabor's Pills. When the couple went outside the family circle, they turned to a variety of helpers: a nearby gentlewoman, neighbors, and two local bonesetters (both women). The Josselins only rarely called upon a physician: once for Ralph during an attack of ague, once to the bed of a dying child, and twice for Ralph in his final illness.

[10] *The Diary of Ralph Josselin, 1616–1683*, ed. by Alan Macfarlane (London, 1976).

The Josselin diary makes apparent two things. First, the family did not clearly distinguish between trifling ailments which could be safely relegated to home remedies and more serious ones for which they felt it imperative to call in a physician or surgeon. Parents often consulted a physician or surgeon for certain maladies in their children, and especially accidents, such as fractured limbs, genital deformities, or eye conditions that threatened blindness. Miquel Parets in seventeenth-century Spain, for example, recorded the passing of his ten-year-old son who "died [in 1651] of a disease of a bone in his arm following five years of illness which cost me a great many ducats, and during the last year and a half surgeons came daily to look after him."[11]

Second, the Josselin family had its own identity and unique characteristics. Their behavior does not typify "middle-class" families. For instance, the Josselins, perhaps more than others, believed that "the best preventive medicine was a sinless life." Other families and other individuals in similar circumstances made different choices.

Diaries, journals, correspondence, and autobiographies are articulate witnesses, but also highly unusual sources. While we possess some similar documents for the artisan classes, we usually must look elsewhere to discover the medical practices of the great majority of people who were illiterate, failed to keep journals, or never wrote letters. Fortunately, some sources allow us to examine ordinary lives more closely.

The "common people" were not unobserved. Beginning in the sixteenth century, the European lettered elite became curious about popular culture, if often only to deplore its errors and primitiveness. Governments, too, assembled huge caches of information that illuminate the process of medical choice in the early modern world. Most famous was the enquête initiated by the Société royale de médecine toward the end of the eighteenth century which uncovered surprisingly deep reservoirs of superstitious practices. Other elite observers were just as quick to note rampant ignorance and a widespread lack of concern for matters of health among the people. Some archival materials, however, present a different, and more nuanced, picture. While there can be little doubt that superstitions persisted throughout the eighteenth century, notions often labeled "errors" were deeply entangled with religious beliefs and with naturalistic concepts of cure. For example, if we look at the ways ordinary people in a small German territory, Braunschweig-Wolfenbüttel, made medical choices in the late seventeenth and eighteenth centuries, we observe once again how varied

---

[11] James S. Amelang, trans. and ed., *A Journal of the Plague Year: The Diary of the Barcelona Tanner Miquel Parets 1651* (New York, 1991), 69.

were the possibilities available and how mixed (but not irrational) was the logic behind them.

In the early decades of the eighteenth century Dr. Johann Barthold maintained an extensive medical practice in the city of Braunschweig. (While it seems that "Dr." Barthold had never acquired a doctorate in medicine, he had studied at the university at Helmstedt.) People from almost every social group called upon his services. Barthold had a contract with the Tailors' Guild and treated a large number of them, their family members, and their servants. During an eighteen-month period in 1712–14, he saw 329 different patients: 221 were adults (67.2 percent) and 103 were children under fourteen (31.3 percent); 162 were male (49.2 percent) and 112 were female (34.0 percent). Thus, although he saw about three adults for every two children and somewhat more men then women, neither women nor children nor the elderly, for that matter, were unrepresented. He did not have an extensive gynecological practice, only occasionally treating, for instance, a case of the "vapors" (fainting or hysteria). Patients most often saw him for fevers (39.2 percent of all cases) and indeed "ardent or burning fever" formed his most frequent diagnosis. Ninety-one patients (27.7 percent) sought his help for chest afflictions ranging from consumption and pleurisy to "suffocation" and "tightness"; twelve (3.65 percent) saw him for dysentery; and seven (2.1 percent) for head colds. The remaining quarter of his business included scattered cases of epilepsy, rheumatism, arthritis, vertigo, jaundice, dropsy, "hectic," stroke, apoplexy, indigestion, and palpitations (this last only among women). There were a few surgical interventions (sixteen) which included the treatment of stones, hernias, and cataracts, although his practice was far more medical than surgical in nature by a ratio of at least 20:1.

Other documents reveal more of this rich medical tableau. In the small market town of Hehlen (673 inhabitants in 1793), the pastor, Johann Uphoff, recorded causes of death and incidence of illness. Uphoff listed a total of eighty-one people as "ill" during the period 1751–60. Although many villagers saw no one for their problems, just as many went to several practitioners. No physician dwelt in Hehlen, but thirteen people visited or consulted physicians elsewhere, often traveling several miles down the Weser River to the town of Hameln. Eight persons procured medicines and advice from apothecaries in the nearby towns of Bodenwerder and Heyen. Three relied exclusively on home remedies; two purchased medicines from an undisclosed "elsewhere"; and two swore by "the remedies of a man by the name of Meßing in Halle," another small town not far away. Ten turned to a local military surgeon (or *feldscher*) or visited the regimental surgeon stationed in Hameln. Another person saw a surgeon whose name she failed to recall, one woman consulted an executioner, and four persons called on a man named Flentje, who was identified as a shepherd. In forty-three instances the name of the healer was unknown, or Uphoff remarked that the patient had seen "no doctor" or "used no medicine."

As these accounts suggest, people often moved from one healer to another in longterm quests for cure, even for ailments they perceived as not particularly dangerous or life-threatening. When Frau Bökel developed lumps in both her breasts while suckling her son, she probably first tried a series of popular remedies: rubbing the breasts with butter or oil or applying wet compresses made of butter, wax, rose water, and spirits. Her husband sought out a physician and then went to an upholsterer named Busch who was renowned for his ability to reduce cancers and other ominous lumps "without cutting." Indeed, when Busch applied his special poultices (made with tincture of lead), the complaint cleared up in four weeks. Children, too, often received the care of many practitioners. The four-month-old daughter of a merchant named Treumann suffered from frightening convulsions. Her mother had first obtained medicines from an apothecary and she then solicited the advice of a physician, before turning to a surgeon with a reputation for being able to arrest fits. Unfortunately, nothing helped and the child died. One can use thousands of such stories to show how ordinary people, like their betters, moved through a wide range of healers in search of help. While physicians were not the obvious first choices as healers, neither were they spurned.

In thinking about the process of selecting a healer – which I choose to call, perhaps anachronistically, "medical decision making" – we should bear four points in mind. First, serial and simultaneous consultations were the rule. People rarely satisfied themselves with the advice of a single healer and often conferred with a number of people at the same time, and felt thereby little disquietude or embarrassment. Second, there was a wide range of healers handy. Third, there apparently existed little sense that particular ailments or afflictions belonged exclusively to the territory of a particular type of practitioner, though there were some "specialists," such as bonesetters, lithotomists, oculists, and tooth-drawers. Finally, people rarely seem to have distinguished neatly between minor and major ailments. The first might quickly turn into the second as scabies or "the itch" could turn inward and cause a more perilous "corruption." Likewise, most people linked the external and internal domains of the body, as well as body and soul. Lay and learned medical knowledge assumed that external ailments could become internal ones, that external ailments might need internal treatments, or that an external sign indicated an internal condition.

When did people move outside the relatively close circle of family and friends to seek help from other healers? Their decisions were never totally predictable. Many people struck by grave illness or suffering from serious wounds or terrible accidents never consulted anyone outside their family. Some feared or disdained physicians and surgeons, but some simply did not consider the possibility of external aid, often trusting their own remedies as more efficacious. Geographical isolation, too, of course, might prevent a person from seeing a healer, but considering the vast profusion of choices, as well as the frequency of consultation by correspondence (especially in the eighteenth century), that was probably not the real explanation. It was a strange village indeed that was not home to some sort of local healer, whether bathmaster, root-wife, cunning-man or -woman, or just a neighbor known for his or her skills in, for instance, setting bones.

We must, however, be careful not to slot early modern medical practitioners too readily into tidy categories of "amateur" and "professional" or "learned" and "lay" (see pp. 11–12). An excellent example of how the two worlds met and overlapped can be found in the medical practice of the Elizabethan gentlewoman, Lady Grace Mildmay (1552–1620). Lady Mildmay treated a wide variety of ailments from epilepsy to hemorrhage, syphilis to fright, and flatulence to gout. Her remedies included many herbal medicines, as one might expect, but, in addition, she distilled chemical medicines in far larger quantities than warranted for use solely among her family and servants. She knew the works of the Galenic and Paracelsian writers. She clearly distinguished among diseases of men, women, children, and the aged. Her practice was, in short, "extensive, systematic and at the forefront of contemporary medical knowledge."[12]

Magic, religion, and healing

In the sixteenth and seventeenth centuries, many people put great trust in magical and astrological healers. By the eighteenth century, however, astrological physicians and magical cures had noticeably waned in popularity. Parts of chapter 1 examined the logic behind astrological and magical medicine. Here, however, I want to look more closely at those who used magic and astrology in diagnosis and therapy.

Thanks largely to the works of Michael MacDonald and Ronald Sawyer on Richard Napier, we possess excellent studies of the practice of a man who was at once healer, magus, and cleric. Over a period of almost

---

[12] Linda Pollock, *With Faith and Physic: The Life of a Tudor Gentlewoman, Lady Grace Mildmay, 1552–1620* (New York, 1992), 108.

forty years, between 1597 and 1634, thousands of patients found their way to the small town of Great Linford, Buckinghamshire, to consult him and hundreds more sent letters. Like others influenced by Renaissance neoplatonism (which viewed the physical world as animate and alive), Napier's medical practice blended religion, magic, and natural philosophy.

So what did Napier do when approached by patients for help? After jotting down vital data on each visitor – place of birth, location, and reason for consultation – he noted the precise time of the meeting. He mapped the heavens, recorded the patient's description of his or her problems, and then compared the two, selecting treatments indicated by the stars and current medical principles. He generally prescribed standard therapies, for example, bleeding or purging. He only rarely turned to the use of amulets or exorcism.

Napier's practice raises the question of the general relationship between religion and healing. Mental distress seems to have yielded to pastoral intervention quite frequently. Pastor Alutarius, for example, cured "a melancholic peasant" of his "religiously tinged depression" in Woerden (United Provinces) in 1623. It is, therefore, difficult to draw the line between magic and religion. Anthropologists have pointed out that the western secular attitude often assumes that what "we" do is religion, while what "others" do is magic. Recent historical scholarship has demonstrated how weak the distinction between magic and religion was in the sixteenth and seventeenth centuries. To an appreciable extent, early modern religious and magical practices rested on a similar assumption: that supernatural forces – whether divine or magical – could affect nature. This was true whether one chanted a magical incantation or muttered a humble prayer. Thus, there are clear affinities between religious and magical practices, especially in the realm of medicine.

Christianity has always been a healing religion. Many of the miracles of Christ were curative. Christianity ultimately regarded illness as the wages of sin, either individual or collective, although its manifestations might differ; leprosy punished individual transgressions while visitations of plague scourged a wicked society. On many of these points, little distinguished Protestant from Catholic outlooks. Thomas Becon, much like his medieval predecessors, understood that "sickness and adversity is sent . . . unto the children of men for their great profit and singular commodity." We thus find in Christian thought and practice a close affinity between saving souls and healing bodies. Medicine could provide images for talking about souls and vice versa and the most immediate remedy for the soul – prayer – was also the most important relief for the body. The English church's "Great Litany" of 1544 petitioned God for "pity upon us miserable sinners, that are now visited with great sickness and mortality, that like as thou didst command thy angel to cease from punishing, so it may now please thee to withdraw from us this plague and grievous sickness."[13]

Christian churches taught, and Christians believed, that illness came ultimately from God as punishment for sin. That acceptance did not, however, prevent people from seeking, and being advised to seek, natural cures for illness. By 1500, the Roman Catholic church had long since come to terms with secular medicine. Thus, while clergy emphasized that prayer and penitence were vital to the success of any cure, and while God remained the ultimate arbiter of life and death, churchmen also counseled Christians not to disdain the aid of physicians nor to spurn the medicines of this world.

Although prayer remained the preferred religious panacea for illness, other practices also fell within the sphere of religious healing. Besides praying, one could invoke the aid of Christ, the Virgin Mary, or saints. Although the Roman Catholic church never taught that saints could cure, people nonetheless entreated them to intervene in cases of illness, and associated certain saints with particular diseases or afflictions: Sts. Roch and Sebastian with the plague; St. Antony with plague and anthrax; St. Huburt with mental illness; and St. Laurent with burns. Women in childbed would cry out to St. Anne for assistance, while epileptics journeyed to the shrine of St. Cornelius near Cologne or to that of St. Willibrod in Echternach (Luxemburg). Such pilgrimages, whether to the holy places of particular saints, such as that of Thomas à Becket in Canterbury or to the Marian site in Kevelaer (Germany), could be undertaken to seek a cure or to acknowledge a cure already received. In the latter case, pilgrims might leave an *ex-voto* (a symbolic object) to attest their recovery and express their gratitude. The walls of the churches at the nineteenth-century shrine of Lourdes and at twentieth-century Fatima are festooned with discarded crutches.

Individuals turned to prayers, pilgrimages, and supplications in response to distress or suffering. Epidemics, however, called forth more structured, large-scale religious responses. Supplicative masses and processions counted among the commonest communal reactions to an epidemic outbreak. Processions drew in the entire society or at least its representatives. Images of saints or crucifixes formed the focal point of

---

13 Quoted in John Booty, "The Anglican Tradition," in Numbers and Amundsen, *Caring and Curing*, 249; Andrew Wear, "Religious Beliefs and Medicine in Early Modern England," in Hilary Marland and Margaret Pelling, eds., *The Task of Healing: Medicine, Religion and Gender in England and the Netherlands, 1450–1800* (Rotterdam, 1996), 147–52.

processions that wound their way through the entire city, stopping at, or passing through, all places of religious or civic relevance. In 1651, the tanner Miquel Parets related how

> The city of Barcelona, seeing that Our Lord was so angered with us and that the plague kept spreading, . . . decided to hold a procession and carry the relic of glorious Saint Severus along the entire Corpus route. This procession took place with great devotion on April 30 . . . and was attended by the lord councilors and the governor. . . and the wool weavers, who marched with torches and dressed as pilgrims, as they always do whenever the relic of the glorious saint is brought out. A great crowd came to this procession.[14]

Processions and supplications remained part of the mainstream of religious and communal life throughout the medieval period and, in Catholic areas, long after the Reformation. If Protestants no longer turned to "graven images" or sought the intervention of saints, they, too, did not abandon the habit of public prayer and penance during crises.

The theological affinity of Christianity for healing was personified in religious healers. Throughout the middle ages, and well into the early modern period, clergymen – whether secular or cloistered – practiced medicine. Medieval monasteries long served as repositories of medical knowledge and, more practically, medical care. Religion and healing coexisted not only ideologically but also physically in the body of the priest-, monk-, or nun-practitioner. The separation of functions – between medicine and religion, and between lay and religious practitioners – occurred only slowly, and was conditioned by ideological, theological, and socioeconomic forces. One can trace three major steps in the process: the first taken by the Roman Catholic church itself in the late middle ages; the second resulting from the Reformation; and the final one in the increasing secularization of the middle to late seventeenth century. The separation was never clear and sharp, but the general trend was to define two spheres of activity and to hold them apart from each other: the care of souls and the cure of the body.

Beginning as early as the twelfth and thirteenth centuries, the church itself began to limit the practice of clerical medicine. Mounting disquietude among the upper ranks of the clergy with the healing activities of monks, nuns, and priests partially drove the shift, but the timing also coincided with the rise of the universities and urban growth. Church councils pared away at the medical practice of the clergy, first banning them from doing surgery and then forbidding regular clergy (i.e., the cloistered clergy) the practice of medicine unless they had also attained a

---

[14] Amelang, *Journal of the Plague Year*, 47.

medical degree. The Second Lateran Council of 1139 ordered that "monks and canons regular are not to study jurisprudence and medicine for the sake of temporal gain."

Still most people accepted that possession or bewitchment could cause illnesses, especially those characterized by bizarre or intemperate speech (or, conversely, muteness), convulsions, or uncontrolled body motions. For these, the spiritual healer remained the practitioner of choice. Priests performed exorcisms and attempted to lift spells, as did cunning-men and -women whose white magic was viewed as an effective response to malevolent forces. At the same time, the Catholic church remained extremely active in running charitable institutions, including the hospitals and the nursing orders that cared for the poor.

The Reformation of the sixteenth century worked to transform the relationship between magic and healing on the one hand, and between religion and healing on the other. The Protestant attack on the miraculous powers of priests included an assault on their ability to heal. Likewise, Protestants decried the whole range of what they termed "superstitious practices": the use of the sacraments or sacramental objects such as the communion wafer to work wonders; the veneration of saints; pilgrimages; and exorcisms. Of course, Protestants did not deny the power of God to heal, but emphasized that prayer and repentance were the only proper spiritual recourse for the ill. More practically, the Protestants stressed the importance of pastoral counseling. The Dutch Reformed church, for example, appointed "comforters of the sick" (*ziekentroosters*) whose primary task was to visit the ill, pray with them, and help them try to make sense of their pain and suffering, although they also gave medical advice. Protestant clergymen crafted special prayers for the occasion of sickness and placed them in prayer books. Both Catholic and Protestants believed that only a good man – i.e., one of conscience and right belief – made a good physician. Protestant theologians, too, helped strengthen the claims of learned physicians by advising the sick to use medicines and consult physicians in illness. Martin Luther, for instance, taught that "God created medicine and provided us with intelligence to guard and take care of the body so that we can live in good health."[15] Likewise, Reformed teachings tended to undercut beliefs in non-natural origins of disease, for example, by bewitchment. One famous opponent of witchcraft persecutions, the Dutch Protestant, Johan Wier, insisted that diseases supposedly caused by witches could be traced to natural origins.

---

[15] Martin Luther, quoted in Carter Lindberg, "The Lutheran Tradition," in Numbers and Amundsen, *Caring and Curing*, 178; see also Wear, "Religious Beliefs," 161.

The Catholic church in the sixteenth century underwent its own reformation and revitalization, variously called the Counter- or Catholic Reformation. In the course of this movement, the church accelerated its retreat from claiming special healing powers for its clergy. In 1626, for instance, the Congregation for the Propagation of the Faith (the part of the church in charge of missions) forbade priests in Bulgaria to "dispense medicines – and in particular laxatives – to the sick, whether they be of the Faith or not."[16] Exorcism, too, was no longer accepted as the unquestioned prerogative of the clergy and the Catholic church discouraged its use. Nonetheless, in the decades after the Reformation, some elements within Catholicism used both exorcism and healing to retain souls for Mother Church and to convince strays to return to her bosom. Particularly the Jesuits were involved in exorcism and perhaps this accounts, at least in part, for their success as missionaries. As Ramon Gutiérrez has demonstrated in a fascinating study of the introduction of Christianity into the north American southwest, the Jesuits adeptly manipulated the magic of pueblo Indians to their own – and their church's – great benefit. Jesuits in Naples actively encouraged belief in miracle cures linked to their missions. In addition, the French *dévots* (members of the laity dedicated to ideals of Counter-Reformation religiosity) pushed programs of reform that included medicine.

Religious healing and healers, sanctioned neither by the Roman Catholic church nor by established Protestant churches nor by secular authorities, of course persisted. Matthew Ramsey, for instance, tells the story of the "saint of Savières," an erstwhile shepherd named Pierre Richard. In 1767, when already in his fifties, he began curing with holy water and at the height of his popularity reportedly treated hundreds each day. As Protestantism in the late seventeenth and eighteenth centuries experienced waves of revivalism, in the forms of Pietism in Germany (a mystical and inner-directed religious movement within Lutheranism) and Methodism in England, the role of religion in healing began to expand once again. At the strongly Pietist-influenced university at Halle (in Prussia), the university clinic educated theological students to minister to the sick. The university also established a pharmaceutical industry and dispatched medications throughout the world. Missionaries educated in Halle, like Batholomaeus Ziegenbalg (1682–1719) who went to India, and Henry Melchior Muhlenberg (1711–87) who missionized in America, practiced medicine along with their theology. John Wesley (1703–91), the founder of Methodism, criticized the standard medical

---

[16] Quoted in Marvin R. O'Connell, "The Roman Catholic Tradition Since 1545," in Numbers and Amundsen, *Caring and Curing*, 120.

practices of his day and developed his own method of "physick." The first edition of his *Primitive Physick* appeared in 1747 and continued to be printed until 1880.

To sum up: in the early middle ages, religion, magic, and healing coexisted within the framework of Christianity. Toward the end of the middle ages, however, the Catholic hierarchy tried to disentangle religion from healing without abandoning the latter altogether. The Protestant and Catholic Reformations of the sixteenth century produced churches that focused more singlemindedly on the care of souls than the cure of the body. By the middle of the seventeenth century, most clergy were reluctant to attempt supernatural cures. Still, religious healing did not disappear simply because established churches began to distance themselves from its practice. Clearly in many regions religious and magical healing tended to hold on longer, although it is far too simple to accept that countrypeople or the "small folk" of early modern Europe were particularly benighted and clung pigheadedly to superstitious practices, while more knowledgeable urbanites forged ahead, accepting the modernizing and secularizing tendencies of the new science of the seventeenth century and the Enlightenment of the eighteenth.

Cures that relied on magic and religion were, however, only one option. As we have seen, there was little tendency in early modern Europe to spurn medicine and few people satisfied themselves with magical or religious cures entirely. The breadth of other choices was great: local healers of many kinds; midwives; traveling practitioners; surgeons; apothecaries; and physicians. These men and women filled important niches.

Local practitioners

Early modern Europe supported a wide range of practitioners who met the medical needs of their communities. As a crude rule of thumb, there were probably more practitioners on the ground in the eighteenth century than in the seventeenth, and larger population agglomerations tended to have more resident practitioners than smaller places. This rule is, however, very imprecise and was subject to almost infinite regional variations. For instance, Groningen actually had *more* physicians in the seventeenth than in the eighteenth century. More prosperous areas usually supported a larger number of practitioners. Special places like Bath in England and Spa in the Spanish/Austrian Netherlands, for instance, attracted a disproportionate number of healers.

The medical providers here termed "local practitioners" were those who resided in one locality – whether a neighborhood, city, market town, or village. While the density and assortment of practitioners varied, most

7.1 Surgeon Norton's House, Golden Square, London, with an advertisement for his "assistant and successor," John Hayman, 1786.

places had several resident healers who drew at least part of their living from medicine. Some people, of course, practiced only in the spirit of good neighborliness. Such local practitioners also included people who over the course of our period tended to be more and more frequently designated "irregulars" – the cunning-folk discussed above, executioners, and those who possessed talents in one or another procedure, such as bonesetting. In addition, however, many local practitioners had undergone a more or less rigorous apprenticeship in a guild system: apothecaries, bathmasters, surgeons, and barber-surgeons. Midwives also belong in this group, but they will be dealt with separately in the next section.

Two variables deeply conditioned the situation of local practitioners: first, the economic niche they occupied within their village or neighborhood, and, second, their social and communal relations with their colleagues, competitors, and clients. To understand "medical practice" in early modern Europe, it is essential to remember that medical decisions turned on many factors, not all (or perhaps not even most) of which were strictly "medical." Doctrinal orthodoxy and church membership could count, and so, too, did one's standing in the community. A "good man" or a "good woman" made for a good practitioner and merit hinged upon a perception that such people fulfilled the community's social, moral, and economic expectations. It also helped, of course, to be tightly coupled to a native hierarchy by ties of blood, marriage, or property. Villagers proved reluctant to patronize healers who drank to excess, blasphemed, chased women, or ran up debts. As most practitioners, especially in villages and market towns, never made a living through medical practice alone, their qualities as house-father, husbandman, debtors, creditors, and churchgoers were essential parts of their identities as *medical providers*.

The world of towns and cities offered more openness than did the countryside, and choices in urban environments were always greater. More physicians, surgeons, and barber-surgeons lived in towns and, by the middle of the eighteenth century, a new consumer society had taken root in metropolitan areas. Medicines were among the most widely advertised and distributed of the growing number of consumer products and, in fact, medical advertising took the vanguard in this new market surge. Newspaper columns bulged with come-ons for proprietary medicines, including many sure-cures for venereal diseases, often under euphemistic names such as the Lisbon Diet Drink. Perhaps the most famous and successful of the mail-order medicine vendors was the Frenchman, Jean Ailhaud. Ailhaud advertised his purgative powders (*poudres d'Ailhaud*) extensively, and he and his son constructed distribution networks that spread over France and reached into the Germanies, commissioning agents and establishing depots in strategic places, such as Strasburg. Not only irregulars and market specialists like Ailhaud exploited advertising techniques. The darling of the French court, the Dutch physician Jean-Adrien Helvétius, puffed his own remedies in print and, by the 1720s, was manufacturing over 100,000 doses a year.

Mail-order and long-distance marketing on a national or international scale, however, probably only became common by 1750, though long before then medicine peddlers were to be found busily hawking their wares across the continent. Some peddlers and mountebanks – the oil-peddlers (*Ölitatenkramer*) of central and eastern Europe or the *orviétan* sellers in France, for example – specialized in specifics, offering theriac or oil of turpentine, as well as an assortment of tinctures. Other colporteurs carried a wider selection of goods and sold distillates, tinctures, pills, and powders along with household items such as ribbons, cloth, knives, combs, pots, pans, and sieves.

One could find apothecaries and their shops, however, in all cities, most towns, and even many villages. Apothecaries were responsible for the sale and distribution of medicines, *simples* and *composita*, herbal and chemical. Simples included herbs and other single ingredient medicines. Composita, as the name suggests, were compounds mixed up in advance or on the spot. Composita were sometimes intimidatingly complex and a sixteenth-century recipe for "a most precious and excellent balm" called for, among other things, sixty-eight herbs, twenty types of gum, six laxatives, and twenty-four different roots.[17]

Pharmacopeias, at least until the middle of the eighteenth century, continued to contain arcane ingredients, such as powdered unicorn's horn. Many of these remedies, as well as the once perfectly respectable ones of theriac and mithradium (both used to treat plague), disappeared or were expunged from official lists by reforms introduced in the eighteenth century. Apothecary ordinances often designated what apothecaries were supposed to stock. The 1763 "Instruction" for apothecaries in Delft forbade them to mix and sell certain antiquated remedies, or those which over the course of time had come to be regarded as useless, for instance, "mithradatium, theriaca, diascordium, philonium Romanam, and aqua vitae Mattioli." The same rules required Delft apothecaries to stock thirty-one specific remedies including a wide range of "spirits," "salts," and "oils."

City, territorial, and, later, national governments regulated apothecaries and, in most places, specifically denied them the practice of medicine. Nor were they permitted to prescribe medicines without the order of a

---

[17] Pollock, *With Faith and Physic*, 103.

physician. Typical, for instance, was the medical ordinance for Amsterdam from 1519 which prohibited anyone – including apothecaries – to dispense medicines except on a physician's explicit, preferably written, instructions. Almost all medical ordinances distinguished between the duties of apothecaries and those of physicians and surgeons. Apothecaries, in short, were not to practice medicine.

There were, however, exceptions. In London, after a bitter fight between the apothecaries and the physicians in the seventeenth century, the apothecaries emerged with the right to dispense on their own. Thus they often functioned as general practitioners. If this de jure situation was unknown elsewhere in Europe, de facto it was not. Almost everywhere apothecaries not only compounded and dispensed drugs on the prescription of physicians, they also did so on their own and proffered medical advice with their medicines. Yet little differentiated the *type* of medicine apothecaries practiced from that of physicians. Apothecaries dispensed the same sorts of pills and potions that physicians prescribed. Throughout early modern Europe, therefore, the competition among apothecaries, physicians, and surgeons for customers could be quite fierce. Apothecaries, moreover, in the eighteenth century often found themselves at odds with a newly emergent group of *druggists* as well as with tavern- and innkeepers because apothecaries also distributed distilled and intoxicating beverages, such as brandies and cordials.

The apothecary had a socioeconomic position in the community as well. To set up shop in a guild town, one had to be a master guildsman. Apothecaries' shops were considered lucrative businesses and were substantially taxed. An apothecary was quite often a financial pillar of his community. The taxes the apothecary Dirck Outgaertzs. Cluyt paid in Delft in the sixteenth century ranked him among its most affluent citizens. Not all apothecaries, of course, were wealthy. In small towns and villages, apothecaries seldom belonged to a guild and might lack formal training altogether. Such "corner-apothecaries" (or *Winckel-Apotheker* as the Germans called them) could be very poor and poorly run. Some stocked only a pathetically meager supply of drugs; many ran groceries and taverns as part of their economy of makeshifts.

Surgeons and barber-surgeons

Surgeons, barber-surgeons, and apothecaries probably provided the lion's share of day-to-day medical and surgical care. Surgeons were the most numerous licensed practitioners in early modern Europe in both town and country. As many as 25,000 barber-surgeons may have practiced in France toward the end of the eighteenth century, for example. We have today a rather jaundiced and unbalanced view of early modern surgery. Certainly, almost all surgery was painful and brought with it the real peril of life-threatening infections and tetanus. Surgeons almost never invaded the cavities of the chest or abdomen, and major operations, such as the amputation of legs and arms or mastectomies, were ventured only if deemed absolutely necessary to save life. Probably only 25 percent of patients survived the initial shock and subsequent dangers of amputating a major limb. Yet, despite these grim statistics and the many harrowing tales of surgical "torture," surgery was a success story. Many surgeons possessed enviable skills and indeed, as Sabine Sander has demonstrated for eighteenth-century Württemberg and Toby Gelfand for Old Regime France, often boasted a high degree of theoretical and hands-on training. Some operations such as lithotomy and the couching of cataracts were often (if not quite routinely) successful.

Radical surgery, however, was rare. Military and naval surgeons performed the overwhelming majority of amputations. The best study we have of everyday surgical practices establishes that surgeons, far from being "knife-crazy," were very reluctant to attempt major interventions unless absolutely unavoidable. In such critical cases, they vastly preferred to work closely with a colleague, partly to add experience and partly to spread the blame if things went awry. Most surgical practices were probably pretty much restricted to lancing boils, setting broken limbs, treating contusions, reducing dislocations, and the like.

Surgeons advocated and exercised caution. Richard Wiseman in his *Treatise on Wounds* (1672) noted that

In small and superficial wounds . . . there Nature of her own accord is wont to effect the cure, without the help of any Medicament; from us only is required that the lips of the wound be brought close together by bandage, that neither hair, nor dust, nor any other things fall between them.[18]

Surgeons were, however, not all alike. Three types of surgeons practiced in early modern Europe – surgeons (or master-surgeons), barber-surgeons, and military surgeons. In addition, bathmasters (who were, properly speaking, not surgeons at all) performed minor "surgical" tasks. Bathhouses and the bathmasters to go with them could be found in most places in Europe since the middle ages. Bathmasters usually rented a bathhouse from the commune for a fee and provided a variety of services: they administered warm and cold baths (to men, women, and children), cut hair, pared corns, "cupped," and set leeches. Cupping (like leeching)

---

[18] Quoted in Stephen Jacyna, "Physiological Principles in the Surgical Writings of John Hunter," in Christopher Lawrence, ed., *Medical Theory, Surgical Practice: Studies in the History of Surgery* (London and New York, 1992), 142.

Les Bains de Plombières (Vosges).

7.2 The baths at Plombières, Vosges (France), 1599.

was a form of letting blood, although a far less risky one than opening a vein. It involved heating the inside of a glass "cup" to form a partial vacuum and then sliding the mouth of the cup quickly onto the body's surface. The partial vacuum thus created ruptured small capillaries. Cupping was used as much to prevent illness as to cure.

Bathhouses and bathing were communal activities. Sixteenth-century prints, for instance, depict whole families strolling down the street, clad only in shirts and petticoats, on their way to the bathhouse. Such bathhouses existed in large numbers in the sixteenth century, especially in the German territories, the northern Italian states, and Scandinavia. The outbreak of the "great pox" in the sixteenth century, however, undercut their popularity and bathhouses quickly fell into disrepute in many places, although bathmasters continued to clip hair, cup, and leech (activities which, of course, soured their relationships with the barber-surgeons).

As the name should suggest, the barber-surgeons were generally licensed to cut hair in addition to performing *minor* surgical operations, such as cupping, leeching, lancing boils, and pulling teeth. Many barber-surgeons also let blood. Although definitions of what barber-surgeons were legally permitted to do varied throughout Europe, they frequently came into conflict with the surgeons over the execution of surgical operations. Much depended on what was considered "minor" surgery. Barber-surgeons often overstepped legal boundaries and infringed on the province of the surgeons by letting blood or performing more complicated operations. This sort of "poaching" also worked in reverse: barber-surgeons constantly complained about surgeons who cut hair and thus interfered with *their* livelihood.

These conflicts over boundaries of legal and illicit activities were ubiquitous and in fact determined much of the daily life and even the identity of surgeons: i.e., surgeons defined themselves as separate and distinctive from barber-surgeons and bathmasters. Military surgeons were also involved in these territorial squabbles. Technically military surgeons were permitted only to treat soldiers and were specifically forbidden civilian practice. While on furlough and on reduced pay, they practiced wherever they could, drawing howls of protest from their nonmilitary colleagues.

Another variety of surgeon closely related to the military surgeon was the marine or naval surgeon. These men confronted not only the injuries of battle, but the manifold health hazards that accompanied long, slow voyages, demanding work conditions, and the deleterious consequences of close confinement, monotonous and inadequate diets, insufficient water, and poor hygienic conditions. An insufficiency of vitamin C caused scurvy and was a common shipboard health problem. Usual, too, were ruptures and hernias as well as the inevitable falls and other injuries typical of the seafaring trade. Syphilis, verminous infestations, and typhus can be added to a catalog of major and minor ills to which seafaring flesh was prey. Indeed, typhus was often known as "ship-fever" (also "jail-fever") because it spread so rapidly in confined populations.

Life aboard ship was not especially healthy, but we need not overestimate seafaring mortality. Take, for example, the history of the Dutch East India Company. The one-way trip to or from the East Indies lasted anywhere from sixteen to thirty weeks (and occasionally longer). Yet, overall death rates were never especially high. In the hundred-year period from 1694 to 1793, mortality averaged 6.8 percent annually. That figure included a shocking toll of 40 percent in 1781/82 (mostly due to typhus). In other years, mortality fluctuated between 2.2 percent and 16.9 percent.

Midwives

More Europeans came in contact with midwives than with any other medical practitioner. Historical writing about midwifery, however, has concentrated on the question of the "disappearance" of the midwife from the birthing chamber and her replacement by *male-midwives, surgeon-midwives*, or *accoucheurs* (and later obstetricians). Much of this literature has an Anglo-Saxon orientation and has focused on events of the middle to late eighteenth century. This model stresses the impact of the introduction of obstetrical forceps in the early seventeenth century by the Chamberlen family and the subsequent rise of the man-midwife, while perpetuating the Sairy Gamps image of the illiterate, dirty, drunken, and incompetent midwife. More recently, scholars have questioned the widespread applicability of this version of history. First, they do not see the triumph of the man-midwife in such absolute terms. Second, studies of midwifery outside England and America have shown that physicians and surgeons never consistently disputed the midwife's role. Moreover, until well into the nineteenth century (and into the twentieth century in many places), midwives continued to deliver the majority of babies, although there is no denying that among certain social groups (royalty, aristocracy, and, later, the haute bourgeoisie) and in certain countries (France and England, for instance) the man-midwife or surgeon-midwife had become quite popular by 1800. Timing is also important. The era of midwifery reform and the rise of the man-midwife occurred in the eighteenth century. For the preceding centuries, midwives were (almost) unchallenged in the birth chamber.

Before embarking on a discussion of midwifery in early modern Europe, one should recognize that childbirth is not a pathological process: that is, pregnancy is not an illness. Feminist historians first argued that, by defining childbirth as a medical event, it more easily became the province of male physicians and surgeons. The majority of births (one historian estimates over 90 percent) were uneventful whether attended by a physician, a midwife, or a stork. Still, some births (perhaps as many as 3 percent) were difficult and an ability to turn the child in utero could spell the difference between a live birth or tragedy for mother or child or both. Likewise the forceps, despite the dangers of introducing infection, tearing delicate membranes, or injuring the child, could result in the live birth of otherwise undeliverable children. Thus, the answer to the old question of whether man-midwives or midwives were the better birth attendants, is not simple. Some midwives were indeed dirty, ignorant, and dangerous; some man-midwives saved lives with their forceps; and some births were doomed to disaster no matter who attended.[19]

The definition of who was a "proper" midwife is not clear-cut. Midwifery ordinances specified a course of training or at least an examination of a midwife's skills by secular or religious authorities. Of course, in some places the position of midwife might be a very informal one. One small German town in the middle of the eighteenth century had no "real" midwife; rather the women "helped one another in turn." Such conditions were hardly unique. By the eighteenth century, however, as part of a widespread attempt to reform midwifery, the delineation of training, examination, and licensing became stricter and more thorough. Nonetheless, the general framework remained the same. Most midwives learned their craft as informal apprentices to older, more experienced women, as surgeons and barber-surgeons did (although there were no midwifery guilds). Sometimes this training was casual; mothers or aunts passed on their acquired knowledge to daughters or nieces. This was probably the commonest form of instruction in most villages and small towns, and perhaps even in cities as well. Midwifery ordinances, especially those issued in the eighteenth century, formalized training, often setting the length of apprenticeship, specifying with whom an apprentice could train, requiring midwives-in-training to attend anatomical demonstrations and lectures, and mandating that they be examined by a master-midwife before they could receive a license. In France in the middle of the eighteenth century, under the protection of the king and with a royal privilege in her pocket, the talented midwife and charismatic teacher, Madame du Coudray, traveled the length and breadth of France giving instruction in the art and craft of midwifery. Her "road-show" and mission lasted about twenty years and in that time she and her entourage trained hundreds of women.

---

[19] Adrian Wilson, "William Hunter and the Varieties of Man-Midwifery," in W. F. Bynum and Roy Porter, eds., *William Hunter and the Eighteenth-Century Medical World* (Cambridge, 1985), 343–69.

Some towns and cities determined the number of certified midwives, dividing the urban landscape into districts and apportioning a midwife to each. Midwives were generally forbidden to use surgical instruments, although they were expected to keep certain implements on hand, such as enema syringes and, especially in German-speaking areas, birthing-chairs.

The most important of the midwife's tasks was, of course, attending births. Generally a pregnant woman would make arrangements in advance with the local midwife and then call her when the labor pains began. The midwife was supposed to go to the woman promptly, ascertain the progress of labor, and, if delivery seemed reasonably near, not depart until the birth was accomplished. The family of the woman plied the midwife with food and drink (preferably not intoxicating) while she was on duty. Midwives did physical examinations, using their hands and fingers to ascertain the state of cervical dilation, straightened twisted limbs, and lubricated the birth canal with oils or fats to ease the passage of the child. The midwife was also expected to offer moral and psychological succor. Madame du Coudray instructed her pupils to

console [the woman] as affectionately as possible: . . . but you must do it with an air of gaiety that gives her no fear of danger. Avoid all whisperings [in the ears of others], which can only make her nervous and make her worry about bad things. You must speak to her of God, and engage her in thanking him for putting her out of peril. Avoid letting her do anything that will depress her.[20]

If complications ensued that exceeded the midwife's skills, or if it became apparent that a child could not be delivered without surgical intervention, or if a child had to be extracted in pieces to save the mother's life (and, despite lore to the contrary, the life of the mother was almost always chosen over that of the unborn child), she was to call a surgeon without delay. In difficult cases, she might also consult with another midwife.

After the child was born, the midwife tied off and severed the umbilical cord, cleaned the newborn (making sure membranes and blood had been removed from the mouth), and administered strengthening potions if the child seemed weak. In many places, she was required to perform an "emergency baptism" (in German, *Nottaufe*) on a feeble and sickly child that seemed close to death. The midwife might also swaddle the child for the first time. The midwife then delivered the afterbirth. If hemorrhage ensued, she would massage the abdomen to try to stop the bleeding.

---

[20] Quoted in Nina R. Gelbart, *The King's Midwife: The History and Mystery of Madame du Coudray* (Berkeley and Los Angeles, 1998), 69, 45.

Midwives were allowed to use bracing cordials and teas, but were to refrain from administering drugs of any kind, although some certainly did so anyway. Midwives also dressed wounds to the vagina and surrounding tissues and would sometimes stitch lacerations with a needle and thread.

In the days after the birth, the midwife would return to check on the progress of the woman and her infant. Although childbed fever occurred rarely until births in hospitals or with instruments became more routine, it was not unknown and was almost always mortal. There was nothing a midwife (or anyone else) could do to halt its fearsome progress. Such fatal complications usually accompanied traumatic and exhausting births, but midwives who attended births with soiled hands or whose clumsiness caused more tearing than necessary certainly contributed. Midwives assisted women (especially those having their first child) in beginning breastfeeding and treated sore breasts with hot compresses or lotions. Other mixtures were applied to help "toughen" nipples. If a woman suffered from postpartum constipation, the midwife administered an enema with the enema syringe. The midwife might also launder soiled linen, cook for the household, and generally help out around the house. The eighteenth-century Maine (USA) midwife, Martha Ballard, took on all these chores, although often, one suspects, impelled by a sense of Christian charity.

For their assistance at births, midwives were paid a fee, generally specified in midwifery ordinances where they existed, but habitually determined by custom. Wealthier clients paid more than less well-to-do ones, and communities and parishes would often foot delivery bills for very poor women or families on relief. In addition, the midwife earned extra payment for performing supplementary duties. Many rural mid-wives received chickens, bread, grain, garden produce, or the like rather than cash as part or all of their fees. In addition, the midwife was responsible for carrying the child to the church to be christened and she enjoyed gratuities for this; prosperous or socially prominent parents and godpar-ents presented midwives with gifts at the ceremony. Few midwives lived from midwifery alone; the vast majority were midwives "on occasion" and their earnings from midwifery made up only a part of their total income.

It is frequently asserted that the social status of midwives was low. If we look at what most midwives earned from midwifery, and consider that sum as their total income, then most of them would have hovered on the brink of sheer destitution. However, because midwifery only comprised part of their income, the economic status of midwives diverged. Many were indeed poor. In fact, appointing a woman as midwife to a village was one way of keeping her off poor relief. Many midwives, however, were the wives of artisans, and their fees supplemented the family's income.

Midwifery was, however, for most of our period not a "career choice." (There were, of course, significant exceptions to this rule.) Some midwifery ordinances, and common practice as well, stipulated that midwives had to be beyond childbearing years themselves as well as to have borne children. While many midwives fit the picture of age and indigence, others were younger women and more financially stable. Some, like Madame du Coudray, never married or bore children. Still the percentage of older, widowed (and thus impoverished) midwives was probably highest in rural areas. In towns and cities, especially by the end of our period, more and more women received quite extensive theoretical and practical training and were choosing midwifery as an occupation. These changes inevitably caused the average age of midwives to decrease while their status and income rose.

Physicians

The final practitioner this chapter addresses is the physician. This priority may seem curious, but it reflects the reality of medical practice in early modern Europe. Most people did not, as a matter of course, turn to physicians. One hastens to qualify this statement, however. First, the availability of physicians was not the same everywhere. In cities, where physicians tended to settle, where there were hospitals, and where parish and municipal forms of poor relief existed, a wide segment of the population (even the poor) probably had some contact with university-trained practitioners. As we saw in the previous chapter, cities often appointed a city physician among whose duties might be that of physician-to-the-poor. Guilds, too, sometimes contracted with physicians (and other practitioners, too, of course) to administer medical assistance to their members.

Second, it is simply not true that early modern people shunned physicians and harbored an deep-seated antipathy toward them. Some, of course, expressed skepticism about, and even enmity to, physicians. Contemporary prints and the works of many novelists, playwrights, and satirists, such as Molière in *The Imaginary Invalid*, frequently targeted physicians.[21] One must wonder, however, if the mistrust of physicians was not more a fashionable phenomenon among some of the elite or a useful literary and pictorial trope than a deeply rooted and widespread conviction. In places where there were physicians, patients consulted them as part of a typical range of practitioners, even if they did not prefer

---

[21] For an excellent discussion of Molière as medical commentator, see Laurence Brockliss and Colin Jones, *The Medical World of Early Modern France* (Oxford, 1997), 336–44.

physicians to other healers. In other words, although physicians were not "privileged," they remained one of the practitioners a person might call upon to help remedy his or her afflictions.

Third, the number of physicians tended to increase throughout Europe in the eighteenth century. By the end of that century many people spoke of a glut, rather than a scarcity, of physicians as part of a general superfluity of those in learned professions. As more and more physicians settled outside major population centers, as once small towns grew, and as states began to appoint officers of health, people gained greater familiarity with physicians. We must also remember that many medical consultations were done by correspondence (especially in the eighteenth century), thus increasing the number of patients a physician might "see" and treat. Practitioners with local or national reputations maintained a huge medical correspondence with patients and with fellow physicians.

Why, then, might a person choose a physician over another healer? This question is easy to pose, and devilishly difficult to resolve. Surely part of the answer lies in individual preference. Status differences might also have played a role, although, as we have seen, a neat formula that equates the use of physicians with the European elites and relegates the rest of the population to the mercies of "other" practitioners is far too crude to catch reality. Fashion might explain the popularity one physician enjoyed over another, although it also explains enthusiasm for faddish cures, such as balneotherapy, electrotherapy, and Mesmerism. People were discriminating in their choices. When they did not consult physicians, it was not because they feared the expense or felt culturally alienated from such learned men, but rather because they perceived that physicians were good for some things, yet not for others. Parents rarely called in a physician (or any other type of healer, for that matter) when their offspring fell ill with smallpox, for instance, not because they considered their children unimportant or replaceable, but because they quite rightly discerned that there was little a physician could do. The same was true during certain epidemics, such as of dysentery, where the disease progressed swiftly. Still many people consulted physicians for assorted types of "fever" (especially recurring fevers), for myriad chronic or slow-moving diseases like dropsy, cancer, vision problems, and gynecological complaints such as the "whites" (a nonvenereal vaginal discharge).

What did physicians do? How early modern physicians examined patients might seem strange to us today. First, physicians generally went to see the patient, rather than the other way around. Second, the standard parts of the physical examination we have come to expect – listening to heart and lungs with a stethoscope; taking the temperature with a thermometer; palpitating the abdomen; percussing the thorax; doing a digital rectal examination; monitoring the blood pressure with a sphygmomanometer; testing blood, urine, and stool specimens – were all absent. A physician might indeed glance at the patient's urine, spittle, or stools, examine a furred tongue, or feel the pulse, but he observed signs other than the basically quantitative measures and deviations from norms physicians today use to determine health or illness. Descriptions of physical phenomena differed and the physician of yesteryear drew other meanings from them. Take the pulse, for example. Few doctors counted beats per minute, rather they evaluated the pulse qualitatively: it was rapid, weak, pounding, or tremulous. An eighteenth-century English physician noted in a pleurisy patient, for instance, a pulse that was "rapid and full but not particularly hard." Fever patients had a "fluttering" pulse.

For the early modern physician (as for most people), the complexion and temperament presented reliable indicators to health and illness that could be perceived on the body's exterior and, especially, on the face. A late seventeenth-century English practitioner read death in a countenance where "the Nose is sharp, the Eyes hollow, the Temples fallen, the Ears cold and drawn in." The physical examination, therefore, depended on correctly deciphering *external* signs. William Brownrigg, who practiced in Cumberland in the eighteenth century, often recorded the appearance of patients. Mrs. James Milham, who suffered from "inflammation of the intestines," was "[a] pretty young woman of 18 with a beautiful complexion and a dainty figure." Brownrigg was not merely admiring her shapely form; her complexion and "daintiness" reliably indicated her predisposition to certain afflictions and her receptivity to particular treatments.[22]

In their examinations, physicians used their five senses unassisted and unamplified by instruments. Only in the nineteenth century did the stethoscope (invented by R. T. H. Laennec in 1816) and the clinical thermometer (the "fever-stick") come into use. An early modern physician gauged fever by touching the brow or feeling a chest; he evaluated stools and urine by sight, by smell, and occasionally by taste (the urine of a diabetic patient is sweet). He might indeed palpitate a hernia, a lump, or a fibrous growth, but seldom did he probe orifices (especially female ones) with an intrusive finger. He listened to the patient's heart and breathing, but far more often he paid attention to what the patient had to say.

[22] Quoted in Fissell, *Patients, Power, and the Poor*, 32; *Medical Casebook of William Brownrigg*, 61, 100.

The patient's narrative of illness was the most important part of the physical examination. Details related by the patient orally were used to form diagnoses, determine treatments, and shape prognoses. Patients emphasized what they felt and observed going on within their own bodies. The language of their narratives very often corresponded to the words a physician himself might use (although few patients employed Latin terms). The early eighteenth-century German physician, Johann Storch, shared a vocabulary with his female patients: they spoke of the body as a vessel of fluids, for instance.

Because of the overwhelming significance of the patient narrative (and, of course, because of the distance of some patients from practitioners), consultation by correspondence was common and became more so in the eighteenth century with the spread of literacy and the improvement of postal services and transportation networks. Patients, family members, or friends wrote to physicians and physicians communicated with their peers about obdurate or interesting cases. Patients often provided exhaustive detail. In 1739, Mrs. Christian of Unerigg (the grandmother of Fletcher Christian, the *Bounty* mutineer) sent Dr. Mead an extensive case-history of her persistent diarrhea (and Mead forwarded it to Dr. Brownrigg):

S[r] [Sir]
  I am 42 years old, mother of 5 Children at 26 till which time I had a very good Health, but after that I often miscarried, . . . [and] that brought the Hysterick Illness upon me, which affected me with a lowness of Spirits, a bad appetite and sometimes a violent pain in the right side, or else the Toothake. I slept very little which brought me to the use of Laudanum but tho' I have used it 15 years I seldom take more than 20 or 25 drops . . . Ten years ago I had the Measels, [from] which I hardly recovered. That quite altered my very nature, for before that I was always costive [constipated], but since that have been very subject to a looseness, which is my greatest trouble at present . . . always the worst when I was with Child . . . I drank Tea made with the Woods a long time, but could not find any alteration from it. It is near two years since I bore my last Child, and my appetite has never been so good as it was before, and my Looseness and other Ailments have been worse . . . Very often the day before I am loose, I am very much loaden and dull, then perhaps I have five or six Stools, but not allways very loose, but it is more than I can bear as I eat little; then I take Laudanum and am fine after it . . . Tho I am naturally chearfull and have very good Spirits, and when I am well of an easy temper, yet when I am ill, my Spirits are greatly affected . . . For the last year I have taken a Drachm of toasted Rhubarb once in a month or five weeks; I am always better and lightsomer after it; but it makes no Alteration as to the looseness. I was so grievously troubled with the Tooth-ake for many years, that at last I chewed Tobacco . . .

> I take my illness to be Hysterick and a bad habit of Body, and I think if
> any thing could help my Stomach and bring me to be regular in going to
> Stool, every other Complaint would vanish in course.[23]

This excerpt from a considerably longer letter shows how fastidiously
Mrs. Christian monitored her condition. She traced her afflictions back
many years, furnished a history of symptoms, and chronicled her own
attempts at cure. Her perceptions were visceral: she spoke of being
"loaden and dull" and of how the illness dampened her "Spirits." She
offered her own diagnosis and proposed a course of treatment: she
believed that the "reason of this bad habit I take to be falling with Child in
ten days time after the Measels went off" and regarded her illness as
"Hysterick" in nature. She felt that it would cure her to be made "regular
in going to Stool."

Dr. Mead found nothing peculiar in her description, nor did either
Mead or Brownrigg suggest that she was presumptuous in her attitude or
mistaken in her analysis. Neither took offense at her advising them.
Indeed, after careful consideration, the two doctors agreed that "the
whole habit of body seems to be concerned in this Indisposition." Dr.
Mead judged it necessary to rectify that "habit of body" before the
"Discharge from the Intestines can be brought into right order." He recommended a purgative of ipecac, a "conserve of red roses," and an
"emetic draught" (to make her vomit). Brownrigg, commenting on the
case, noted that the vomits did not agree with her and "that the other
Remedies were not unpleasant but sometimes seemed to bind her too
much, and then she w[ould] have a swelling in her face, and flying [migra-
tory] Pains until the Diarrhoea returned."[24] The language of Brownrigg
and Mead, and their insights, do not differ in any significant way from
those of Mrs. Christian, except for a moment when Brownrigg speaks of
"Leucophelgmatick Swellings"! Both physicians felt perfectly comfort-
able about prescribing from her account. The continuation of the correspondence shows Mrs. Christian to be an active participant in her
treatments and, for example, when she complained that a prescribed
decoction (an extract got by boiling) did not agree with her, the medica-
tion was changed.

The cases of Mrs. Christian and of the many women who spoke to Dr.
Storch reveal several characteristics typical of the medical practice of
early modern physicians. Physicians depended heavily (if not exclusively)
on patient narratives. Physicians conducted physical examinations
(although perhaps the better word is *observations*), but these did not much

---

[23] Ibid., 128–29.   [24] Ibid., 130.

resemble twentieth-century ones. Patients exercised a fair degree of say in how they were treated and physicians amended treatments or suspended them when patients complained that something disagreed with them. Of course, this was not a perfect world of patient–physician cooperation. Obviously some physicians pooh-poohed the opinions of their patients, or, perhaps more often, thought their patients lied to them or concealed information (as patients sometimes did). The point is that a narrative based on the patient's insights and judgments was a central part of the medical consultation whether done face-to-face or by letter.

In concluding this chapter on medical practice, we may want to ask ourselves what patients expected from the healers they consulted. Perhaps this seems a foolish question: surely all people sought an end to their ills. But did they? Early modern medicine was unable to cure and could provide little relief for most illnesses and ailments. Opiates could deaden pain, but the side effects were risky and the chance of accidental death or addiction great. Surgeons could help in certain cases, by extracting bladder stones, couching cataracts, lancing boils, and amputating smashed limbs, but the dangers of infection and gangrene remained considerable as was the agony most surgical interventions produced. Yet people did not abandon medicines and healers, nor did they inevitably become resigned to illness, pain, and death. The accounts presented in this chapter demonstrate how vigorously people pursued health. Few abandoned the quest entirely. They might, of course, turn to prayer as well as physick for assistance, or seek help from a cunning-man or -woman as well as a doctor, but they did not deny the possibility of cure.

Some historians, however, have suggested a rather different interpretation: that early modern people did not go to practitioners with the same goals in mind that we hold today. A recent magisterial treatment of medicine in early modern France concluded that "the majority [of French men and women] were . . . fatalists and stoics. They might crave release from their ills, but they also recognized that the length of their days was measured by God. It made little sense to change physicians repeatedly in a vain attempt to defeat divine nemesis. It was irrational as well as unseemly."[25] Illness and suffering could also be interpreted positively, as marks of divine favor, for instance. Most of us today, on the other hand, view health as a positive good and an objective to be attained, and pain as an evil to be avoided. According to those, however, who draw distinct lines between us and our ancestors, no such ideals or expectations existed in the early modern period. People were accustomed to experiencing a succession of minor and major ailments, as well as intermittent or even

[25] Brockliss and Jones, *Medical World*, 305.

constant pain, throughout their lives. When they approached practitioners, they might have sought psychological support rather than physical
aid. Thus, they went to practitioners to have their own diagnoses
confirmed and to get a sense of their prognosis: was the illness deadly?
Temporary? Incapacitating? Minor?

It is indeed difficult to decide which of these two accounts comes closer
to being correct. The truth probably lies somewhere in the middle. Early
modern people had different expectations of healers than we do, but they
also had their own idea of what health should be and desired it greatly.
Although it seems fairly clear to us that early modern medicine was powerless to cure, it was not completely impotent. Laudanum, hot compresses, and some herbal remedies were effective in relieving symptoms.
Good nursing care, cleanliness, and proper and sufficient food must have
often made the difference between those who survived an attack of
influenza, for example, and those who did not. Finally, the sense of "doing
something" was a excellent psychological prop and that alone might have
justified "going to the doctor" for many people. In that, our early modern
ancestors were probably much like us.

Conclusion

The history of medicine can be written many ways. One can decide to relate a compelling tale of progress, dwell on the titillating details of quaint or gruesome practices, or, as I have done here, take the past on its own terms and stress the links between the history of medicine and the historical mainstream. Some scholars (by now, fortunately, a dying breed) still regard medicine in early modern Europe as something best forgotten. Those were the "bad old days" of ignorance, misery, and unrelieved human suffering in the face of capricious and ubiquitous disease. It was a dark age of superstition and error. Here and there, it is true, glimmered a hopeful development, and here and there an isolated genius preternaturally endowed with a unerring sense of "the right way" labored to lift the veil of superstition. This handful of intrepid men, scientists perhaps before "science" was born, were pioneers, who kindled the fire of knowledge and passed it down through the ages to us, their true descendants. Yet even while acknowledging these points of light, the "gloom-and-doom" school regards the vast majority of medical providers as worse then useless, creatures who inflicted unnecessary pain and suffering on their patient-victims. Theory was sterile and scholastic, utterly divorced from practice, and wrongheaded because it was not based on the twin gods of "modern medical science": experimentation and observation.

This book has pointed out the fallacies inherent in such views of early modern (and, for that matter, medieval) medicine. We have seen that the idea of a universal form of "science" and a generally agreed upon way of "doing science" was not born with the "Scientific Revolution" of the seventeenth century. No sharp schism characterized epistemology then, and men like William Harvey and Isaac Newton were as much heirs of an older world as founders of a new one. Likewise, the often postulated breakthrough toward clinical and scientific medicine that purportedly happened in the late eighteenth century was not (as Foucault suggested) a sudden rupture, but the result of multifarious conditions and forces, some of which can be easily traced to medieval precedents.

Throughout this book we have concentrated on characteristics of continuity and change. The period from 1500 to 1800 was not an undifferentiated whole. Neither can "Europe" be understood as a single mass. Medicine was embedded in the larger forces acting on early modern society and cannot be divorced from them. Demographic growth and decay, religious turmoil, sectarian squabbling, the European geographical "discoveries," the forging of the great colonial and trading empires, wars, natural disasters such as famine, social change, urbanization, political upheavals, the rise of a consumer society – all deeply affected the medical world of early modern times. Regional and geographical differences have also proved significant. And, while this book has concentrated to a large degree on European-wide similarities, European-wide influences and movements, like the Enlightenment, played out differently in different places.

Some of the polarities once used to emphasize the differences between those times and ours have likewise been shown to be not very useful. Pronounced urban/rural differences did exist: urban areas *tended* to have more practitioners of all kinds than in rural areas; public health policies *were* more forcefully implemented; hospitals, asylums, and other institutions *were* mostly located there. Nonetheless, the isolation of rural areas and the benightedness of their inhabitants have been considerably exaggerated. Likewise we have observed just how often the lines between popular and elite (or academic) medicine blurred. I have emphasized the broad common ground the two inhabited. Moreover, recourse to magical or even superstitious explanations was not confined to an uneducated, brutish herd.

Finally, one of the most persistent stereotypes in medical history – the paucity of practitioners in early modern times – has been shown to be fallacious. The landscape literally swarmed with them in every conceivable form: physicians, surgeons, midwives, cunning-folk, bonesetters, dentists, lithotomists, bathmasters, apothecaries, pastors, and ordinary people who busied themselves with medicine either as part of their normal household chores or as expressions of good neighborliness. Ideas of what constituted a "good healer" turned on many variables and medical choice was always to a degree idiosyncratic. Medical promiscuity pertained to practically everyone in early modern Europe and, although social position and fashion could cleave differences, a simple division based on status or social group is wrong. Monarchs and milkmaids both consulted root-wives and physicians. Concepts of professionalization played little role in such selections. Far more important, especially in the eighteenth century, was the growing world of consumer choices and the proliferation of products, services, and information that finally undermined an older corporate world.

Finally, this book has assiduously avoided speaking in terms of an "us" and "them" dichotomy. While it is true that "the past is a foreign country, they do things differently there," one must be careful not to overvalue variance. It is not that they were "wrong" and we are "right," or that they were "ignorant" and we are "knowledgeable." Historical dynamics affect us as much as they did our ancestors. Neither we nor they, however, are the hapless dupes of larger forces that we barely perceive and cannot control. Rather, our forbears' struggles are the stuff of history and it is our job as students of the past to seek to understand and esteem their solutions and not merely judge them.

Further reading

MAJOR JOURNALS IN THE HISTORY OF MEDICINE

Bulletin of the History of Medicine
Journal of the History of Medicine and Allied Sciences
Isis
Medical History
Medizin, Gesellschaft und Geschichte
Social History of Medicine

GENERAL AND REFERENCE

Brockliss, Laurence and Colin Jones. *The Medical World of Early Modern France.* Oxford, 1997.

Bynum, W. F. and Roy Porter, eds. *Companion Encyclopedia of the History of Medicine.* 2 vols. London, 1993.

Medical Fringe and Medical Orthodoxy, 1750–1850. London, 1987.

Cartwright, F. F. *A Social History of Medicine.* London, 1977.

Clark, E., ed. *Modern Methods in the History of Medicine.* London, 1971.

Conrad, Lawrence, Michael Neve, Vivian Nutton, Roy Porter, and Andrew Wear. *The Western Medical Tradition, 800 B.C. to A.D. 1800.* Cambridge, 1995.

Corsi, Pietro and Paul Weindling, eds. *Information Sources in the History of Medicine and Science.* London, 1983.

Cunningham, Andrew and Roger French, eds. *The Medical Enlightenment of the Eighteenth Century.* Cambridge, 1990.

Faure, Olivier. *Maladies et médecines.* Lyons, 1993.

Fischer, Alfons. *Geschichte des deutschen Gesundheitswesens.* 2 vols. Berlin, 1933.

Foucault, Michel. *The Birth of the Clinic: An Archaeology of Medical Perception.* New York, 1973.

French, Roger and Andrew Wear, eds. *The Medical Revolution of the Seventeenth Century.* Cambridge, 1989.

Herzlich, Claudine and Janine Pierret. *Illness and Self in Society.* Trans. by Elborg Forster. Baltimore, 1987.

Hunter, Lynette and Sarah Hutton, eds. *Women, Science and Medicine, 1500–1700: Mothers and Sisters of the Royal Society.* Stroud, 1997.

Jones, Colin and Roy Porter, eds. *Reassessing Foucault: Power, Medicine, and the Body.* London, 1994.

234

Kiple, Kenneth F., ed. *The Cambridge World History of Human Disease*. Cambridge, 1993.

Lachmund, Jens and Gunnar Stolberg, eds. *The Social Construction of Illness: Historical, Sociological, and Anthropological Perspectives*. Stuttgart, 1992.

Leavitt, Judith Walzer. "Medicine in Context: A Review Essay of the History of Medicine." *American Historical Review* 95 (1990): 1471–84.

McGowen, Randall. "Identifying Themes in the Social History of Medicine." *Journal of Modern History* 63 (1991): 81–90.

McKeown, Thomas. *The Role of Medicine: Dream, Mirage, or Nemesis?* Princeton, N.J., 1979.

Nutton, Vivian, ed. *Medicine at the Courts of Europe, 1500–1837*. London, 1990.

Oxford Concise Medical Dictionary. 4th edn. Oxford, 1994.

Pelling, Margaret. *The Common Lot: Sickness, Medical Occupations and the Urban Poor in Early Modern England*. London and New York, 1998.

Porter, Roy. *The Greatest Benefit to Mankind: A Medical History of Humanity from Antiquity to the Present*. London, 1997.

"The Patient's View: Doing Medical History from Below." *Theory and Society* 14 (1985): 175–98.

Porter, Roy and Miklas Teich, eds. *The Scientific Revolution in National Context*. Cambridge, 1992.

Porter, Roy and Andrew Wear, eds. *Problems and Methods in the History of Medicine*. London, 1987.

Shapin, Steven. *The Scientific Revolution*. Chicago and London, 1996.

Sheils, William, ed. *The Church and Healing*. Oxford, 1982.

Wear, Andrew, ed. *Medicine in Society: Historical Essays*. Cambridge, 1992.

Wear, Andrew, R. K. French, and I. M. Lonie, eds. *The Medical Renaissance of the Sixteenth Century*. Cambridge, 1985.

Webster, Charles, ed. *Health, Medicine and Mortality in the Sixteenth Century*. Cambridge, 1979.

MEDIEVAL BACKGROUND

García-Ballester, Luis, et al., eds. *Practical Medicine from Salerno to the Black Death*. Cambridge, 1993.

McVaugh, Michael. *Medicine Before the Plague: Practitioners and Their Patients in the Crown of Aragon, 1285–1345*. Cambridge, 1993.

McVaugh, Michael and Nancy Siraisi, eds. *Renaissance Medical Learning: Evolution of a Tradition*. Philadelphia, 1990.

Siraisi, Nancy. *Medieval and Early Renaissance Medicine: An Introduction to Knowledge and Practice*. Chicago, 1990.

1 SICKNESS AND HEALTH

Appleby, Andrew B. *Famine in Tudor and Stuart England*. Liverpool and Stanford, 1978.

Bynum, W. F. and V. Nutton, eds. *Theories of Fever from Antiquity to the Enlightenment*. London, 1981.

Bynum, W. F. and Roy Porter, eds. *Living and Dying in London*. London, 1991.

Fissell, Mary E. *Patients, Power, and the Poor in Eighteenth-Century Bristol.* Cambridge, 1991.

Jewson, N. D. "The Disappearance of the Sick-Man from the Medical Cosmology." *Sociology* 10 (1976): 225–44.

"Medical Knowledge and the Patronage System in Eighteenth-Century England." *Sociology* 8 (1974): 369–85.

McKeown, Thomas. *The Origins of Human Disease.* Oxford, 1988.

Porter, Roy. "Lay Medical Knowledge in the Eighteenth Century: *The Gentleman's Magazine.*" *Medical History* 29 (1985): 138–68.

Riley, James C. *Sickness, Recovery and Death: A History and Forecast of Ill Health.* Iowa City, 1989.

2 EPIDEMICS AND INFECTIOUS DISEASES

Alexander, John T. *Bubonic Plague in Early Modern Russia: Public Health and Urban Disaster.* Baltimore, 1980.

Amelang, James S., trans. and ed. *A Journal of the Plague Year: The Diary of the Barcelona Tanner Miquel Parets 1651.* New York, 1991.

Arrizabalaga, Jon, John Henderson, and Roger French. *The Great Pox: The French Disease in Renaissance Europe.* New Haven, Conn., 1997.

Biraben, Jean-Noel. *Les hommes et la peste en France et dans les pays européens et méditerranéens.* 2 vols. Paris, 1975–76.

Calvi, Giulia. *Histories of a Plague Year: The Social and the Imaginary in Baroque Florence.* Berkeley and Los Angeles, 1989.

Carmichael, Ann G. *Plague and the Poor in Renaissance Florence.* Cambridge, 1986.

Crosby, Alfred W., Jr. *The Columbian Exchange: Biological and Cultural Consequences of 1492.* Westport, Conn., 1972.

Darmon, Pierre. *La longue traque de la variole: les pionniers de la médecine preventive.* Paris, 1986.

Dols, Michael. *The Black Death in the Middle East.* Princeton, N.J., 1977.

Hopkins, Donald. *Princes and Peasants: Smallpox in History.* Chicago, 1983.

Miller, Geneviève. *The Adoption of Inoculation for Smallpox in England and France.* Philadelphia, 1957.

Quétel, Claude. *History of Syphilis.* Trans. by Judith Braddock and Brian Pike. Baltimore, 1990.

Ranger, Terence and Paul Slack, eds. *Epidemics and Ideas: Essays on the Historical Perception of Pestilence.* Cambridge, 1992.

Razzell, Peter. *The Conquest of Smallpox: The Impact of Inoculation on Smallpox Mortality in Eighteenth-Century Britain.* Sussex, Eng., 1977.

Slack, Paul. *The Impact of Plague in Tudor and Stuart England.* London, 1985.

Twigg, Graham. *The Black Death: A Biological Reappraisal.* London, 1984.

3 LEARNED MEDICINE

Ackerknecht, Erwin H. *Medicine at the Paris Hospital, 1794–1848.* Baltimore, 1967.

Broman, Thomas H. *The Transformation of German Academic Medicine, 1750–1820.* Cambridge, 1996.

Debus, A. G. *The Chemical Philosophy: Paracelsian Science and Medicine in the Sixteenth and Seventeenth Centuries.* 2 vols. New York, 1977.

Grell, Ole Peter and Andrew Cunningham, eds. *Medicine and the Reformation.* Cambridge, 1993.

King, Lester S. *Medical Thinking: A Historical Preface.* Princeton, N.J., 1982.

The Philosophy of Medicine: The Early Eighteenth Century. Cambridge, Mass., 1982.

Park, Katharine. *Doctors and Medicine in Early Renaissance Florence.* Princeton, N.J., 1985.

Porter, Roy, ed. *Medicine in the Enlightenment.* Amsterdam and Atlanta, 1995.

Temkin, Owsei. *Galenism: Rise and Decline of a Medical Philosophy.* Ithaca, N.Y., 1973.

4 MEDICAL EDUCATION

Beukers, Harm and J. Moll, eds. *Clinical Teaching, Past and Present.* Special issue of *Clio Medica.* Amsterdam, 1989.

Bynum, W. F. and Roy Porter, eds. *William Hunter and the Eighteenth-Century Medical World.* Cambridge, 1985.

Cook, Harold J. *The Decline of the Old Medical Regime in Stuart London.* Ithaca, N.Y., 1986.

Gelfand, Toby. *Professionalizing Modern Medicine: Paris Surgeons and Medical Science and Institutions in the Eighteenth Century.* Westport, Conn., 1980.

Lawrence, Christopher, ed. *Medical Theory, Surgical Practice: Studies in the History of Surgery.* London and New York, 1992.

Lawrence, Susan C. *Charitable Knowledge: Hospital Pupils and Practitioners in Eighteenth-Century London.* Cambridge, 1996.

Moulin, Daniel de. *A History of Surgery with Emphasis on the Netherlands.* Dordrecht, 1988.

Nutton, Vivian and Roy Porter, eds. *The History of Medical Education in Britain.* Amsterdam and Atlanta, 1995.

Rosner, Lisa. *Medical Education in the Age of Improvement: Edinburgh Students and Apprentices, 1760–1826.* Edinburgh, 1991.

Sander, Sabine. *Handwerkschirurgen: Sozialgeschichte einer verdrängten Berufsgruppe.* Göttingen, 1989.

Wilson, Adrian. *The Making of Man-Midwifery: Childbirth in England, 1660–1770.* Cambridge, Mass., 1995.

5 HOSPITALS AND ASYLUMS

Digby, Anne. *Madness, Morality, and Medicine: A Study of the York Retreat, 1796–1914.* Cambridge, 1985.

Granshaw, Lindsay and Roy Porter, eds. *The Hospital in History.* London, 1987.

Macalpine, Ida. *George III and the Mad-Business.* London, 1991.

MacDonald, Michael. *Mystical Bedlam: Madness, Anxiety, and Healing in Seventeenth-Century England.* Cambridge, 1981.

Porter, Roy, W. F. Bynum, and M. Shepherd, eds. *The Anatomy of Madness.* Vol. I: *People and Ideas.* Vol. II: *Institutions and Society.* London, 1985.

Mind-Forg'd Manacles: A History of Madness from the Restoration to the Regency.
London, 1987.

Risse, Guenter. *Hospital Life in Enlightenment Scotland: Care and Teaching at the Royal Infirmary of Edinburgh.* Cambridge, 1986.

Tenon, Jacques. *Memoirs on Paris Hospitals.* Ed. with an introduction, notes, and appendices by Dora B. Weiner. Canton, Mass., 1996.

Wilkinson, Catherine. *The Hospital of Cardinal Tavera in Toledo.* New York, 1977.

6 HEALTH AND SOCIETY

Cavallo, Sandra. *Charity and Power in Early Modern Italy: Benefactors and Their Motives in Turin, 1541–1789.* Cambridge, 1995.

Cipolla, Carlo. *Miasmas and Disease: Public Health and the Environment in the Pre-Industrial Age.* New Haven, Conn., 1992.

Public Health and the Medical Profession in the Renaissance. Cambridge, 1976.

Frank, Johann Peter. *A System of Complete Medical Police: Selections from Johann Peter Frank.* Ed. by Erna Lesky. Baltimore, 1975.

Gentilcore, David. "'All that Pertains to Medicine': Protomedici and Protomedicati in Early Modern Italy." *Medical History* 35 (1994): 121–42.

Goubert, Jean-Pierre. *The Conquest of Water: The Advent of Health in the Industrial Age.* Cambridge, 1989.

Grell, Ole Peter and Andrew Cunningham, eds. *Health Care and Poor Relief in Protestant Europe 1500–1700.* London and New York, 1997.

Hannaway, Caroline. "Veterinary Medicine and Rural Health Care in Pre-Revolutionary France." *Bulletin of the History of Medicine* 51 (1977): 431–47.

Heller, Robert. "'Priest-Doctors' as a Rural Health Service in the Age of Enlightenment." *Medical History* 19 (1975): 361–83.

Henderson, John. *Piety and Charity in Late Medieval Florence.* Oxford, 1994.

Huisman, Frank. *Stadsbelang en standsbesef: gezondheidszorg en medisch beroep in Groningen, 1500–1730.* Rotterdam, 1992.

Jones, Colin and Jonathan Barry, eds. *Medicine and Charity Before the Welfare State.* London, 1991.

Jütte, Robert. *Poverty and Deviance in Early Modern Europe.* Cambridge, 1994.

Martz, Linda. *Poverty and Welfare in Habsburg Spain: The Example of Toledo.* Cambridge, 1983.

Riley, James C. *The Eighteenth-Century Campaign to Avoid Disease.* New York, 1987.

Rosen, George. *From Medical Police to Social Medicine: Essays on the History of Health Care.* New York, 1974.

Russell, Andrew, ed. *The Town and State Physician in Europe from the Middle Ages to the Enlightenment.* Wolfenbüttel, 1981.

Weiner, Dora. *The Citizen-Patient in Revolutionary and Imperial Paris.* Baltimore and London, 1993.

Wilkinson, Lise. *Animals and Disease: An Introduction to the History of Comparative Medicine.* Cambridge, 1992.

7 PRACTICE

Beier, Lucinda McCray. *Sufferers and Healers: The Experience of Illness in Seventeenth-Century England.* London and New York, 1987.

Digby, Anne. *Making a Medical Living: Doctors and Patients in the English Market for Medicine, 1720–1911.* Cambridge, 1994.

Duden, Barbara. *The Woman Beneath the Skin: A Doctor's Patients in Eighteenth-Century Germany.* Trans. by Thomas Dunlap. Cambridge, Mass., 1991.

Friedson, Eliot. *Profession of Medicine: A Study of the Sociology of Applied Knowledge.* New York, 1989.

Gélis, Jacques. *A History of Childbirth in Early Modern Europe.* Trans. by R. Morris. Oxford, 1991.

Gentilcore, David. *Healers and Healing in Early Modern Italy.* Manchester, 1998.

Jütte, Robert. *Ärzte, Heiler und Patienten: medizinischer Alltag in der frühen Neuzeit.* Munich, 1991.

Kleinman, Arthur. *Patients and Healers in the Context of Culture.* Berkeley and Los Angeles, 1980.

Larson, Magali Sarfatti. *The Rise of Professionalism: A Sociological Analysis.* Berkeley and Los Angeles, 1977.

Lebrun, François. *Se soigner autrefois: médicins, saints et sorciers aux 17e et 18e siècles.* Paris, 1983.

Lemay, Edna H. "Thomas Hérrier: A Country Surgeon Outside Angoulême at the End of the Eighteenth Century." *Journal of Social History* 10 (1976/77): 524–37.

Lindemann, Mary. *Health and Healing in Eighteenth-Century Germany.* Baltimore, 1996.

Loudon, Irvine. *Medical Care and the General Practitioner, 1750–1850.* Oxford, 1986.

Marland, Hilary, ed. *The Art of Midwifery.* London and New York, 1993.

Marland, Hilary and Margaret Pelling, eds. *The Task of Healing: Medicine, Religion and Gender in England and the Netherlands, 1450–1800.* Rotterdam, 1996.

Nagy, Doreen Evenden. *Popular Medicine in Seventeenth-Century England.* Bowling Green, Ohio, 1988.

Numbers, Ronald and Darrel W. Amundsen, eds. *Caring and Curing: Health and Medicine in the Western Religious Tradition.* New York, 1986.

Pelling, Margaret. "Medical Practice in Early Modern England: Trade or Profession?" In *The Professions in Early Modern England,* ed. by Wilfrid Prest, 90–128. London and New York, 1987.

Pollock, Linda. *With Faith and Physic: The Life of a Tudor Gentlewoman, Lady Grace Mildmay, 1552–1620.* London, 1993.

Porter, Dorothy and Roy Porter, *Patient's Progress: Doctors and Doctoring in Eighteenth-Century England.* Stanford, 1989.

Porter, Roy. *Health for Sale: Quackery in England, 1660–1850.* Manchester and New York, 1989.

Porter, Roy, ed., *Patients and Practitioners: Lay Perceptions of Medicine in Pre-Industrial Society.* Cambridge, 1985.

Ramsey, Matthew. *Professional and Popular Medicine in France, 1770–1830: The Social World of Medical Practice.* Cambridge, 1988.

New Approaches to European History

Index

Page-entries in bold type indicate the first use of a term and its definition. Titles of medical works are not listed. The index includes proper names of historical figures, but generally does not identify modern historians or their works.

7274